SANDWICHED

SANDWICHED

A Memoir of Holding on
and Letting Go

LAURIE JAMES

Published 2021
Printed in the United States of America
Print ISBN: 978-1-63152-785-2
E-ISBN: 978-1-63152-786-9
Library of Congress Control Number: 2021902054

For information, address:
She Writes Press
1569 Solano Ave #546
Berkeley, CA 94707

She Writes Press is a division of SparkPoint Studio, LLC.

To my four daughters:
may you know your mother better than I knew mine.

"Courage does not always roar. Sometimes courage is the quiet voice at the end of the day saying, 'I will try again tomorrow.'"

—MARY ANNE RADMACHER

PART ONE

৩৩৩

one

I was young, about seven, when I stood inside Gene's wooden sailboat at the Portofino Marina in Redondo Beach. Gene was a friend of Mom and Dad's. I tucked my uncombed blond hair behind my ears and put my hands on my hips. I was wearing my brother's hand-me-down, blue-and-white-striped, Hang Ten T-shirt. I was unhappy about something I didn't have words for, but I'd carry this un-nameable feeling throughout much of my life. Ken and Will, my two older brothers, were out in our dinghy, motoring around the harbor and fishing. Mom and Dad were having an afternoon drink with two other couples on a boat nearby. I sat down on Gene's boat and curled up, wrapping my arms around my knees. I watched my parents laugh with their friends. This aloneness seemed like an all-consuming feeling, as if I were empty and didn't belong to my family. It seemed as if my aloneness was something permanent and unchangeable. Just then, Gene stepped on the boat and patted the seat next to him. "Come over and join me."

I'd known him all my life and was happy to have his company. I moved close to him, and he put his arm around me. He must have noticed my sad expression, but his comfort didn't ease the hollowness I felt. It didn't seem like anyone could.

૮ઠૃ

Now, I was a few months shy of my twenty-fifth birthday. My friend Stacy begged me to go to a club with her. Our favorite DJ was playing at a local pub. I was a white girl who loved to dance and thought I had rhythm. I'd let the music travel through my body, stirring me to move. Music made me feel alive. I'd been sneaking out my bedroom window to go dancing since I was sixteen. My friends and I would throw on our scanty thrift-shop outfits, alter our IDs, and push my VW bug down my parents' driveway so we could drink and smoke pot before going to the hot clubs in Hollywood: The Florentine Gardens, Whisky a Go-Go, and The Odyssey.

That night, Stacy sat on my couch, her big green eyes peeking through her curly red hair. "Come on, Laurie," she said. "Let's go to Houlihan's and have a drink, and if it's boring, we can come home."

"All right." I decided to shift my mood and hoped the night would promise to be better than the last one.

I wanted to erase the memories of last night and the blind date that had gone wrong. A girlfriend had set me up with her boyfriend's friend David. The four of us went to the Dodgers game, and by the end of the night, my date was so drunk I had to help him walk to the car. He bragged about himself as he scooted close to me. I inched closer to my door. When we got home, I went to the bathroom and when I came out, I found him sprawled on my bed. I told David's friend to take him home. I was done entertaining losers. I'd met too many over the last year. I was ready to meet my husband-to-be, and that guy wasn't him.

As I got dressed that night, I thought about my girlfriends' weddings and marriages—they seemed to be happy and content. I wanted that too—to be married and happy. So I was searching for "my guy." I had been dreaming about the husband I'd start a family with since I graduated from college. If I didn't find someone soon, I was sure I'd never find anyone at all. All the failures I had been dating were jeopardizing my grand plan to have my first blue-eyed child before I was thirty. If my future husband and I had kids when we were young, we'd still have the energy to raise them and be in good health by the time they were grown. Then we could relax and enjoy the rest of our lives.

Although I wouldn't categorize myself as the "princess" type, there was a part of *that* fantasy that I sought. If I found "the one," I'd find the security and love I'd lacked much of my life, and we'd live happily ever after. I was determined to have a better marriage than my parents, and I wanted my kids to feel more secure than I'd felt growing up. The right person would make all that come true. I was sure of it.

Despite the disaster of my blind date the night before, I didn't want to miss out on any potential fun with Stacy. I curled and teased my permed blond hair, put on black suede shorts and a tapestry vest, and dabbed Calvin Klein's Obsession on my wrists. I didn't need to meet "my guy" that particular night. I was just looking to lift my mood.

"You look hot, and I like your shorts," Stacy said as we got in the car. Her ruby-red lips smiled.

"Thanks, you look great too." A flood of excitement washed over me. Stacy and I always amused ourselves dancing and flirting with cute guys together.

We arrived at the half-empty Irish pub. High-top tables surrounded the hardwood dance floor, and mirrored Irish beer labels hung on the walls. We ordered a drink and watched the bar fill up with people. As everyone trickled in, we checked out each cute dude.

"There are a lot of guys here tonight." I sipped my vodka and cranberry juice, eyeing the lineup. Stacy nodded in agreement. I liked it when the odds were in my favor—the perfect recipe for an entertaining night. Thirty minutes and one drink later, a cute, tall blond guy walked up and asked me to dance. I hesitantly followed him to the floor, smiling back at Stacy. I danced with him for two songs, thanked him, and went to the bathroom—my usual move when I was ready to ditch someone. The night was young, and I didn't want to be tied to one guy the entire night. On the way back to my table, I noticed Stacy talking to two guys, so I joined her. Neither of them was my usual go-to surfer blond, but I had nothing to lose. I was only looking to have a few drinks and a good time.

"Hi, I'm David," one of them called out to me.

I laughed at the coincidence of him having the same name as my blind date the night before. This David was tall, with dark hair, brown eyes, and freckles on his thin face. He wore a plaid, button-down shirt, jeans, and Topsiders—more preppy and reserved than the guys I usually dated. I introduced myself and told him about my previous night's blind date, and we both laughed.

After we talked for a while he asked, "Would you like to dance?" His big brown eyes sparkled as he held my gaze. I agreed, and one song led to the next. I was intrigued.

Stacy and I spent the majority of the evening with David

and his friend Tom. We laughed, drank, danced, and talked about our commonalities. David liked to ski and sail like I did, and we lived a few miles from each other in nearby beach towns. Before I knew it, the DJ was calling last dance. David grabbed my hand. "Come, join me."

He led me to the dance floor, wrapped his arms around my waist, and I rested my arms on his broad shoulders. He was the perfect height, over six feet tall. The kindling between us was simmering, but I shied away from him. I wasn't interested in getting too close to anyone that night. As the song finished, his eyes met mine and he kissed me on the lips. I pulled away at his sudden move.

"I'll be back," I told him and headed to the restroom. I took my time primping in the mirror, hoping David and Tom would leave. As I walked out, I looked for Stacy and motioned her toward the door. After David's move, I wanted to keep my distance, but he caught my eye as I walked to the door. Maybe my blind date the previous night had skewed my perception of this David, but that night, fun was the only thing on the menu.

He caught up to me and grabbed my arm. "Can I get your phone number?" My eyes drifted away. I was hoping to escape without talking to him.

"I don't think so." I impatiently waved at Stacy.

A determined look crossed his face. "Well, can I at least walk you to your car?"

"Sure." I resolved to stay aloof.

David and Tom asked if we wanted to go back to their place. I shook my head. "I don't think so, but thanks for a fun night."

David smiled. "You can't get mad at a guy for trying."

"No, you can't." I smirked as I got into my car.

David shut my door and waved as we pulled away.

As we drove out of the parking lot Stacy asked, "Why didn't you want to give David your number? He seemed cute and really into you."

"I know, maybe a little too into me," I snickered.

I liked more of a chase with men who interested me. Even though I was looking for a future husband, and David was witty, smart, had an MBA and a good job at a large aerospace company, and owned his home, my first impression told me he wasn't "the one."

The following Thursday I received a call at work. "There's someone named David on the phone for you," my colleague said. I froze, thinking it was the blind date from Friday night. I'd given him my number to coordinate our meeting time.

My clammy hands picked up the phone.

"Hi, this is David. Remember me?"

Expecting a different voice, I stuttered, "Who?" My heart was palpitating.

"Don't hang up on me," he urged. I realized it was the David I'd danced with Saturday night.

"How did you get my number?" I felt a pit in my stomach. Was he stalking me?

He continued, "You told me where you worked in Los Angeles, so I looked you up."

Flattery and trepidation twisted inside me. What was his real intent? No guy had gone to such lengths to seek me out.

David went on, "I don't want you to get the wrong idea. I

just had a really great time with you the other night and thought it was worth giving it one more shot."

My concerns began to fade as he continued to tell me the lengths he'd gone to find my office number. But could I really trust his intentions? I'd been burned before and didn't want to be a notch on his bedpost, like I'd let myself be many times. I wanted to do things differently this time.

He went on. "I'd really like to see you again. You pick the time and place, and I'll be there."

His flattery worked, and I agreed to meet him again. I suggested Tequila Willies, a local watering hole—I knew it well from the many happy hours I'd spent there with friends. It had a large outdoor bar area with multiple ways out. I chose that bar in case our second meeting went south and I needed a quick exit strategy.

We met the next day—Friday night. Tom, his friend, was at the front door, and I wondered why he was greeting me. Before I could ask where David was, he said, "David's running a little late. Can I buy you a drink until he gets here?"

Disappointed, I agreed, wondering if he was going to be like the rest of the guys I'd recently dated—they were either unavailable because of other involvements or expected instant gratification. At the bar we ordered drinks. I wondered why David was late. The bar was full of laughter as it always was at the beginning of a weekend. Most of the tables were occupied, and I looked around for a place for us to sit. I picked up my margarita and turned to face the door. It was dark inside, but then I noticed the silhouette of a tall man walking toward me, the bright sunlight illuminating his frame. As my eyes adjusted, I realized it was David. My heart fluttered as I saw the big smile on his face. He looked handsome in his blue suit and red tie, and even more handsome once I noticed the large bouquet of flowers in his hands. I began to see him in a new light. Heads turned to watch David. I kept my gaze on him, and my smile grew bigger. He handed me the bouquet. Everyone's eyes were on me now, probably wondering why I was the lucky girl receiving that beautiful bouquet.

"I was going to send these to your office, but decided to give them to you in person to thank you for meeting me again."

His air of confidence was suddenly attractive.

I inhaled the aroma of the Stargazer lily protruding from the center as my sentiments softened toward him. I cradled those flowers for the next two hours as if they were a delicate child. Tom made himself scarce as David and I got to know each other. We flirted, laughed, and talked about his recent business travel to New York. He wanted to know what I thought of working in the male-dominated produce business, and after a while asked when we could see each other again. Before I knew it, we were saying our goodbyes—David had plans that evening. He walked me to my car, and I gave him my phone number. We agreed to go for a bike ride and play racquetball on Sunday, two days later. He pulled me close and kissed me. This time I embraced him, surrendering to our chemistry and grateful for his persistence.

When I came home, I put my flowers into a vase and arranged them perfectly. I floated around the house the rest of the evening, unable to take my eyes off my beautiful bouquet. I continued to find reasons to walk by and smell them—each time feeling my stomach flutter, wishing tomorrow were Sunday.

two

The next date was a success, and the one after that too. He was different from any guy I'd dated. He was a man who knew what he wanted. He was a problem solver and very career oriented—all of which were on my list. Our physical connection developed quickly. I loved the way he touched me when we locked eyes and how he held my hand when he led me to the bedroom. I enjoyed the feeling of his soft skin against mine. I felt secure and wanted as he held me when we made love. Afterward, we'd lie in each other's arms and fall asleep, intertwined. I quickly became smitten and knew this was the kind of guy I wanted to marry.

A month after David and I started dating, he broke up with his girlfriend and we became exclusive. Three months later, we spent our first weekend away together in Santa Barbara. The morning after we arrived, we made love, and I couldn't hold in my feelings any longer. I put my hand on his broad chest and looked into his eyes. "There's something I want to tell you."

"Oh, what's that?" The softness of his face tightened.

"I'm falling in love with you." My eyes drifted away, not knowing if he'd return my sentiments.

He smiled, put his hand under my chin, and drew me toward him so he could see my face. "I'm falling in love with you too. In fact, I've known for a while." His dark eyes shone.

His response gave me the courage to ask, "So what kind of future do you see us having?"

He kissed me on the forehead and replied, "One with you in it."

I had told David I was adopted, that my eldest brother, Ken, struggled with addiction, and that my middle brother, Will, had divorced our family in his early twenties. I thought my parents should have split up years ago since they had fallen out of love and seemed to fight more than they talked. I didn't know much about David's childhood or his family, and I had a few unanswered questions. Why didn't he marry his last girlfriend he'd dated for two years? Did it bother him that I was seven years younger than he was? Why did he think his first marriage at age twenty-two had failed after three years? And what was his childhood like?

Those questions bounced around in my head until the car ride home. We stopped in Malibu to watch the sunset and sat on a park bench. I nestled under his arm as we watched the pastel colors of the sky fade to gray. I asked him my questions. He told me he knew he didn't want to marry his last girlfriend and was waiting for the right time to tell her. Our seven-year age difference didn't matter to him. His marriage failed because they were both too young—her parents were very Catholic, and his mother was Jewish, but ultimately, he'd caught his ex-wife in bed with another man. He didn't have a very happy childhood. His dad worked two jobs while he was growing up. His parents fought, and he had only a few happy memories. Some of them included having Sunday dinners with his younger brother, parents, and an aunt and uncle he was close to, Ruth and Harold. His mother would sometimes hide in her room for weeks at a time. When I pressed him further on his childhood, he changed the subject, so I let it go. We'd shared enough for that weekend, and I was pleased to hear his reasonable responses. He seemed happy now, and even though he was more reserved than most of the men I dated, his intelligence and secure job gave me the confidence that he'd be a good provider, a trait my dad didn't have. After our weekend away, I was enamored and pleased with the direction our relationship was going. It seemed possible that David was "the one."

Two months after our trip to Santa Barbara, I brought David home for a barbeque so he could meet my parents. Mom quickly took a liking to him, but she liked everyone. Dad sat in his chair drinking his beer. David asked him questions about his work, but he responded with short answers, not inquiring about David in return. Later, I asked Dad what he thought. "I guess he's okay. It's hard to know after only meeting him one time."

Dad was an introvert and rarely started any conversation unless he was approached. He spent most of his time working and was a glass half-empty kind of guy. As a teenager, my brother Will nicknamed him "Eeyore," which stuck. Mom was the opposite. She was optimistic and saw the good in everyone, sometimes to a fault. After meeting my parents, David assured me that he liked them.

A few weeks later, I met his parents for the first time at a restaurant for dinner. They were very different from mine—reserved and proper where mine were casual and relaxed. I learned that his parents had met in Brazil while his mom, Irene, worked for the United Nations, and David's dad, Ray, lived there with his family since he was a child. After they married, and shortly before David was born, they moved to Los Angeles to be closer to his Aunt Ruth and Uncle Harold. Harold was Irene's older brother, and he and his wife had recently moved to Los Angeles from England. We were compatible enough.

That winter, David asked if I'd join him Christmas morning for breakfast at his parents' house. I agreed, excited that he wanted to share the holiday with me. It would be the first Christmas I'd spend with a boyfriend, and I was eager to see how he celebrated the holidays with his parents. We drove to Yorba Linda, a suburb of Orange County, an hour away. We arrived at their single-story tract home with its perfectly manicured shrubs and knocked on the door.

"Come in, come in," David's dad Ray said with a smile. He was slim, dressed in slacks, a neatly pressed plaid, button-down shirt, a sweater vest, and slippers. David and his dad shared the same long thin face and large sharp nose—their resemblance was clear. As we walked into their sparsely decorated home, their small entryway was empty and the air was stale and still. My impulse was to open a window to let in the fresh air, but I didn't want to appear rude. David's mom walked out of the kitchen, wiping her hands on a dishtowel.

"Hello, dear," she said with her lingering British accent. She and David kissed on both cheeks.

I greeted David's mom. "Hi, Irene, it's good to see you again."

We exchanged kisses, and I set our lox and bagels down on the table in their family room that overlooked a small empty patio. Irene put the flowers David had brought in a vase. Lox and bagels was a meal that had never crossed my family table as I grew up. I would have preferred eggs and pancakes with syrup, but I guessed that wasn't part of either of his parents' upbringing. David's mom was Jewish, his dad Christian. Irene guided us into their family room. As I looked into their dark living room, there was only a single floor lamp next to the fireplace and nothing else. Why hadn't they furnished and decorated their living room? His parents owned a small wholesale business and appeared to be financially stable. My childhood home was a modest three-bedroom, one-bath house, but it was always decorated with furniture, drapes, and tchotchkes. I didn't want to pass judgment. I was falling in love with their son. Why should I care how his parents chose to live? I took note and planned to ask David more about it later.

We sat down at a table for four located in their fifties-furnished family room. I faced the patio and waited for Irene to pass the platter of lox and bagels to Ray, then me—each of us picking our sides. I added extra tomatoes, onions, and capers to help make the lox more palatable. David's mom took half a bagel and ate it quietly while David and his dad talked about work. I nervously followed suit, sitting quietly. I finally understood where David's reserved traits came from.

"So, tell me again what you do for a living?" Irene finally asked as she pushed back a strand of black hair.

I told her I was in the produce industry and sold citrus to restaurant purveyors and small grocery stores in Los Angeles, but I was looking to switch jobs in the near future. I asked her about the small wholesale business that she and David's dad owned. She told me she handled the French-speaking customers from Quebec since she spoke fluent French. She showed little excitement about their business and didn't seem to have many hobbies. I struggled to find something in common with her, and awkwardness settled in. With little else to say, I finished my bagel as we both listened to David and his dad's conversation. I hoped the result of the breakfast would be that they liked and approved of me.

After eating, we drank tea and made small talk about the weather and traffic. Finally, David said, "Well, we should let you get back to your day."

We said our goodbyes and left—the brisk air outdoors woke me up like an alarm clock. I wasn't sure what impression I'd left on David's parents.

Once we were in the car David turned to me, "I think they like you."

"How could you tell?"

He smiled and put his hand on my leg. "I could just tell."

I wasn't convinced. His parents' reserved approach was so different from what I was used to. It was hard to read them, but I trusted David. He was loyal to his family, and he seemed different from his parents, especially when he was with me. He had his serious side, but he was fun loving, and I appreciated his well-rounded style.

On the car ride home, I asked him how long his parents had lived in their house and why it was void of furniture and decorations.

He raised his eyebrows. "Well, that's a very good question. They've lived there over five years, and we didn't have much money growing up. Since my mom was raised during the Depression, I think she feels more comfortable living minimally." He took a long pause. "And the furniture you saw in my parents' family room was given to them by my Aunt Ruth and Uncle Harold when they redecorated their house twenty years ago."

I caressed David's arm as we drove home, feeling closer to him. Even though his own house was a bachelor pad he shared with two roommates, it was better decorated than his parents' house. David and I seemed like-minded despite the few differences, and I was excited to see where our relationship would take us.

After the holidays, David and I started spending most weekends together, and we continued to talk about what our future might look like together. He generously offered to help support me financially as I transitioned into the recruiting business later that year. We talked about how many kids we wanted together—I wanted two and he wanted three, but we agreed to take them one at a time. I'd never before felt the kind of love that I felt with him. The unnamed feeling that had accompanied me all my life melted away.

three

David invited me to join him in Maui for our one-year anniversary as a couple. It was my first visit to Hawaii, and I couldn't wait to see him when I got off the plane. He had arrived a few days before me for a conference. I saw his tall dark head above the crowd in the baggage claim area. When we caught each other's gaze, he walked toward me, and I ran into his arms. We embraced and he put a lei around my neck, grabbed my bag off the carousel, and led us to the convertible that took us to our hotel room. I put my arm out the window and closed my eyes as the warm tropical breeze blew past my face. David told me he'd arranged for us to ride bikes at sunrise from the top of the Haleakala Volcano, which rises 10,023 feet above sea level. "It's going to be fun and the sunrise is supposed to be spectacular."

Even though I was adventurous, I grumbled about starting my first day of vacation at four in the morning. I'd envisioned a leisurely morning of sleeping in and having breakfast by the pool, followed by snorkeling in the neighboring cove. When the alarm went off, I rallied and did my best to put on a smile. We checked in with the guide and jumped into the van with a half dozen other cyclists. Sleepy-eyed, I sipped my hot coffee as the van traveled up the windy road into the thick gray clouds. I hoped the caffeine would improve my attitude. As we approached the top, it started drizzling, and the temperature dropped. I kept expecting the clouds to part so I could experience what Mark Twain described in *Roughing It* as "the sublimest spectacle I ever witnessed." We donned our rain jackets, got out of the van, and walked toward the edge of the crater while the staff unloaded our bikes. Shivering, I looked over the railing and scanned the caldera. It was a cinder desert landscape of black, red, and brown that swirled into the dull fog. The clouds darkened the sky, and the drizzle quickly turned to rain. Fog filled in the volcano. I pulled my hood over my head and put my hands in my pockets. A chill traveled down my spine. I thought of the warm covers I'd crawled out of and wished I were back in our room snuggled up next to David.

"What are we doing here?" I mumbled under my breath. I turned to David to tell him I was heading back to the van, but I paused as his dark eyes focused on me. He had a look of determination on his face. He took my hands and pulled me closer. "This is the dawn of a new day, as we stand together on top of the world, and the beginning of a new life together. As we reach greater heights." He paused, pulled a little black box out of his pocket, knelt down, and opened it. "Laurie, will you marry me?"

"*Yes,*" I replied, fully awakened by his proposal. He put the diamond ring on my finger. He stood up, and I wrapped my arms around his neck and kissed him with more heart than ever before. We embraced, his body warming mine and it felt like the clouds around us had disappeared. The moment was truly ours.

We walked back to the van where our bikes were ready. With my new ring and a new life ahead of me, I was ready to take the ride alongside David down the next road called marriage. Even if we had to endure a little weather, we were in this together. I was convinced that our strong love and commitment would prevail over any challenges that might come our way. I was sure David was different from Dad. He was strong, well educated, and took care of me. My marriage was going to look different than my parents' marriage. Ours would be more loving and meaningful, and I could count on David for better or worse, richer or poorer.

The rest of the day I wore my ring with pride, but that afternoon before we went to the beach, he asked for it back. "This was just a loaner, and I don't want to lose it while we're on vacation. When we get home we'll pick out your stone and setting together."

I reluctantly agreed, feeling like a kid getting my bag of candy taken away after eating only one piece. I decided I didn't want to lose the ring either and focused on enjoying my first trip to Maui with my new fiancé. The rest of the week we slept in, made love, snorkeled in the clear blue waters off Molokai, toured the island and its many beaches, and enjoyed romantic dinners in Lahaina. It was the best engagement a girl could ask for.

Our last night in Maui, David arranged for us to have dinner as the sun set behind Lanai. The painted sky looked magical as the deep oranges, pinks, and purples painted the clouds. David grabbed my hand and looked deep into my eyes, smiling. I gazed back as our hearts connected. At that moment, I felt I deserved my happiness.

꙳

The morning of our wedding, I woke up in my hotel room at the crack of dawn, my stomach in knots, as waves of joy, anxiety, and ambivalence took their turn. Months shy of my twenty-seventh birthday and two years after we first met, I was marrying David. It was mid-September, and we had arranged for a beautiful outdoor ceremony at the Malibu Lake Mountain Club. David loosely affiliated himself as a Jew and I a Lutheran, so the venue was perfect for us.

At breakfast, I forced down a couple of bites of toast, but my nerves had taken over my appetite. In the dressing room my hairdresser curled my hair and applied my makeup. My bridesmaids popped a bottle of champagne to help calm my wedding day tensions.

Amber, my maid of honor and closest friend from high school, lifted her glass: "Here's to many happy years together."

The champagne made my stomach churn and my head throb. The ceremony was quickly approaching. My bridesmaids helped me into my off-the-shoulder fitted dress and pinned on my veil. I saw our guests arriving. My knees grew weak. Was I feeling the typical wedding day jitters, or was my anxiety trying to tell me something? At twenty-seven, was I really supposed to make a lifelong decision? How did I know David was my forever after? Does anyone ever really know?

"I'm not sure about this." I sat down in a white wicker chair —my mind jumping from thought to thought. My nerves always caused me to be clumsy, and I didn't want to trip on my dress, fall flat on my face, or make a fool of myself as I walked down the aisle.

The chairs were aligned in perfect rows with colorful flowers and white ribbons decorating the aisle—the untouched runner trailing down the middle was ready for Dad to walk me down and hand me over to David. I grabbed the glass of champagne, my hands shaking as I took one last gulp. Amber turned to me and asked, "Are you okay?" with concern in her brown eyes.

"Yeah, I just need to stop shaking." I pursed my lips and tried to breathe out my anxiety. Even though everything was going as planned, I wanted my wedding day to be perfect for my guests and more importantly for David and me. I worried that our guests wouldn't like the food or the DJ, or they'd think the evening was boring. The last thing I wanted was to be the talk at the water cooler the following Monday.

Dad knocked on the door. "Are you ready?" My heart pounded harder. Amber handed me my bouquet of flowers with a Stargazer lily front and center—the same kind of flower David had given me in the bar that first day. She helped straighten my train as I walked down the steps toward my guests.

The warm fall air wrapped around my body. I looked past our guests, who were seated under the large oak trees that shaded the lawn, searching for David in the distance. I kept my eyes on him. He was standing under the floral arch next to our minister, Georgie. A smile came across his face when he saw me. His smile eased me for a second, until I approached the edge of the grass, and the wedding processional song began. I gripped Dad's arm tighter as I teetered on the uneven runner. I took a deep breath and began my journey down the aisle to become Mrs. David James.

We had a twenty-minute ceremony that I hardly remembered afterward, and vows I could barely say. The ceremony was followed by too many pictures, a long line of guests to greet, and a dinner that I barely ate. One of the best parts was waltzing to our song, "Everything I Do, I Do It for You" by Bryan Adams.

After we cut the cake and changed our clothes, we climbed into a limousine to start our new life together, sipping champagne on the drive to our hotel. My body vibrated with adrenaline from the day. The champagne quickly went to my head after having little to eat.

I thought about how smoothly the day had gone despite my fears, and I was pleased that our guests had enjoyed themselves. It was time to start my new life with David. We were leaving for Cancun in the morning, and all I wanted to do was embrace my new husband and relax in his arms, but I'd saved a surprise for him, a little limousine foreplay. We rolled up the back window for privacy on our long ride to the hotel. I wanted to make sure David knew that I'd take care of his needs, to show him I was all in, and I would be the best wife I could be. I trusted he'd give me the same in return. This was a new beginning for us—for me. With David by my side, I was no longer adrift in the world.

When we arrived home from our week-long honeymoon in Cancun, I moved into David's fifties beach bungalow bachelor pad. We opened our gifts, wrote thank you notes, and I experimented with new recipes using our kitchen gadgets. I found places for our cherished gifts, made curtains for the bay windows, washed the fingerprints off the walls, and started watering the grass and plants in the front yard. I wanted our house to be a home. David hadn't put any time or money into his house since he'd bought it three years prior. During our first year of marriage, we began talking about building our dream house where we would raise our family.

I was working for an employment agency, placing technology professionals in corporations across the Los Angeles area. David's salary was twice mine, so he suggested living on his money and saving mine. He'd withdraw money from the bank biweekly and give me my sixty dollars of spending money for the next two weeks. I looked to David for guidance and trusted his opinion—something I rarely, if ever, saw Mom do with Dad. David had an MBA, and he'd backpacked through Europe after college. I yearned to travel like that, but I'd never had the guts or money to do it. I looked to David for his wisdom, knowledge, and financial astuteness.

As I was growing up, Mom handled all the household finances. Dad never seemed to understand the importance of getting paid in a timely manner by his clients and took months to repair the rental properties they owned—losing out on many months of rent. Mom would get so mad at Dad that her face would turn beet red, and I thought she'd explode. David was more frugal than I thought we needed to be, but I wasn't going to question him. He had a plan for us, and I was confident he'd look out for me.

A year after we wed, we decided to start our family, and I quickly became pregnant. My body stretched in ways I'd never thought possible, and after thirteen hours of labor, our first child was born. We named our brown-eyed little girl Emma, and when I first held her in my arms, I didn't know how I could let anyone else care for her when I went back to work. In the first few weeks of her life, she developed jaundice, and I came down with mastitis in both breasts. I wanted to be a mother, but nothing could have prepared me for the sleepless nights, her evening colic, and the constant diaper changes and feedings of that first year. Bleary-eyed and exhausted by my new responsibilities, I forged ahead and went back to work as a part-time executive recruiter after four months despite my sleep deprivation.

When Emma was eight months old, we moved into a small two-bedroom apartment while we built our dream house. After work and before I picked up Emma at our sitter's, I'd stop by the stores and pick out appliances, tile, hardware, and carpet, bringing home samples to get David's opinion. He continued working long hours as he moved around within his company and built his career. I was comfortable overseeing the construction of the house, caring for Emma, and doing the housework. We hired a professional to build our home, unlike Dad who had remodeled our house himself, one room at a time, after work and on the weekends. He never finished one room before starting another. Each room was left with a door missing or floor molding on only half the walls, which irritated Mom. My brothers and I would fight to use the tiny shower and bathroom in our motor home during the month Dad was remodeling our only bathroom, and if we didn't get in there before Dad did, we brushed our teeth in the kitchen sink. David and I were doing things differently—working together to build our new house and life together—and I was grateful.

We moved into our new home when I was five months pregnant with our second daughter, Heather. Our traditional two-story house had four bedrooms, four baths, a living room, and a family room. It was painted Swiss coffee white inside and out—not a lick of color anywhere. When I first saw it, the house looked sparse and cold to me, and after we moved in, our furniture looked small and ratty, so we painted the kitchen and family room buttermilk yellow and bought new furniture and matching floral window treatments for those two rooms. The rest of the house stayed stark white and unfurnished. I made the main living space feel like home and assumed we'd finish decorating the rest of the house in the coming years.

Heather came into the world two months after Emma turned two and slept through the night within the first month, while Emma continued wandering into our bedroom asking to sleep with us. David was against "the family bed" concept, but I would have done anything for a good night's sleep. It was an important commodity, and my exhaustion and frustration were taking a toll on me. Desperate for a solution, I asked Mom's friend Georgie, our minister and family therapist, for a suggestion. She told us to put both Emma and Heather in the same room, and within a week Emma stopped waking up at night. It turned out that the solution was a simple one that made sense to me. None of us wants to be alone. As my sleep deprivation subsided, so did my frustrations, and our lives were finally settling down. At last, I was becoming the mom and wife I wanted to be.

One evening when Heather was able to crawl, I sat on the floor in the family room, Legos sprawled out on the floor.

Emma was building a tower, and Heather had pulled out every toy from the toy box. My heart swelled with joy. We were raising our family in a beautiful home, the girls were happy, and I had a hard-working, loving husband. I was living the life I'd always dreamed about—I didn't need anything else.

four

Every time my mother, Elizabeth (Betty), came to the house, her blue eyes would sparkle as my daughters, her only grandchildren, ran into her arms. She'd visit every couple of weeks, and more often during the summer when she wasn't teaching. She'd babysit so David and I could have a date night out. She'd sometimes help me when David worked late, or when I had plans with my girlfriends. She accompanied us traveling when we combined a vacation with David's work travel. Having her with our family gave me an extra set of hands, which was comforting and helpful. I came to rely heavily on her.

When Mom went back to teaching after I started kindergarten, she became one of the first special education teachers in Los Angeles. She developed the curriculum for the El Monte Unified School District, where she worked for over thirty-five years. She loved working with the kids, but often complained about the increase in paperwork that was required of her. Mom had grown up in Des Moines, Iowa, and met my dad, Jim, in Wisconsin where she was teaching. They moved to Southern California a year after they got married. Dad introduced Mom to camping, canoeing, and skiing—activities she hadn't experienced growing up in the forties and fifties, but she quickly took a liking to the outdoors. Over time, she became the more adventurous of the two and hiked Mount Whitney at age fifty-five.

Early in her marriage, Mom had finally become pregnant after many tries, but she delivered a stillborn baby girl at eight months—the baby's umbilical cord was wrapped around her neck. That must have been excruciating news for her to bear. I could only imagine how difficult it must have been to carry a baby almost full-term and have your hormones produce milk without having a child to feed or hold in your arms.

After that, Mom and Dad decided to adopt children. I never knew if that was the doctor's recommendation or their decision. As I was growing up, I was aware that Ken, Will, and I had been adopted from different families. None of us looked alike, but I didn't recall a specific conversation about the adoptions. As a child, I'd often wondered who I was and where I'd come from. I spent years as a young child trying to fit in with my brothers, dressing like a boy, playing with trucks, looking to connect with them, but most of the time I felt like a misfit—as if I didn't belong to this family.

Mom never talked to me about her stillborn baby or the pain she carried with her, no doubt wanting to protect me, but as a child I felt her self-protection. When I became an adult and a mother, I wished she'd told me about her past. Knowing more about her would have helped me make sense of my childhood instead of having to knit together the conversations I'd overheard and the secondhand information from Dad's stories and those of Mom's best friend, Nancy. Mom's words might have brought me closer to her.

I tried to imagine the look on Mom's face the first time she held me after I'd spent three days in the hospital being changed and fed by the nurses. In the sixties, most adopted babies stayed in the hospital alone for at least that long before they went home with their parents. Dad said he was the first to hold me, but it was Mom's reddish-orange lipstick that might have caught my eye, accentuating her warm smile. She gave me the first loving contact I had after I was born. I imagined her brown hair shaping her warm smile as she cradled her youngest in her arms, the only daughter of their three adopted children. I must have been wrapped in her warmth as she held me.

Mom reassured me I was loved when I was young, but I always felt an emotional distance. I wondered if it was because she'd already lost one baby girl and feared losing me too. I spent a lot of time with Mom trying to close that gap by sailing with her and listening to her conversations with neighbors and friends.

Dad told me the story of how we all became sailors at a young age. When I was a baby and my brothers were still toddlers, my parents purchased their first sailboat. Mom and Dad had gone down to the Redondo Beach marina looking to buy a large canoe, and it was then that they met John Stiles. John was selling his seventeen-foot sailboat, which was in pristine shape. John was a former ship's captain, turned Budweiser truck driver after he developed hearing loss in one ear. He had a warm, kind smile, and I imagine that Mom and Dad took an immediate liking to him. Dad told me they didn't look at any other boats, and bought John's because he offered to include sailing lessons with their purchase. The next boat Mom and Dad bought they named *Laurie Too*, after me. Over the years, Mom fell in love with sailing, holding the tiller in her hand while Dad held a beer in his.

One warm summer morning just shy of Heather's first birthday, David turned to me and said, "I couldn't sleep the other night, so I got up and started surfing the Internet."

"Yeah, so what were you surfing for?" I asked.

He sheepishly turned to me. "I got to thinking . . . what would be something interesting to search for?" His eyebrows shot up. "I pulled out your adoption papers and looked up your birth mother in the white pages."

Did he really have the nerve to look her up? When I was in my late twenties, I'd asked Mom for my adoption papers, and my birth mother's last name was listed. I'd told David during our courtship and many times after we started having kids that I had no desire to find my birth parents.

Suddenly feeling like I'd been hollowed out with an ice cream scoop, I said, "Please tell me you didn't . . ."

"Well, you'll never believe this, but when I looked up her last name, there were only two Storstrands: Daniel, who lives in Colorado and Mary, who lives in Irvine . . . and she'd like to meet you."

Stunned at his audacious intrusion, I snapped, "What? How do you know that?"

David's nose wrinkled like a little boy ashamed to admit what he'd done wrong. "Well, because I spoke with her."

"You didn't!" My body tensed as his words cut through me. How could he disregard my wishes and contact her without my consent?

I turned to him in disbelief. "You're kidding me, right?"

"Don't you want to know your medical background now that we have kids?"

An emotional chill settled in as I stared into his eyes. "Don't even think about trying to find my birth father, or I will divorce you."

Seething, I stormed down the hall and grabbed the girls out of their room on the way downstairs to the kitchen. I went through the motions as I started to make oatmeal. Heat crawled up my neck as I tried to make sense of what my husband had done. Although my childhood had been far from perfect, I had two parents who loved me, and I loved them in return. I didn't want Mom to think I was going to replace her with my birth mother. The oatmeal boiled over as I stared at the blue flame under the pot, the shock seeping in that David had broken through my stated boundaries, and that he had gone so far as to contact her. What was I supposed to do with that? What would I tell Mom? A sudden urge to call her washed over me. Even though it seemed irrational, the thought that she'd somehow find out or that David would tell her made me feel sick. I needed to protect her. She was leaving in two days for Cranberry Island, Maine, to go sailing and would be gone for a month with limited access to a phone. I didn't want to hurt her—she'd already lost a baby girl. I didn't want her to think she was losing me too.

I fed the girls their breakfast, and when David tried to kiss me goodbye before he left for work, I turned my cheek away. I couldn't dismiss what he'd done.

After he left, I called Mom and asked if we could get together for lunch. I had the day off from my part-time recruiting job with a pharmaceutical company in Irvine. Her happy voice said, "Yes, I'd love to see you."

Neither Will nor Ken had found their birth parents, but Will and I had filed for our identifiable information from the state when we were eighteen. I didn't know exactly how to tell Mom what had happened, and I didn't want her to be angry with me.

After dropping the girls off at my babysitter's, I met Mom at a café near her home. After we sat down at our quiet table for two, Mom said, "This is such a pleasant surprise." Flushing, she smiled warmly.

I smiled in return as the pit grew in my stomach. We ordered our lunch and after the waitress left I said, "There's something I need to tell you."

"Oh, what is it?" She must have seen the stress written across my face.

"David told me this morning that he'd located my birth mother and made contact with her without discussing it with me first."

"Oh?" Her eyes widened with surprise.

"Yeah, and I'm pretty unhappy with him right now," I said, holding back my tears.

Mom reached across the table and touched my hand. "Don't be mad at David. He didn't mean to be hurtful."

My eyes began to tear. Even if David's actions weren't meant to be hurtful, he had invaded my privacy and crossed a line that I'd made clear to him. I wanted Mom to take my side, but she didn't say anything else. I knew she was just trying to help ease the tension between us, but I needed her in my corner.

Toward the end of lunch she said, "If there's ever an opportunity to meet your birth mother, I'd like to thank her for the gift she gave me." Her eyes held my gaze, and I felt her sincerity.

"I'll let you know what I decide to do." I was relieved that she took the news so well.

For the next several weeks, two thoughts consumed me. Should I meet my birth mother, Mary? How could I manage the deep-bellied resentment I felt toward David? I was torn. I'd never had a desire to meet Mary, but now I felt boxed in. How could I be true to myself and not hurt her? Was I protecting Mom from more pain? Was there an unconscious reason why I didn't want to meet Mary?

I would never act against someone's wishes, especially not my spouse's. David had gone against my requests about my birth mother, and I still burned with fury. It was his job to protect me, not to rip my heart open and leave the pieces on the floor. For the next few weeks, I repeatedly brought up the subject to give David an opportunity to repair the situation and apologize, but with each conversation he'd respond defensively, "I did it so you could find out your medical history," or "I thought I was doing you a favor." Each time, my insides roiled like a storm.

Since we had been unsuccessful resolving this issue on our own, I reached out to Georgie. We'd met with her twice before she married us as part of her ministry services. She told me not to make a big deal of the situation. I was bewildered by her comment. Why was I the one who had to acquiesce when I was the one who'd been betrayed? Did she say this because we had two little kids in the house? I left our session even more confused.

I stewed about the conflict for several more months, but I never received the apology I wanted. I eventually came to the conclusion that Georgie's rationale was old-school thinking— it was better not to keep creating conflict, but that didn't keep my bitterness from slipping out unexpectedly when David did or said something that annoyed me. I began to feel as I'd felt as a child, and for the first time in seven years, the loneliness that had been dormant since we married began to surface.

As the weeks went on, aggravation, guilt, and empathy for Mary ran through my veins. I didn't know what to do. If I decided to meet Mary, I was betraying myself, but when I put myself in Mary's shoes, a feeling of devastation set in. She'd wonder why the child that she'd put up for adoption didn't want to meet her. Still feeling trapped by David's choice to contact her, I eventually had an uncomfortable phone conversation with Mary, and she asked me out to lunch. I accepted her invitation.

Agreeing to meet her brought up a plethora of questions: Would it feel like I belonged to her, or would it feel like I was encountering an aunt I'd never met? Would I recognize her and share similar mannerisms? Would there be an instant connection, or would my indignation toward David block me from being open to her?

The morning of our meeting, I woke up nervous and unsure about my decision. A tidal wave of emotions carried me in every direction. I arrived at the restaurant and pried my sweaty hand off the steering wheel. Time slowed as I approached the doors; I saw her standing outside. I knew immediately who she was—with her five-foot-six frame, short blond hair, and deep blue eyes. The soft marionette lines around her mouth showed under her pale makeup. I saw my exact coloring, my nose, and my forehead. There was no denying our resemblance.

I wiped my clammy hands on my pants before I shook hers. Then we awkwardly hugged. "It's so nice to finally meet you," she said, warmly looking at me.

"It's nice to meet you too." My body tensed with my false words.

We sat down at a table by a window and talked about the weather and traffic as we looked at our menus.

Mary put down her menu and held my gaze. "So, I have to tell you, I've waited for this moment for a very long time." Her soft voice continued, "I wasn't sure it would ever happen." She beamed at me across the table.

My stomach twisted tighter. I was unable to share the same sentiments, but I gave her a nod and asked her if she'd eaten at the restaurant before. Our food eventually arrived, but I ate very little. I pushed my shrimp Louie salad around as I listened to her tell me about her life.

She had grown up in California, her parents had passed away young, and she wasn't currently married. I took a sip of my iced tea to wash down the lump in my throat before asking about my birth father. Her face became sullen as she told me they'd met in Germany when he was a lieutenant in the army and she was working as a civilian on the same base. When Mary told my birth father that she was pregnant, he said he had a girlfriend back home to whom he was promised. Sadness welled up in her eyes. "I asked if we could marry just for a while and then divorce . . . but he said no."

"I'm so sorry," I replied, unsure of what else to say.

As we continued to talk, my consciousness hovered above my body, watching a scene in a movie play out. Was this really happening?

She continued, "You were the only child I ever had."

My spine straightened as I worried about the implications of her statement. I wasn't prepared for a full relationship with her, and I perceived that was what she wanted.

I told her that a loving family had adopted me and taken good care of me. She smiled affectionately. I wasn't prepared to tell her about the dark moments in my childhood that I'd pushed out of my mind, not wanting her to regret putting me up for adoption. Instead, I told her about my career, marriage, and recent life as a mother. As we walked out of the restaurant, she asked if she could see me again.

My words caught in my throat. "I don't know . . . maybe soon."

She said she'd call me, and I nodded, unable to confess that I wasn't ready for more. Even though our resemblance was uncanny, I didn't feel like I belonged to her either.

As I drove home, my jumbled thoughts and mixed emotions kept me from seeing anything clearly. Did I want anything from Mary? Was I correct in sensing that she wanted more of a relationship with me? I couldn't tell if meeting her had alleviated my indignation toward David or added more fuel to the fire that sat deep inside me. The white lines that divided the highway blurred as tears fell down my cheeks. I didn't know what I was going to do with David's unwanted gift, but I had to propel myself forward. My family's future was at stake.

five

During the months following my meeting with Mary, I heard one adoption story after another. They popped up on the evening news, in conversations with friends, and on talk radio. One person searched her entire adult life and still hadn't found her birth mother. Another found her biological mother with little effort, and it was a Hallmark reunion. I wondered if I might have felt differently about meeting Mary if it had been on my terms.

I invited Mary to meet Mom one Saturday afternoon a few months after our first lunch. It wasn't an easy decision, but I was looking for this second encounter to help me define this new relationship and what it meant for me. Mom had expressed interest, so I wanted to follow through.

Mom arrived early wearing a baby-blue polo shirt and long khaki shorts. Her short silver hair was parted on the side, and her pink-rimmed glasses sat high on her nose. Mom wrapped her arms around Emma and Heather as soon as she walked in. The girls asked her to play with them, and she agreed. She sat on the floor with the girls while I straightened up my already tidy house.

When the doorbell rang minutes later, my stomach

churned. I invited Mary in, and Mom walked up behind me. "It's so nice to finally meet you," she smiled warmly, reaching to hug Mary.

David came downstairs and introduced himself to Mary before leaving for the afternoon. I'd asked him to make himself scarce. I didn't want his presence to skew my perception and decision. More importantly, I wanted to avoid him saying something that might cause me to be snarky in front of everyone.

My heart beat faster as Mom and Mary walked toward the family room. Emma and Heather continued playing on the floor with their Barbies—blissfully unaware of whom they were about to meet. Mary pulled out gifts for each of them, and they ran over to grab them. I prompted the girls to thank her as they ripped open their toys.

I invited the two mothers to sit on the couch while I went to the kitchen to get tea and cookies. I needed to keep moving to ease my nerves. They spent the next hour getting to know each other while I listened quietly. Mom told Mary about Ken and Will, our sailing adventures, and our travels to ski resorts throughout the western United States. Mary told Mom she liked skiing too, but had given it up after her hip surgery. She talked about her childhood and her family's interior design business.

Toward the end of the visit, Mom put her hand on Mary's shoulder and said, "Well, I can't thank you enough for the wonderful gift you gave me." Mom's eyes grew wet with tears.

"It seems like she ended up with a good family," Mary replied with an affectionate touch on my arm. The warm sentiments passed through me as I wiggled uncomfortably in my seat. There was so much about our family that Mary didn't know. Would she feel the same way if she knew the hidden parts of my childhood?

After Mary left, my body slowly stopped vibrating. I asked Mom, "So what did you think?"

"She seems like a lovely woman," Mom smiled.

I nodded in agreement. Our afternoon together had given Mary the comfort that a good person had raised the only child she ever gave birth to, and Mom was able to show appreciation for the opportunity to adopt me. I was relieved that I'd taken care of my guilt-driven obligations around my adoption, but it didn't help me reconcile my emotions. I hoped that time would help untangle the complex knot of feelings that remained.

The following month, Mary called and asked if she could take me to the Getty Museum and to lunch for my birthday that November. David encouraged me to go, and I reluctantly agreed, even though I would rather have spent that Saturday with my girls after working all week. That day we wandered around the museum, and at lunch we made small talk, but I felt a pull to get home. As she dropped me off she asked, "When can we get together again?" Dread washed over me. I had anticipated that question all day.

My heart palpitated as I found the courage to say, "I have two small kids, and I'm working." I looked out the window before glancing back toward her. "I'm not ready for this relationship right now."

Mary's head hung low. "I understand. I gave up that right when I put you up for adoption thirty-two years ago." The sadness in her blue eyes left me with guilt.

"Let's stay in touch through cards or a phone call once a year," I suggested. The last thing I wanted to do was hurt Mary, but it was too late. The pain in her eyes was evident. Even though I was still bitter about David contacting her, I knew both Mary and David wanted me to want more. I couldn't keep living this lie for them. I gently separated from her that day, and when I got home, I lay on the floor next to the children. I was relieved with my decision, but my resentment hadn't dissipated.

David and I took Emma and Heather to visit his Aunt Ruth and Uncle Harold one spring Saturday, six months after I'd first met Mary for lunch. Although my unhappiness toward David was subsiding, residual feelings were still simmering inside. That day, I bottled them up and put on a good face for our visit.

Harold and Ruth were both in their mid-seventies and had become like a third set of grandparents to our girls. They'd moved to the States in the early fifties from England for the warmer climate. Harold had developed a degenerative hip disease in his late twenties, so the temperate climate eased his joint pain. Growing up, David, his brother, and their parents had spent many Sunday dinners together with his Aunt Ruth and Uncle Harold. They were their only relatives who lived nearby. Ruth and Harold couldn't have children of their own, so they all had remained close through the years.

We drove up the steep driveway to their Beverly Hills home for our monthly visit. I unbuckled the girls from their car seats and handed Emma a bouquet of flowers. She ran up and rang the doorbell of the midcentury home. When Ruth opened the double doors she said, "Well, look who's here." Her orange lipstick accentuated her wide smile. "It's so good to see you, love," she added, her English accent still thick.

Emma handed Ruth the flowers, then ran past her. We kissed each other on both cheeks. She looked her usual put-together self, with brown painted eyebrows, and her short blond hair perfectly coiffed. Ruth wore her usual weekend attire—a beige cardigan over a blue silk blouse, knit pants, and her Ferragamo heels.

Emma ran into Harold's legs for a hug. "Can we go swimming?"

Harold's warm brown eyes shone, and he replied, "Of course. Have your mum change you into your suit."

Harold loved our kids as if they were his own grandchildren. A few years earlier he'd told David and me that he and Ruth would pay for all our children's college education. That was a very generous gift, given how expensive it was to raise children.

I took the girls into the bathroom and helped them change into their swimsuits before putting on mine. Their pool took up most of the backyard of their home, which nestled into a hillside. The girls and I swam while David sat and talked to Harold on the chaise lounge chairs a few feet away. Harold wore a blue-and-white-checked shirt under his navy blue V-neck cardigan, and his walking canes were propped next to him. I overheard David say, "I'm thinking about changing positions within my company."

David was deciding if he should take a new position at a small division within his company, and he respected Harold's opinion—something he didn't have with his own father. Harold had been a successful businessman turned philanthropist—supporting Los Angeles Philharmonic, Los Angeles Opera, Center Theater Group, and a research lab in London that was looking for a cure for spinal paralysis.

We got out of the pool and changed just in time for their housekeeper, Lily, to bring out cookies, tea, and juice for the girls. Lily's homemade walnut cookies were our favorite.

Toward the end of our conversation, Harold put his arm around Ruth. "We are going to celebrate our fifty-fifth wedding anniversary this year."

Ruth's face beamed as she put her hand on his leg.

"And you will always be my bride," Harold said affectionately.

"Oh, stop it," Ruth giggled.

"Wow, congratulations. That's a milestone to celebrate," I replied as I watched Harold give her a peck on the lips. David and I had been married less than five years—fifty-five seemed like a lifetime. Their love and adoration for each other was inspirational. I wanted to adore David again, for my sake and for our family's sake. I sat there wondering what it would take for me to forgive David for making contact with Mary. I wanted to let go of the anger that was bogging me down like quicksand. It was time to move on and try to find a way to like him again, to have fun and give my marriage another chance.

Six

During the next ten years, my life was filled with tears, miracles, apprehension, joy, and marital tribulations. One challenge began with David persistently nudging me to have a third child. While Heather was a baby, I'd ignored his requests, saying, "I want to wait until Heather's two before we even discuss a third child." I was happy with our two daughters, and the thought of having three children two years apart seemed daunting. It had been almost a year since David had found my birth mother, and time had helped to heal our relationship. We'd been getting along, and even though I never received the apology I'd hoped for, it seemed that he'd seen the hurt and turmoil he'd caused me. I was grateful that he'd recognized the results of his actions, and that contributed to resolving my discontent.

One summer day, I picked up the girls early to take them to the beach. For the last two years, I'd been working as a contractor, recruiting information technology professionals for a pharmaceutical company in Irvine. That day our babysitter, Michelle, put Heather in my arms and said, "Heather used the potty for the first time today."

Michelle looked comfortable in her jean shorts and T-shirt. My silk blouse and wool skirt instantly became tight and itchy. I smiled and said, "That's so great, Heather." I kissed the top of her head as my insides twisted with envy. I wanted to be the one helping her use the potty for the first time. I could go back and have a career later in life. These special times with my girls would end soon enough as they grew up.

Before having kids, I never thought I would want to stay home with my children—I'd always planned to continue my career. I didn't want to completely rely on a man for support, but once I held Emma in my arms, I could feel the tug to stay home. When I left for work every day, I often felt conflicted.

A few weeks after Heather used the potty for the first time, I was reading in bed when I turned to David. "Maybe we should consider having that third child." The timing seemed to be right.

David sat up against the headboard and looked at me, his big brown eyes open wide. "What did you just say?"

"I'll consider having a third child if I can stay home with the kids."

The responsibility of raising our children would continue to fall on me. I didn't want resentment to linger inside me if I kept working and took care of three kids, while David dedicated his usual sixty hours a week to his job.

He looked heavy in thought. "I don't think you'll be happy staying home with the kids."

"My contract is winding down. So let me give it a try for the next couple months, and we can discuss it more."

That night we made love, letting our decision to expand our family consume us.

The next morning, David agreed with my trial period of

staying home. Over the next couple of months, we talked about the new car we'd need, hiring help one day a week, and how we'd live on one income comfortably. David put a spreadsheet together so we could see our future in black and white, and he agreed it could work out.

The first two months I stayed home were suffocating. I missed the interaction with other adults and the break it gave me from the nonstop meals, diaper changes, and entertainment I needed to provide. If I found myself in the bathroom alone without a child in tow, it became the highlight of my day, but I adjusted to this different life. I made friends through Emma's preschool and met neighborhood moms at the park. That summer, Mom and I took the kids sailing, and I did arts and crafts with the girls at home. We developed a routine, and I began enjoying my time raising my girls.

Similar to my first two pregnancies, I became pregnant a month after I stopped birth control, and at my twelve-week checkup, David joined me for my first ultrasound. I expected this ultrasound to be routine. I planned to mention my heightened exhaustion to the doctor, but I expected him to tell me it was from chasing a two- and four-year-old around. The bubbly brown-haired female technician called me in and walked us down a long hallway to a small dark room. I lay down on the table and pulled up my maternity shirt. The technician pulled out a bottle of gel and said, "This may be a little cold," then squirted it on my already large belly. I hadn't been this big at twelve weeks in previous pregnancies.

I tensed up as she moved the cold camera around my stomach. She stopped, pressed on one side, then the other. I recognized the sound of the heartbeat and took a deep breath. She continued moving it around and took pictures. She held down the camera on my stomach. "I think I hear two heartbeats."

Time slowed down as I tried to understand her words.

"Yes, look there's one here." She then moved the wand to the other side. "And here . . . congratulations . . . you're having twins." The technician's smile widened.

"What?" I was unable to compute what she was saying. How could I be pregnant with twins? I hadn't taken fertility drugs. Having twins had never entered my mind.

David sprang to his feet as his voice boomed, "Ah-ha-ha! Show me again!" A grin of pride crossed his face.

I sarcastically said, "Wait, what are you congratulating me for? I already have two children at home." Neither of them heard me.

When the doctor came into our room, I sat there numb with shock. I hadn't planned for this. *We* hadn't planned for this! How could I care for two small babies at one time? The doctor must have seen my blank face as he assured me everything was going to be okay, but he wasn't the one who'd be caring for these children.

David walked me to my car as tears streamed down my face. He asked, "Are you okay to drive?" David had come from work and we'd driven separately.

My lip quivered as I nodded yes, unable to speak. He helped me get into the car and shut my door.

Tears began to pour down my face on the car ride home. Oh, my God, what am I going to do? *Oh, my God, what am I going to do*? I remembered how hard it was caring for one newborn. How could I manage two?

Over the next several months, I'd break out in tears when

my anxiety got the better of me. I couldn't predict the time or place. Tears would come during the most inopportune times— at a restaurant with friends, at the park with another mom, or at the grocery store in aisle six. I did my best to keep my distress from Emma and Heather. I didn't want them to see me upset, but I'm sure they felt it. Every spreadsheet and conversation David and I had put together was ripped up and thrown in the trash. I was going to need full-time help, a Suburban to hold all of us, and a new attitude once these babies were born. In the meantime, I was having a pity party for one.

Normal gestation for twins is thirty-six weeks. Katie and Jessie were born at thirty-eight weeks after a difficult pregnancy. I'd put myself on bed rest for two months from a complication called TTTS (twin to twin transfusion syndrome) that fortunately corrected itself. I was hospitalized twice for preterm labor and at the time of my delivery, I had gained over fifty pounds. The last month of my pregnancy, I could barely eat, sleep, breathe, or walk, and I was ready to crawl out of my own skin with misery. Every time one of the babies' arms or legs moved, I thought my stomach might rip open. At our last doctor's appointment David suggested, "Why don't we spend a relaxing Fourth of July together as a family and then schedule the C-section."

He must have been blind. Didn't he notice my huge belly, swollen ankles, and hormonal attitude? I looked at the doctor and laughed. "When's your first available appointment for my C-section? I need these babies out now."

Our doctor grinned. "I think she's ready."

꿍

My C-section was scheduled for a few days later, and I couldn't have cared less that I'd be spending the holiday in the hospital. During the delivery, David held my hand as the twins were being born. A look of amazement crossed David's face, and then I saw a purple head above the curtain. I instantly felt nauseated, unable to enjoy the anticlimactic birth of my healthy identical twin daughters.

As the nurse laid each baby on my chest, waves of nausea passed through me. I smiled as I examined each of their tiny features—imprinting their differences in my mind. Jessie's face was thinner, and her eyes were set slightly closer. Katie's face was rounder, and she weighed almost a pound more than her identical twin sister, a result of the complications in utero. The nurses quickly swooped them away so they could be weighed, measured, and their respiratory systems checked. Those few minutes with the twins went by far too fast. I wanted to marvel a little longer at the miracles David and I had created.

During the first year of Katie and Jessie's lives, sleep became a precious commodity—neither David nor I ever had enough. I tried keeping the twins on the same feeding schedule, but once they developed chronic ear infections, there were months when I slept in two-hour increments. I tried letting them cry it out, but quickly gave in since none of us were sleeping. Mom saw my struggles and offered to help. We quickly discovered to our dismay that the twins would only allow David or me to feed and care for them.

I tried napping during the day while the nanny was there, but my to-do list of feedings, laundry, meal preparations, shopping, and drop-off and pickup times for Emma and Heather's different schools occupied me. I often wished I could purchase sleep while I was at the grocery store. I would have paid top dollar for it during the first year of Katie and Jessie's lives.

David offered to take a couple of feedings during the week to help out, but one evening at dinner he said, "I fell asleep in a meeting again today, this time with the president."

After that, he helped me with the twins only on weekend nights.

During the week after the nanny left, I was alone with all four kids until David came home, and by then the kids were asleep. There were many nights those first two years of the twin's lives that were variations of this:

After hurrying through everyone's baths, I'd sit in the rocking chair and read Katie and Jessie's favorite book, *Goodnight Moon*. Once they fell asleep, I'd put the twins in their cribs. I'd rush through reading to Emma and Heather, tuck them in before crawling into bed myself, weary from the long day. I'd turn on the TV and click through a few channels before turning it off, unable to focus on a show. Tears of sheer exhaustion would sometimes soak my pillow. I'd hear Mom's voice as I drifted off to sleep: "You are given what you can deal with, and can deal with what you are given." Many nights, it didn't seem like I was handling any of it well, rather like a robotic parent who had gone haywire without an off button. I'd close my eyes and plead with a god I wasn't sure existed: "Please allow all of us to sleep through the night and give me the strength to get through tomorrow." Some mornings I'd wake up refreshed, realizing my wish had been granted, and other mornings I'd add up the interrupted hours of sleep to see if they equaled six. If they did, I knew I could make it through another day.

I begged David several times to come home earlier to help me with the girls in the evening. He'd oblige for a few weeks before slipping back into his old routine. Frustrated after several failed attempts, I eventually stopped asking. I'd remind myself to be grateful that we had the financial means for me to stay home to raise our girls, but when David would come home late and complain about how bored he was at yet another work dinner or another business trip he had to take, a pang of sadness would bubble up. I knew he was building his career, but at times I'd wished he'd chosen more time with his family.

As the kids got older, and I was back on a better sleep schedule, I began enjoying the girls and the traditions we were creating as a family. One of those rituals was Sunday morning breakfast. David would enlist the girls to help him make pancakes and then take them to the park to play. I cherished my weekend breaks, and I loved that David wanted to spend time with our girls on his days off. The girls loved their weekends too. It was the only time they were allowed to watch television during the school year. Sunday mornings, Emma and Heather would wake up and hurry downstairs to watch *Lizzie McGuire*, one of their favorite shows. Katie and Jessie would crawl into bed with David and me and snuggle before we all went downstairs. David would pull out the ingredients for pancakes and assign each daughter a different job, rotating their responsibilities each week. One helped stir the Bisquick batter, another poured the pancake mix on the griddle, and the other two would set the table.

One day David said, "Emma, it's your turn to cook the pancakes this morning before we go to the park."

Emma hopped up from the couch and onto the step stool and said, "Don't overcook my pancakes. I like them light."

The other three sat on their stools and said in unison, "Mine too."

David helped Emma take them off the griddle before they became too brown. Emma took the plate and set it on the counter—all the girls grabbing at the lightest ones—and not one pancake was left. Heather pulled apart her pancake and said, "Look, it's ooey-gooey inside."

Katie and Jessie separated theirs too, sticking their fingers in the middle of the pancake and eating the uncooked batter inside. Katie said, "More ooey-gooey pancakes, please." Her smile widened.

The sweet smell of fresh pancakes and maple syrup, and the smiles our morning routine brought to the kids' faces on those Sunday mornings was better than any worship service I'd ever attended. There was no better way to fill my weekend mornings.

Somewhere along the way, David decided to stop wearing his wedding ring. He had gained fifteen pounds and had told me it was pressing on a nerve on his ring finger. I asked him repeatedly to wear his ring, even suggesting we could buy him a new one, but each time he found an excuse. "It's a waste of money," or, "I'm committed to you, and a ring shouldn't matter."

I wore my ring with pride. Even though I didn't sense that

he was cheating on me, it stung that he didn't want to wear his ring. Did he not view our vows the same way I did? After running out of convincing arguments, I let that go too.

As the kids became involved with organized sports, theater, dance, and volleyball, our weekends began shifting from quality time together to time apart spent on soccer fields, at Girl Scout and father–daughter YMCA Adventure Guides outings, and inside gymnasiums. We continued to divide our responsibilities and our kids' activities, but as our family time together lessened, I insisted on Sunday night dinners together, keeping some family time on the books.

David and I both had grown up in middle-class families; our fathers worked two jobs while our mothers stayed home when we were young, trying to give us a better life than theirs had been. I was thankful that we were giving our girls a better childhood than we'd had. When David and I were first married, I found it attractive that he was frugal and more responsible with our finances than Dad ever was. I used to joke, telling our friends, "There's the retail price, the sale price, the wholesale price, and then there's the James price." David took pride in his frugality, but kids were expensive, and our community had become more affluent over time. Even though our net worth continued to grow, David questioned my credit card purchases monthly. "What are you buying that's causing your credit card bill to be so high?"

I tried to appease him, justifying my purchases and my place in our marriage. When he'd ask for details, I'd walk him through the bill and explain each item, reminding him that I clipped Sunday coupons and shopped for most of the kids' clothes at Target, Gap, and Old Navy. I kept the hand-me-downs that were in good shape for the younger kids. I enjoyed the hunt of a deal almost as much as David did, but as our lives became busier, time became its own commodity. After years of this pattern, I eventually began pushing back on his questioning. "If you're looking at the bill, you can see my purchases. We are a family of six, you know." Or when I was really frustrated, I'd say, "You're welcome to do the shopping for the kids." I knew he hated shopping, and I hoped he'd stop doubting my judgment.

Many evenings when we were getting ready to go out, he'd question what I was wearing. His shopping radar was always on, wanting to know if I'd bought something new. I'd sigh and reply, "Yes," as my stomach clenched.

I wanted him to say, "You look beautiful tonight," like he used to do in the early years, but his probing would continue.

In the beginning, I'd tell him where I shopped, always pointing out that I'd purchased the item on sale and how much I'd saved, but later on, I'd take the tags off my clothes and hang them up in my closet before he came home from work. Or I'd tuck my shopping bags behind my hanging clothes. I was tired of him interrogating my purchases. Couldn't he see that I was being responsible with our money? Our financial dance strained our time together. I wanted him to trust that I had similar goals for our future as he did, and that I was his partner, not his foe.

When my girlfriends and I would get together over drinks, we'd let off steam by sharing our husbands' annoyances. I figured mine were a normal part of marriage. Little did I know that these small fissures were the early warning signs that would later shake my marriage to its core.

PART TWO

❧

Seven

One Saturday morning in April, I was sitting at my desk paying our bills before taking Heather to her American Youth Soccer Organization soccer game. At age thirteen, she still enjoyed playing recreational soccer, unlike many of her friends who'd transitioned to more competitive club teams. Startled by the ring of my phone, I saw that Nancy, Mom's best friend, was calling me.

"I don't want to alarm you, but I took your mom to the emergency room."

"What happened?" I asked, concerned. During the last year, Mom had been showing early signs of memory loss. She'd survived breast cancer and we'd just gotten her rheumatoid arthritis back under control.

Nancy continued, "She was at my house and started throwing up, then her breathing got really heavy and erratic, so I thought it was best to take her to the hospital."

"Shit. Is she okay?" Acid flooded my stomach.

"Yes, they have her resting, but you may want to come see her."

I stood up and paced around my office. Mom was too young for anything more to happen to her. Besides, I still needed her.

"I'll be there as soon as I can." I started down the hall to
my bedroom. We agreed that I'd call Dad and she'd call my
brother Will. I rarely spoke to Will outside of birthdays and
holidays, but Mom's health was in question and he had a right
to know. In that moment, I needed efficiency and help.

"Okay, that's great. I'll stay at the hospital with your mom
until you both arrive."

"Thanks," I said, somewhat relieved. "I'm so glad you were
with her."

"Me too." Nancy portrayed an unusual sense of calm instead of her normal nervousness.

David walked out of our bedroom wearing his weekend T-
shirt and khaki shorts. The twenty pounds he'd gained during
our seventeen-year marriage was noticeable. "Who was that on
the phone?"

"That was Nancy. She's at the hospital with my mom, and
I need to get out there."

"Okay, what happened?" He paused to look at me, concern
on his face.

I told him what Nancy said and turned to get ready. "Will
you watch the girls? I gotta go."

"Of course, go see your mom." He wrapped his arms
around me for a moment.

I stopped at my desk to clean up my papers before leaving.
I stood for a moment and stared out my office window, thinking about my conversation with Nancy. The trees were swaying
in the spring breeze and I suddenly felt like one of the leaves
being blown by a force I couldn't control. I didn't like what was
happening to Mom. She was too full of life for her health to
fail. Even though both of us had been sad when we sold the

sailboat four years ago, she was still eager to travel and loved staying active.

Heather walked upstairs to change for her soccer game. I explained what was going on and gave her a hug, wondering if Mom would be able to continue helping me with the girls or if this was a turning point, a change I wasn't prepared for.

After an hour's drive, I arrived at the Arcadia Methodist Hospital, the same hospital where I was born. I didn't know what to expect. As I walked into the small waiting room, I noticed the corners of the wallpaper were peeling away. There were only a few people waiting in the gray vinyl chairs. An Asian couple sat against the far corner with their two young sons, who were playing with their Teenage Mutant Ninja Turtle action figures. It was early in the morning, and I knew the room would be full by evening. The sterile smell clung to my nose and turned my stomach as I approached the registration desk. When I noticed no one was behind the glass window, my impatience set in. I needed to see Mom. Now. A young woman eventually greeted me. The few minutes I'd waited felt like a lifetime. "Can I help you?" she asked calmly.

"Yes, I'm here to see my mom, Elizabeth Byrne. She's already been admitted."

"Hold on, ma'am. Let me check." She looked at her clipboard.

"Yes, I see her paperwork here. Um, she's in bed twenty-nine, down the hall and to the left. I'll buzz you in."

My heart pounded as I grabbed the door, unsure what I was about to see. Hospitals made me queasy. I walked through the door, passed the nurse's desk, and let my eyes wander to see people behind the closed curtains. I wondered why they were there and what ailments had brought them in. I turned the corner and saw Mom in bed with her eyes closed. Her short gray hair lay flat on her head looking as if it hadn't been combed in a week. Her colorless face blended into the white pillowcase. I hugged Nancy, who looked uneasy in her denim dress and turtleneck.

Nancy had become Mom's teaching assistant after she left the convent at age forty. I'd first met Nancy when I was a teenager. She was the first nun or ex-nun I'd met, and timidity was etched into her face. She was kind, too kind, almost tripping over herself to help others. Mom was fond of Nancy, and they quickly became friends. She often celebrated birthdays and holidays with us since her only sister lived hours away. Nancy eventually went back to school and became a teacher, staying close to Mom and our family through the years.

I turned to Mom and noticed wires and tubes coming out from under the tan hospital blanket that covered her. An IV bag and monitors beeped regularly by her bedside. My nausea returned, forcing me to sit down in the chair next to her bed. As my queasiness slowly subsided, I told her I was there and held her hand. She seemed relaxed, going in and out of consciousness. Nancy stood next to her bed and held Mom's other hand.

"You got here quick," Nancy said, sounding surprised. I think she expected me to take longer. She knew my weekends were filled with activities for the children.

"Yeah, traffic was light. How is she?" I bent over the bed to give Mom a kiss on the cheek. She opened her blue eyes and gave me a dopey smile. I looked to Nancy with worry.

"Oh, they've given your mom some morphine to help with pain."

"Really?" I said, alarmed that she'd had such a strong drug. "Was that necessary?"

"It's pretty common, actually."

A curly haired nurse arrived with a machine on wheels. "I'm going to do an EKG on your mom to see if we can figure out what's going on."

The nurse hooked Mom up to even more wires. She left them on for a few minutes and then unhooked her. She left, saying she'd be back soon. Within a few minutes, my brother Will and Dad showed up. I stood up and hugged Will—noticing less stubble on top of his shaved head and his Scottish skin more wrinkled than I remembered.

Will gave Mom a soft kiss on the cheek. He said hello, and received a dopey smile in return.

I turned to Dad and put my arms around him, but he didn't hug me back. He mumbled, "Hello."

Standing a few feet from the bed, Dad turned toward Mom, waved and greeted her, but he didn't touch or kiss her. Dad rarely showed affection toward Mom. When we were young and Mom would hug Dad, he'd say, "Not in front of the kids."

Mom's eyes opened to slits and she gave him a warm smile. At seventy-eight, Dad had been carrying around an extra fifty pounds for twenty years. I was becoming more concerned about his health too, especially after his triple bypass heart surgery eight years prior. He wore his usual Dickies work pants with a blue plaid shirt that matched his eyes. Dad liked his shirt unbuttoned halfway down his stomach—a seventies trend that he had yet to give up. He wore his scar from his heart surgery like a badge of honor.

Will sarcastically chuckled, "Will you button up your shirt?" Dad shrugged his shoulders and let out a sigh, "I like it this way."

Will snickered under his breath, "We're in a hospital, not a bar."

Growing up, the only time we'd ask Dad for permission to do something was when Mom wasn't around. Even then Dad would say, "Okay, I guess, but double-check with your mother when she gets home." Dad left all the parenting decisions to Mom. He preferred to spend his free time after work in his garage sanding and refinishing furniture for friends or working on the latest room remodel in our house. It seemed that Will still held resentment toward Dad. I had tried to let mine go, accepting Dad and his shortcomings.

Will stood next to Dad with his hands tucked into the front pockets of his jeans, looking unsure of what to do.

I asked Nancy, "So now that we are all together, exactly what happened this morning with Mom?"

Nancy told us that Mom drove to her house to run errands, and Mom was running late as usual. When she finally heard Mom's car pull up, Nancy looked out her front window and noticed the right front wheel of the car on her lawn. Nancy grew more concerned as she watched Mom get out of her car and stumble up the front porch steps. She quickly opened her front door, guided Mom to the kitchen table, and helped her sit. Nancy knew something was wrong, so she made some breakfast, but Mom said she felt sick to her stomach. She ran to the bathroom and threw up. Nancy called Mom's doctor who told her to take Mom to the emergency room immediately. That's when Nancy called me.

"Well, I'm glad she was driving to your house and not to mine," I responded with a sigh of relief.

"Yes, thanks for being there, Nancy," Will chimed in.

"What did Will say?" Dad asked, moving his head closer to me to hear my response.

I checked to make sure Dad's hearing aids were in. He'd been wearing them for ten years, but he still couldn't hear.

"He was just thanking Nancy," I raised my voice.

"Oh, okay. You know I don't always hear everything and don't want to miss anything important."

Will snickered with irritation and turned away from him. "We know."

I didn't like Dad's hearing loss any more than Will. I never knew how much he actually heard, which left me with little confidence that he'd be able to care for Mom properly after she was released from the hospital.

Nancy left us, and for the next couple of hours we all took turns sitting with Mom since there wasn't room for all three of us around her bed as we waited for a doctor to give a diagnosis. I was pleased that Will and Dad were there to help. The last time David's mom was in the hospital after she took a fall, she didn't tell anyone until after she had come home. His mom said she didn't want to burden him and didn't want anyone to see her bruised face. Wasn't that what families were for? To help celebrate each other in the good times, but also to be there when times got tough.

After several hours, the doctor finally came in. "We still don't have a diagnosis for your mom, but we'd like to admit her so we can monitor her overnight and run a few more tests tomorrow."

The doctor stayed tight-lipped, but based on her symptoms, I speculated that it was a heart attack. I was relieved, knowing she would be in better hands at the hospital than at home. Leaving Dad in charge of anything important was always a crapshoot.

I looked at my watch; it was almost five in the evening. Will and Dad's eyes looked glazed over. "Take Dad home, I'll stay with Mom," I offered.

"Are you sure?" Will's face brightened.

"Yeah, it doesn't make sense for all of us to stay now that they are going to admit her. Go feed Dad, and I'll call you on my way home."

Will and Dad said their goodbyes, and I perched myself on Mom's bed and took hold of her hand. I asked her if she understood what the doctor said, but she seemed too confused from the drugs and trauma to answer. My nausea had subsided, but I still had little appetite. Mom opened her blue eyes, smiled, and squeezed my hand, mumbling something indecipherable. Tears filled my eyes and I gripped her hand tighter. This wasn't the way I envisioned Mom's later years. She was too vibrant and full of life to fall ill.

Mom had retired from being a special education schoolteacher five years earlier and enjoyed being a substitute teacher after that, picking up extra days when she could. She spent her time on the things she loved most—volunteering at her church, traveling, going on women's retreats with her friends, and visiting the girls and me.

When Mom would babysit the girls, she'd help them with their homework, make breakfast for dinner, and let them stay up late and watch TV. Those things irritated David, and they'd bothered me in the beginning, but I realized that we should let those unimportant details go. I told David, "That's the cost of having Mom watch the girls for free." David's Mom, Irene, would help out occasionally too, but Irene didn't express the same level of interest in seeing her grandchildren as Mom did.

As I waited for Mom to get transferred to her room, anguish crashed over me as if I were being swallowed whole. Mom was always so strong and insurmountable. Many years earlier, she'd pulled through a hysterectomy and a bleeding ulcer. After her recent cancer and arthritis challenges, I thought we were in the clear. What was happening?

Mom had raised Ken, Will, and me, and dealt with Ken's drug and alcohol abuse and unruly behavior since he was thirteen, all while working. Mom took care of Dad, helping him run his hardwood flooring business that had made little money for the family. When I was a teenager, she went back to school to get her master's degree so she could earn more money, and managed their two rental properties. Her older years now were her time to enjoy the life she'd worked so hard to earn. I imagined she'd grow old and beautiful, still driving out to visit me into her mid-eighties. It seemed her body was keeping the score of her life, and it felt like a cruel game. Mom had always been my lifeline and my support system. I knew there was so much more she wanted to do. Worry churned in my gut. I needed her to be well and whole, not just for her sake, but also for my family and me.

cᕒᴐ

On my drive home, I called David to let him know I was on my way. Then I called Will and gave him an update. After I hung up, I thought about our upcoming spring break trip a week away. I'd made plans to take the four girls up to our condo in Mammoth that we'd owned for the last four years. We planned on spending five days skiing, building snowmen, sledding, and having dinners with friends. David had decided to stay home and work, so I had invited my good friend Sharon and her daughter, Grace. I had also offered to let Emma and Heather's friends stay with us. Mom's sudden admittance to the hospital weighed on me. I'd made a commitment to others, and I felt overwhelmed by the sudden responsibility of the guests I'd invited and the uncertainly that lay ahead with Mom. Would I have to disappoint the girls, Mom, or me?

When I exited the off-ramp, I thought about how I'd taken to skiing at such a young age. Dad first put me on wooden skis when I was six, and I've craved flying through the snow on skis ever since. Dad had learned to ski when he was in the army stationed in Germany during the Korean War. Dad taught Mom how to ski when they first met in Wisconsin, and they decided to teach us kids how to ski too. When I was around ten, Mom and Dad decided to take us to a different ski resort every spring break. They loved to explore new ski towns and try out new resorts. I felt lucky to be the recipient of their curiosity. Dad liked to tell the story about how he taught me how to ski and within the first couple of years, I'd be waiting at the bottom of the hill for him after each run.

As I entered high school, skiing became an escape. It was

something I could do and be in complete control of myself. Skiing gave me a sense of freedom as I glided over the snow, carving a turn when I wanted, always leaving me with a grin on my face. After sailing, skiing was the other activity I could do to escape my worries as I floated along with the wind in my hair and the crisp breeze awakening me. It was a euphoric experience, and one I wanted to share with my family, just as Mom and Dad had shared those sports with me. When I was in college, instead of joining a sorority, I joined the ski team and raced at a club level for three years. After we had kids and before we bought our condo, I became a part-time ski instructor for a year, which allowed the four girls to take free group lessons. I quickly realized I preferred to teach my own girls how to ski, not someone else's whiny children.

When I walked through the front door, I found Katie and Jessie snuggled up together on the couch watching *High School Musical* with David. Heather and Emma were at sleepovers. Exhausted, I poured myself a cold glass of wine and warmed the plate of food David had left me in the refrigerator. I nestled myself in between David and Katie and let out a sigh. Katie shushed me. I kissed the top of her head and smiled at her quietly, happy to be home with my family. As I settled in, I thought about Mom alone in the hospital. Even though she probably would prefer to sleep in her own bed, I could get some rest knowing she was in better hands.

eight

The first weekend Mom was in the hospital, I phoned her internist every day to ask questions, but he'd give curt answers. He seemed annoyed and said there was no new information. After three days, we still didn't have a definitive diagnosis for Mom. Will and I had been asking Mom and Dad to find a new doctor for the last couple of years. Neither of us liked this one's wait-and-see approach to health care. We wanted a more proactive doctor, someone who would tell them what they needed to do to optimize their health as they aged.

On the fourth day, I tried a different approach. After dropping the kids off at school, I drove to the hospital to see Mom and try to get some answers from her cardiologist. He was the same doctor who had been caring for Dad since his open-heart surgery eight years prior. I timed my arrival for his rounds. I still thought Mom had had a heart attack, but I was looking for confirmation. I wanted to find a course of treatment so I could finalize my decision about the trip to Mammoth six days away.

I entered Mom's modern private room and gave her a hug and kiss, thankful that she had good insurance.

"How are you?" I asked. She looked better; her cheeks were rosy, and her eyes seemed clear.

"I'm fine. Ready to go home, that's for sure," she said with an impatient smile.

Her voice was strong, and I was happy to see that she had bathed.

"Well, let's see what the doctor says." I hoped for good news too.

She looked at me with anxious eyes. Mom never sat still for very long.

"You look a lot better than you did Saturday." I paused. "Your color is back."

"When were you here?"

I tried to appear calm. "Do you remember what happened last Saturday?"

"No, not really." She looked confused.

"Do you know how you ended up in the hospital?"

"No." She didn't seem to remember I'd been there.

I turned toward the window before she could see my uneasy expression. Nancy had warned me in the emergency room that Mom might not remember the trauma, but her lack of memory left me concerned. Her memory had been slipping during the last year. I'd found late notices scattered around their house and then their electricity was turned off. I helped her put their utility bills on auto pay. Nancy mentioned that Mom had had trouble putting on her clothes and she was struggling to find words.

I started to tell Mom what happened on Saturday when Dr. Smith, her cardiologist, walked in. His gentle demeanor immediately put me at ease. He wore a plaid coat and tie over a white dress shirt. Looking at Mom kindly, he said, "Well, how are you doing this morning, Betty?"

Mom sat up a little taller. "I'm feeling pretty good, and I'm ready to go home."

"That's good to hear, but we would like to keep you in the hospital until we can treat you. One of your arteries is ninety percent blocked and that's most likely what caused you to have a mild heart attack on Saturday. We would like to schedule an angioplasty procedure. Do you know what that is?"

We told him we didn't.

He went on. "This would involve temporarily inserting and inflating a tiny balloon where your artery is clogged to help widen it. The surgeon would then place a small wire mesh tube called a stent to help prop the artery open and decrease its chance of narrowing again."

Mom frowned and looked like she was trying to respond.

I asked, "How routine is this?"

He explained it was a standard procedure. "It has minimal side effects, and based on your mom's medical history, I don't expect any complications."

We talked about scheduling, and my tension traveled to my stomach. Mom was sensitive to medication and anesthesia, something we'd discovered from her many surgeries over the last twenty years.

The doctor went on. "I will have my staff contact you as soon as possible, but we would like your mom to stay here until then so we can monitor her."

"So, I can't go home?" Mom said with dismay, not seeming to comprehend the seriousness of her situation.

He said, "No, Betty. We would like you to stay here just in case something happens between now and the surgery."

I held my emotions in check as we discussed more details

about the procedure. As Dr. Smith was leaving he said, "Give my best to your dad."

I said I would, trying to sound cheerful, though we'd hoped for different news. I helped her settle back into her bed as we digested the details in silence.

On my way home from the hospital, I stopped at Trader Joe's to do my weekly grocery shopping. I grabbed a cart and pushed it toward the flowers, looking for something to brighten my day. I turned and saw my friend Ellie standing beside me. "How are you?" I asked her.

Ellie smiled. "I'm good. How are you?"

She had a daughter the same age as Emma, and I'd met her when our kids started kindergarten. "Well, not so great." I bit my lower lip.

"Why, what's going on?"

Tears welled up in my eyes as I told her what had happened to Mom the last few days. I was relieved to tell her my worries.

She gave me a sad look. "Oh, I'm so sorry. I hope your mom is okay."

"Me too," I replied, "I hope this isn't what I have to look forward to in my forties. I feel like I'm just starting to enjoy my freedom now that Katie and Jessie's school days are a little longer."

"I know, I'm sure it's nice now that the twins are self-sufficient and in fourth grade."

She paused in thought. "I was just talking to someone the other day about how much fun we had at your fortieth birthday party." She grinned. "You sure know how to throw a great party."

Fondly remembering it, I smiled. "Thanks, that was a really fun night."

I'd received many compliments the first few months after my party, and it felt good to know people still thought about that night. I'd thrown an eighties-themed dress-up party with a DJ playing all our favorite music from that era. Everyone dressed up in fun costumes.

As we said goodbye, I pushed my cart down the produce aisle thinking about what Ellie didn't know about that night. Only a few friends knew about my marital struggles. I had kept most of them to myself, afraid of what others might think.

The September before my birthday four years ago, I'd told David that I wanted to throw a milestone party to celebrate. I'd created the plan in my head to invite my closest friends and throw the party at our house. We could have it catered, set up some tables in the backyard, and get a DJ. David had wanted only a small family celebration for his fortieth birthday, even though I offered to do something special for him.

"Okay, what's all this going to cost?" He sent me a glance as he washed his dinner dishes at the sink.

What? Why was he putting a price tag on this? We had the money. Was he going to make a big deal of this?

"I don't know exactly. I just came up with the idea a few days ago. Why?" My face flushed. His question left me feeling the same way I did when he asked me about my clothes purchases.

"Well, get prices for everything and then let me know."

He didn't share my excitement, and I didn't like the idea of reporting back to him, but I was happy he was open to my idea. Over the next couple of weeks, I got bids from two local catering companies, I talked to DJs, and went to Costco to research prices.

Excited about my party, I assembled a handwritten outline of what the party would cost for forty couples. I methodically chose a weekend morning after we made love, he'd eaten breakfast, and the kids were being entertained in the other room. I took my list to him in his office.

"So here's the estimate for my party. Take a look." I handed it to him as he leaned back in his office chair.

He glanced at it and asked a couple simple questions. Then he said, "It seems like a lot of money to spend on a party, but if that's what you want, go ahead."

I hugged him with delight. "Thank you, it's going to be so much fun."

I hoped that when he saw how happy I was to have the party, he'd share my excitement. As I made my way downstairs David added, "I think you should add 'no gifts' on the invitation."

"Why?" I liked giving and receiving gifts.

"Because I don't think it's appropriate for an adult birthday party."

I paused, trying to understand his point of view. "I'm okay leaving that off the invitations."

I knew that in his family, gift giving had always been a challenge. Most holidays when we'd ask his mother what she wanted for Christmas or her birthday, she'd often say with a straight face, "World peace." We'd often buy her something anyway, and she'd usually return it, claiming that it didn't fit right or she didn't need it. Well, I wasn't his mother. I wanted to let my guests decide for themselves.

Over the next month, I sent out invitations, hired the DJ, and met with the catering company to finalize the menu. I rented tables, linens, outdoor heaters, and a hardwood floor to turn our family room into a dance floor. Each time I checked off a task for the party, my excitement grew.

There was still plenty to do the Saturday of my party, and I was looking forward to David's help since I'd done everything else leading up to the day. I needed a playlist for the DJ, the fall leaves from the liquid amber tree in our front yard had to be raked, and the family room furniture needed to be moved out so the dance floor could be set up. I asked David to help move the furniture. He asked, "Can't we get the rental company to do that?" His face tightened.

"No, I told them that we'd have the room cleared out." Why didn't he want to help after I'd done so much?

"Why did you tell them that?" He folded his arms, looking put out.

"Just come help me, please," I said with a frown, wanting him to be more cooperative. My head had been buzzing all morning with the to-do list, worried about getting everything done in time.

He must have felt my frustration rising because he finally said, "Okay, what furniture do we need to move?"

The party came together with minutes to spare. I wore an eighties blue crushed-velvet prom dress, teased hair, and light blue eye shadow thick on my eyelids. David wore a matching light-blue ruffled tuxedo shirt with dark-blue trim—similar to the one my high school boyfriend had worn to my senior prom. I was the prom queen and he was my king. Everything had finally come together as our first guests rang the doorbell.

My close friend Deedee and her husband, Don, were the first to arrive. Deedee and I had met at Sunkist, our first jobs out of college. David and I greeted them with a B-52 novelty shot that my friends and I used to drink back in the day. Her curly hair was teased, and her blue eyes sparkled. We hugged, and she handed me a small Tiffany bag.

"Wow, I can't wait to see what's in there," I said excitedly.

"I hope you like it," Deedee said as she hugged David. Deedee always bought me the most thoughtful gifts.

David quickly chimed in, "You didn't need to do that."

Deedee glanced at me and said, "Oh, yes I did." We giggled in unison.

"What did you get for Laurie?" Deedee asked.

I turned to David. I hadn't asked for anything, but I thought he'd get me something special to reflect my milestone birthday.

"Isn't this party enough?" he grinned before taking Deedee and Don's shot glasses from them.

Did he really not get me a gift? A flash of pain burned beneath my breastbone and I wondered if he, or they, saw the disappointment in my eyes.

The doorbell rang again, and I quickly pushed my hurt aside. I wasn't going to let David's thoughtlessness spoil the evening. Everyone began to arrive in their creative costumes. A group of friends dressed like the band DEVO, another friend as Tom Cruise in *Top Gun*. The best costume was Richard

Simmons, wig and all. Most of the women dressed up like Madonna with short skirts, black tank tops, ripped fishnets, and teased hair in high ponytails. One girlfriend arrived in an old purple eighties thong leotard and black tights looking ready for an aerobics class. Another wore a vintage floral Laura Ashley dress with puffy sleeves that she'd found in the back of her closet.

I bounced around the party, fueled by adrenaline and vodka as I greeted my guests. I introduced friends to each other, and made sure everyone had a drink and felt included, as we danced to Prince, Chaka Khan, Sugar Ray, Cyndi Lauper, and A Flock of Seagulls.

I took a break from the dance floor to see my good friend Sharon. She had a bag of flour from my pantry in her hand and giggled. "What are you doing with that?" I laughed curiously.

"Shhh, watch this," she whispered.

She poured a small amount onto my glass coffee table, pulled out a credit card and made small thin lines. She asked if I had a straw. I found one in the kitchen and set it next to the flour. "Oh, my, you are so bad," I roared. It looked like lines of cocaine.

"Let's watch the expressions on people's faces as they walk by."

We laughed as people's heads jerked back to take a second look. We reminisced about the stupid things we'd done during the eighties and reflected on how lucky we were to be alive.

Toward the end of the evening the cake appeared, champagne was passed around, and then David made a toast, "To my beautiful wife: happy eleventh anniversary of your twenty-ninth birthday. I love you very much."

He turned to kiss me before taking a sip of champagne. Everyone laughed and toasted me. My heart pounded. "Thank you for making my birthday special and helping me celebrate. You all mean so much to me." I kept my comments short, uncomfortable speaking in front of crowds.

My happy evening flew by. Our guests started to leave around eleven, and our house was empty by midnight. David went straight to bed, but I couldn't sleep even though I was exhausted. I began cleaning up so we'd have less to do in the morning. On my way upstairs I stopped and looked at all my presents sitting on a table in our living room. Warmth filled me as I thought about all the friends who'd helped me celebrate my birthday. But then the pain from earlier that night returned as I looked through my gifts. I wanted a gift from David to be in the center of all the others, the one I'd be most excited to open. It would have meant so much more than all the others, because it was from the man I loved who had professed his love to me. Did those words not mean as much to him as they did to me? My sadness deepened as I took off my dress and climbed into bed. I lay there, trying to justify David's decision not to buy me a gift. When he reached out his hand to touch me, I pushed it away. Maybe he had seen the sadness in my eyes when he said he hadn't bought me a gift, and he'd get me one on my actual birthday, which was still two weeks away. I drifted off holding onto that thought.

That day after talking to Ellie, I loaded my car after checking out of Trader Joe's, and the tears that I'd held back while shopping began to fall. When I got home, I scrubbed the refrigerator and put away the groceries as I thought about how David and I professed our love so differently now compared to when we'd first dated. In the beginning, we'd bought each other thoughtful gifts and made an effort to spend quality time together. Now he seemed to profess his love in a way I couldn't grasp—not buying me a fortieth birthday gift or taking any initiative to help plan my party. When had he changed? Unable to pinpoint an event, I pushed the thought aside. I continued my cleaning binge as I sorted out my pantry and moved to the more pressing issue: what was I going to do about my upcoming trip to Mammoth and who should I put first, my mother or my family? I scrubbed and organized until everything was in perfect order, yet I still didn't have clarity on what to do.

nine

Days passed with no decision on whether to go to Mammoth or stay for Mom's surgery. The girls and our friends had planned the trip months ago, and we were all looking forward to a much-needed break. I wanted to split myself in half so I could be there for both. I talked with Nancy, Will, and the voices in my head until I made the decision to go to the mountains. Nancy and Will assured me they'd take good care of Mom. When I called Mom to tell her I wouldn't be there, she sounded strong. "I want you to enjoy your trip with your girls. Don't worry about me, I'll be fine."

When I hung up the phone, I worried that I was disappointing her, but she'd never admit it.

The Sunday morning we left, I decided to stop by the hospital on my way up to Mammoth to ease my guilt and so she could see the girls. All six children—my four and two of Emma and Heather's friends—piled into my Suburban. David stood by the driver's side door, and I reached up to kiss his brown freckled face. The gray from his temples had spread throughout his hair. "Drive safely and say hi to your mom for me," he said. We were all getting older, like it or not.

༄

As I drove to the hospital, I yearned for David's companionship on my trip. I'd become good at juggling many things at once, but over time my responsibilities at home had begun to weigh on me. When I decided to stay home to raise our kids, I knew we were dividing our family responsibilities, but along the way, the division between us had grown too large. I had imagined that we'd come together in the evenings after our long days apart and find solace with each other, sharing the good and bad stories about our days. I envisioned these moments would reunite us, but that was not our current pattern. Instead, I'd sit down for dinner with the kids and leave a plate of food for David. By the time he got home from work, the kids would often be in bed, and we were both tired. He would eat his dinner in front of the TV, and I'd either watch TV with him or go upstairs. Rarely did we find time to connect.

David was a good weekend dad. He helped me take the girls to soccer games and birthday parties, and checked off my honey-do list of handyman work, but I wished that he wanted to be more involved with the girls' activities. I thought he'd make a good soccer coach or a YMCA Adventure Guides leader and be more engaged with our kids. He had strong leadership qualities. He sat on the board of a credit union and managed more than a dozen people at work, but every time I'd bring up these ideas, he'd tell me he couldn't commit with his long hours. So I became the assistant soccer coach and the Girl Scout leader. While I enjoyed volunteering my time and being involved in the girls' activities, I wondered what had happened to the sense of togetherness we'd had when the kids were younger and we'd spent more family time together.

On the way to the hospital my thoughts vacillated between the gap that had grown between David and me and my worry about Mom's health. I felt like I was carrying a five-pound sandbag in each pocket. I tried to guide my thoughts to all the good things in my life: I had four healthy kids and a beautiful home. I lived close to the beach, and we were on our way to our vacation home in Mammoth. I was blessed with great friends, but I wanted my partner to choose his family over his job more often than he did. Sometimes our separateness left me feeling ungrateful for what I had. If it continued to grow, would we find our way back to each other?

We arrived at the hospital, and when all seven of us walked into the elevator, a white-haired elderly woman looked at me with wide eyes. "Are all these kids yours?"

I chuckled. "Four of them are mine and two are friends." The woman shook her head in amazement.

"Wow, four beautiful daughters? You have your hands full."

"Yep," I smiled, feeling the truth of a comment that was often made by others.

As we walked into Mom's room, her face lit up, and she quickly put her glasses on to see everyone better.

"Well geemenently!" she said, grinning from ear to ear. "Come in, come in. Now come give me a hug and kiss." *Geemenently* was one of Mom's favorite words to use when she was excited to see someone.

She had been in the hospital for a week, and on each visit she looked better. She had more strength in her voice and in the grip of her arthritic hands. Her IV had been taken out, and she wore only a heart monitor.

"Heather, come sit next to me and tell me how school is going," Mom said, patting her hospital bed.

Heather made her way past Katie and Jessie and sat next to Mom. At thirteen, her braces protruded from her big smile. Her freckles spread from her button nose across her cheeks, and her long brown hair flowed down her back. Awkward or not, she was always a happy kid and brought me joy.

"School is great, and I'm taking French this year. Seventh grade is the first year we can take a foreign language, and I really like it," she said eagerly. "I'm also going to be in a play in May. If you're feeling better, will you come see it?"

Curious about their conversation, Katie and Jessie bounced over to the other side of Mom's bed, heads bobbing with matching brown ponytails. "We're in the show too. I hope you can make it," Katie chimed in, and Jessie nodded in agreement.

"I wouldn't miss it for the world." Mom grabbed Jessie's hand and held it.

I looked across the room and saw Emma and her friend Tara sitting in chairs next to the window, their heads almost touching as they texted and giggled.

"Emma, come here and tell Grammie about your recent trip to Atlanta with your volleyball team."

Emma was fifteen and scowled at me for interrupting, then put her phone in her back pocket and started telling Mom about the trip and her team, looking excited and vibrant as she relayed how their team had done better than they'd expected.

Mom asked each of the girls questions and listened intent-
ly, showing interest in all their activities. Watching all the kids
visit with Mom confirmed it had been the right decision to
stop by on our way to the mountains. After an hour, I told the
girls to say their goodbyes, and I saved mine for last. I stood
there seeing how life had defined her face, with wrinkles
around her mouth that spread to her pink cheeks. I leaned in
to give her a hug and kiss, stroking her soft skin.

I looked into her eyes. "I'm sure everything will go
smoothly, and I'll check in with Will and Nancy regularly. Love
you." A lump sat in my throat. I wasn't sure I believed my own
words. Would everything go smoothly?

"I love you too. You have fun with the girls, and I'm in
good hands," she said confidently.

"Okay." Tears welled in my eyes. I hoped there was truth in
her words.

I walked behind the kids, wiping the tears off my face before I met them at the elevator. I wanted them to enjoy their
trip and be protected from my worries. The elevator opened
and we all got in, beginning the week-long adventure we'd
looked forward to for so long.

The Sierras came into view after a few hours of driving. The
snow-capped mountains grew larger as we approached Lone
Pine. Small white clouds sat on top of the jagged peaks like
tiny cotton balls against the deep blue sky. I looked in my
rearview mirror and saw the girls' heads huddled together
watching *High School Musical 2*. When Mom and Dad used to
take Ken, Will, and me on ski trips, we didn't have DVD play-

ers to entertain us. We played car games like the alphabet game or I spy. Sometimes Will and Ken would play with me, but more often than not, I'd play a game with Mom or play the alphabet game by myself. My girls seemed far more confident than I was at their age. As I watched them laughing and having fun, I thought back to my own childhood.

I felt out of place in my family as I was growing up, and I didn't belong in my neighborhood either. El Monte had been a middle-class community when Mom and Dad bought their house back in the late fifties. By the time I reached high school, the area had turned primarily Hispanic, with run-down front yards and gangs nearby. Ken had dropped out of school when he was a sophomore, and within a year Mom and Dad kicked him out of the house after he'd been arrested for stealing and dealing drugs. It wasn't long before he moved back home. Will worked first at the local liquor store, and then got a job at Vons. He ignored me during our high school years together, acting as if he didn't have a younger sister, which left me mostly on my own.

When I was old enough to stay home by myself, I'd rummage through Mom's dresser drawers in her bedroom looking at old pictures, cards, and small gifts she had saved. I was searching for clues about who I was and where I fit into my odd family. It was a cycle. When I was unsuccessful, I'd give up for a while, only to resume my curious searching again later.

The summer before high school, Mom and Dad moved their dresser into our den, next to the new sewing machine I'd received as my eighth-grade graduation gift. I'd learned how to sew from Helen Stiles, a family friend and wife of John, who'd taught Mom and Dad how to sail. I liked the creativity of going to the fabric store, picking out material, and making the latest fashion trend my own. Back then I could make the clothes I wanted cheaper than I could buy them.

One day after summer school, I went into the den to finish sewing the gauze drawstring pants I'd been working on. When I was done, my curiosity was piqued again, and I began digging through the dresser I hadn't looked through in years. I opened the bottom left drawer that held Mom's keepsakes and began sifting through the same cards and pictures I'd seen so many times before. A stack of cards tucked in the back corner caught my eye. I pulled a card out of the envelope that was decorated with a baby rattle—the paper had begun turning yellow.

"Dear Betty, Congratulations on your new baby girl, Julie."

I caught my breath. Who was baby Julie? Mom and Dad never mentioned a baby named Julie, but neither of them talked much about our adoptions. I tried to remember when Mom and Dad had told us we were adopted, but my memory was cloudy. This couldn't have been Mom's stillborn. They wouldn't have named the baby yet. I knew Mom had a hard time when she lost her first baby, so I didn't dare bring it up.

Did they change my name from Julie to Laurie? When was this baby brought into their lives? There weren't any dates on the card. My thoughts were coming so fast I felt dizzy. What should I do? I tried to rewind the last few minutes by quickly closing the card, stuffing it back in the envelope, and shoving it in the back corner under all the pictures. I put my hand over my mouth and sat there, trying to make sense of what I had just discovered.

Curiosity got the best of me, so I opened another card, which had a similar message. I continued to dig through the drawer looking for more clues, finding more cards and then a picture of a baby girl. I studied it for a while before flipping the picture over—this child didn't look like me. The baby was smiling, dressed in a pink-and-white gingham dress with chunky arms under her lace sleeves. She had a big smile on her face as if someone were cooing at her. On the back of the picture I read Mom's handwriting: "Baby Julie, 5 ½ months." Did I have my facts wrong? Was this the baby Mom and Dad had lost? How had I missed this in the past? I felt like a steam engine had just rolled over me. How could I tell Mom that I'd been snooping through her drawers and then ask questions about this mystery baby girl? I couldn't even ask her about her stillborn baby she'd lost at eight months gestation before adopting us.

Over the next several months, I thought about the cards and picture and tried to come up with a way to approach Mom. I thought this new information could bring me closer to understanding who I was and how I came into my family, but I never got the courage to ask her. Throughout my adolescence, I searched for more connection with my siblings and Mom and Dad. I tried to feel like it was *my* family, but I was never successful. I didn't want to bring more pain into Mom's life by asking her about something she had kept private. Besides, she always had her hands full trying to parent us kids, managing Ken's unruly behavior, teaching, and helping Dad manage his business.

My desire to know about baby Julie slowly faded through my high school years. I became more absorbed in navigating school, friends, parties, and boys. I often wondered if Will knew about baby Julie or Mom's stillborn, but after years of him ignoring me during high school, my bruised heart kept me from asking him. I needed my older brother to look after me, not discount me. After Will graduated, and I became an upper classman, I spent less time thinking about baby Julie and the way Will had treated me in high school and more about how to get out of El Monte and create a better life for myself. Graduating with a four-year degree, moving to the beach, marrying David, and enjoying the family we'd created reflected my success.

I looked back at my girls as they finished their movie, giggling about their favorite parts. I smiled, remembering when they'd all play house or school together with the neighborhood kids. As they grew into preteens and teens, they spent more time with their friends than each other and fought about wearing each other's clothes or whose turn it was to clean up after dinner. I'd often tell them that the longest relationship they'd ever have was with their siblings, so make it count. As the girls became more independent with school, homework, and outside activities, I continued to look for ways to bring our family together. Teaching the girls how to ski before they were six was one of those ways, like Dad had taught me. I wanted to take what Mom and Dad had created for my brothers and me and build upon it, forming unity in our family and teaching them a lifelong sport they'd be able to enjoy for decades. I wanted my girls to have what I didn't have growing up—connection, confidence, and a more secure family, one they could always count on.

ten

The morning after we arrived in Mammoth, I woke up early and smiled. We had five days of skiing ahead of us and little responsibility. I walked upstairs and weaved through the well-worn furniture in our living room. The girls' Monopoly game from the night before was still spread out on the game table, waiting to be played.

"Good morning," Sharon said as she poured herself a cup of coffee. She wore paisley-print flannel pajamas and her blond hair in two ponytails.

"It looks like it's going to be a beautiful day," I exclaimed, standing in front of our large window looking out at the ski runs that the sun was already warming. The mountain still had plenty of snow that spring. I always welcomed being in Mammoth's fresh air, a nice change from Los Angeles's smoggy sky.

Sharon and I scrambled eggs, made pancakes, and talked while the kids slept.

"I can't believe it's been nine years since I met you at that Christmas party," she chuckled.

"Has it been that long already?"

"Yeah, I'll never forget how crazy red your eyes were and how wiped out you looked." She laughed. We often reminisced about that night.

We had met at a mutual friend's Christmas party. Katie and Jessie were one and a half years old, and I was elated to have a night out. I put on a two-year-old holiday dress, eye shadow, and lipstick, and felt more put together than I had in a long time. David and I each grabbed a glass of wine and walked over to a friend who was engaged in a conversation with another couple. Our mutual friend introduced David and me to Sharon and her husband, Sam. I'd seen Sharon at the park with her daughter, who looked similar in age to my twins. Sharon wore a sleek, modern black dress with a zipper down the front, boots, and funky jewelry.

Sharon's eyes suddenly lit up. "Oh, my God, you're the gal who's always pushing the red double baby jogger around town."

Every day, I took Katie and Jessie for a walk and to the park, sometimes twice a day. We'd all get our exercise, and when we came home, the girls played happily with their toys while I made dinner. During those early years, I was still trying to keep my head above water, and our routine helped maintain my sanity and theirs.

Our mutual friend laughed, and I wondered what Sharon was thinking.

"Yes, that's me." I hesitated. I was giddy to be out for the evening. Could she see how desperate I was for adult interaction? I examined my dress to make sure it wasn't stained from baby food or milk.

"I thought I recognized you," she said, smiling warmly.

The four of us talked and laughed for the next hour, commiserating about the struggles of sleepless nights, diaper changes, and spit-up. David and I mingled with other friends, and as we were leaving, we ran into them again at the door.

"It was great meeting you tonight. I hope to see you around," Sharon said, smiling.

"I'll see you at the toddler park," I exclaimed with a laugh.

After that, we exchanged hellos when I saw her around town, but it wasn't until her daughter, Grace, was enrolled in the same preschool class as the twins that we became closer friends. Our girls clicked as soon as they met, and Sharon and I followed suit. Since then, we'd spent hours at the park and the beach, and recently had begun traveling to Mammoth together. With little time to foster new friendships, we found our relationship a welcome surprise.

At Mammoth that morning after we finished making breakfast, I woke the kids up. One by one, they slowly made their way to the breakfast table. I announced, "Okay, after we're finished with breakfast, no dillydallying. Let's get our gear on and get some runs in before it gets slushy."

I set the tone for the day so we'd get on the mountain while the snow was still good and before it got too crowded.

Heather grumbled as she pushed her pancakes and eggs around in the syrup on her plate.

"Are you okay?" I asked. She struggled with altitude sickness and often needed a day to adjust.

"I don't know," she replied, staring at her food.

I kissed her head as she sat curled up in her chair. She looked pale, and we agreed it would be best if she stayed at the condo that day. I was thankful she was my independent child since I was eager to get back on my skis.

When we got to the lodge, Emma quickly took off to meet up with her friends from school—she knew the mountain well. I found Sharon, Grace, and the twins in line for the chairlift. The girls huddled with their black helmets touching, giggling with happiness.

We loaded ourselves on the chairlift, and I looked at my watch. My heart sank, realizing Mom was probably being prepped for her surgery. Jessie said something and I didn't answer.

"Laur, are you okay?" Sharon asked, putting her hand on my arm.

"Yeah, sorry. Mom's about to go into surgery."

I put my arm around Jessie and gave her a squeeze—something Mom often did on the chairlift when I was Jessie's age. Mom would wiggle closer to me so I could snuggle under her purple down ski jacket and stay warm in the frozen air. She'd grin and say, "Hee-hee, isn't this so beautiful?"

I'd agree with her, but it took me until my late thirties to truly appreciate the beauty of the outdoors. Jessie and the girls seemed to enjoy it more than I did at their age.

As we got off the lift I asked, "Okay, which way, girls?" I let them decide where they wanted to ski. They deserved to have some control over their vacation. I zipped along, enjoying the soft spring snow and the cool mountain air brushing past my cheeks. I stopped at the bottom of the run, watching the girls ski in my tracks, Katie right on my tail.

"That was a fun run," I said zealously.

Katie smiled, "Can we do that one again?"

"Sure." I grinned as I saw the same joy that skiing brought me written across her face.

I guided Grace and the twins around the mountain, taking them on all their favorite runs like Round Robin, Roller Coaster, and Swell. I reached the bottom first and saw their confidence grow with each run. After lunch, I checked my phone on every chairlift ride up, waiting for word from Will. Why hadn't he called yet? Mom should have been in recovery by then.

By three thirty, we were back at the condo and I still hadn't heard from Will, so I called him and asked how it went.

He sighed. "Not that well, Sis."

"Shit." I bit my nails and looked over at Sharon. A flash of concern crossed her face. I was glad she was with me and understood my worry about Mom.

Will went on. "They just brought Mom out of recovery, and she's not doing well. She's extremely disoriented, thrashing around, trying to get out of bed, and trying to pull her IV out of her arm. They finally had to sedate her and strap her to the bed. I couldn't believe it," Will rambled, sounding upset.

I was instantly filled with regret that I'd left her. "You're kidding me. What happened? Was the surgery successful?"

"We're still waiting for the doctor to come talk to us." I could hear he was worried too.

"Do you want me to come home?"

"No, let's just wait to hear from the doctors and see how Mom's doing, then decide."

We agreed to check in later, after he talked to the doctors. I threw my phone down on the bed and stared out the window. What had gone wrong? This wasn't supposed to happen. A scrub jay landed on the aspen tree outside the window and flew off again. I wished I could be that blue jay and fly away from my mounting guilt. Even though my presence wouldn't have changed the outcome of her surgery, I longed to be there to comfort her when she woke up.

For the rest of the night, I put on a good face, made dinner for the kids, and played games, keeping my phone close. Will finally called around nine as he was leaving the hospital. He told me Mom's surgery hadn't been successful. The surgeon couldn't get the stint into her artery because it was too small. Mom was calmer now from the sedation, but a nurse would be stationed in her room for the night to make sure she didn't pull her IV out or wander around the hospital.

A wave of helplessness crashed down on me. I wished I could be like Samantha on *Bewitched*—twitch my nose and be home with Mom.

We agreed to talk in the morning and decide then when I should come home. I called David as soon as I hung up and told him the latest news.

"I'm sorry. So what are you going to do?" I could hear him eating his dinner.

"Will and I are going to see how Mom is doing in the morning and make a decision then."

"Okay, let me know tomorrow." He spoke with a flat voice. He seemed distant, and I could hear him turn the page of the newspaper.

A flash of hurt settled in my gut as I hung up. I knew he couldn't solve my problem, but why couldn't he say, "I'm here for you" or "What can I do to help?" or something sincere. I knocked on Sharon's door looking for a more sympathetic ear, and she invited me in. I sat on the end of her bed, venting my frustrations as she put her book down on the nightstand. I knew she'd help fill the emptiness like she had so many times before.

The next morning, I acted like nothing was wrong, even though uncertainty had me tossing and turning much of the night. I set out for another day on the mountain, wearing my false cheerfulness on my face. I tried to keep the kids' vacation fun while Mom's reaction to her failed surgery occupied my mind.

I'd just pulled into a parking spot when my phone rang. A sinking feeling came over me. It was Dr. Shan, Mom's internist. He usually called in the evenings.

"Your mother had complications during her surgery, and she's not doing well." His thick Indian accent was hard to understand.

"What kind of complications?" I needed details.

He quickly reiterated the same story Will had told me the night before and added, "I just made my rounds, and she's still very confused this morning."

"So there's no real change since last night?" I gripped the steering wheel tighter as I sat in the parking lot.

"No, not really." His voice was solemn.

"What do you think is causing her confusion?"

Sounding impatient as usual, he said, "Well, sometimes this can happen with people who are suffering from memory impairment. Surgery and anesthesia can make it worse."

"I'm sorry, what?"

"Yes, it's not uncommon for this to happen."

I was stunned by his remark. Why hadn't the doctors warned us? Dr. Smith had assured me everything was going to be okay. Dr. Shan knew Mom had been showing early signs of dementia and confusion—he'd been my parents' doctor for years.

I continued asking Dr. Shan questions as they popped into my head, and each time his answers were shorter. He then began adding "Okay?" signaling me that he wanted to wrap up the call. I despised feeling like an inconvenience after our calls. Through the last several years with him, it seemed to me that he lacked respect for women, and I'd witnessed him responding differently to Will and Dad than to Mom and me.

I hung up the phone and slid lower in my seat. "Shit!" I banged on the steering wheel. I looked around my car to see if anyone had heard my embarrassing outburst. Now what? If only we'd switched internists sooner.

I got out of the car and put my ski boots on, stewing in anger. Then it dawned on me—this wasn't the first time Mom had had problems with anesthesia. How was it that I hadn't put these pieces together sooner? I felt so stupid.

I thought back. When Mom was in her early fifties and I was about twenty, she'd had emergency surgery for a bleeding ulcer. The doctor said it was from taking too much Ibuprofen for her arthritis. Over the next six months, she'd suffered mild memory loss and dyslexia, which the doctor had attributed to the anesthesia. My guilt for not remembering this stung deeper. This was my fault now. What had I done?

I caught up with Sharon and the girls and skied with them the rest of the day, but my mind was disconnected from my body. I went through the motions of the day, but I was stuck in a dark forest. I wanted to find my way out and make my way home. If only I could rewind the past week. I put my fake smile back on and tried to enjoy the snow, the girls, and my friend. I hoped my girls didn't know it was an act.

eleven

My daughters stayed behind in Mammoth while I drove into the eye of the storm toward home. Sharon had offered to stay at our condo with the twins and Heather while Emma stayed with a girlfriend and her family. That morning, I left before dawn for my six-hour drive down Highway 395 toward Los Angeles. I planned to meet Will, Dad, and Nancy at the hospital around eleven. When I reached Bishop, the sun rose and turned the white snow-capped mountains shades of yellow and pink. I was one of the only cars on the road, and I found my eyes wandering to the colorful peaks reflecting the morning sun. The stark desert dotted with yellow and purple wildflowers surrounded the pristine mountains. It was my favorite time of year to make the drive, and the view helped to distract me from my unruly thoughts. I was ruminating about Emma stealing my vodka the night before, which added another layer of worry. Fifteen was too young to drink. I'd hoped she would be more in tune with Grammie's hospital visit and my concerns for her. I told Emma she'd have a week of restriction when she returned home. I hoped this wasn't an early warning sign of what might come through the rest of her high school years.

As I admired the vast landscape, my mind drifted to my oldest brother, Ken, and his ongoing problems with drugs and alcohol. It seemed strange, but I was thankful that he was currently serving time in prison. I didn't need him to get wind of Mom's health issues and have him complicate our lives like he had done in the past. Will and I had recently helped Mom and Dad obtain a restraining order against Ken. Between his anger issues and his drug use, Will and I wanted to make sure he didn't prey on our parents as they got older. The only time Ken had stopped drinking and doing drugs since he was a teenager was when he was incarcerated. His current drug of choice was meth, and he'd recently been living on the streets. He couldn't make it through the court-supervised rehab program that would have wiped his felonies from his record, so the court had sent him to prison.

My mind meandered into the darkness of my youth and the turmoil Ken had caused our family. He'd struggled in school since kindergarten, and his problems only grew as he got older. Mom would get calls from his teachers throughout grade school telling her that Ken had picked a fight that day or had disrupted class. When I snooped through Mom's drawers, I found one of his old report cards with Ds and Fs in most subjects and unsatisfactory marks in all areas of citizenship. His grades made me feel better about Bs and Cs on my report card.

As Ken grew up, Mom and Dad continued to worry about the direction he was taking. When he was eleven, they asked for a psychological evaluation, which recommended that Ken continue with extra educational support, behavior modification, and counseling. If those didn't work, medication might help to manage his inability to focus. I don't believe they ever medicated him, and shortly after that, he started self-medicating with alcohol and marijuana.

In Ken's early teens, his angry outbursts increased. Once, I threatened to tell on him for drinking in the den with his buddies when Mom was paying him to watch me. He ordered me to stay in my room, and I told him, "You can't tell me what to do."

Before I knew it, he had picked me up and thrown me against my bed by the window. His aim was off, and I hit the pillow that was between the bed and the window. If I'd landed a few inches higher, the force of my body would have broken the glass.

A few years later, Ken punched Will in the mouth. Will had braces, and the blow impaled his lips. Blood dripped down the sides of his mouth as Mom rushed him to the orthodontist, and it took weeks for his mouth to heal. I didn't have braces, but I feared Ken's wrath just the same.

When I was twelve, I still looked like a little girl—flat as a board and skinny. I had a November birthday so I was the youngest in my class and a late bloomer. I prayed for boobs and curves, but every morning when I'd look at my chest I'd sulk, not seeing any difference from the day before. I wanted to develop like the other girls in school so I could fit in, but I didn't want it bad enough to go to the measures Giovanna Tabone did in eighth grade. One day she was as flat as I was and the next day she had lumpy boobs under her tight T-shirt. We all assumed she'd stuffed her bra with toilet paper and the boys teased her until she couldn't take it any longer. She didn't come back to school for a week after that.

The next year, Ken stopped calling me by my childhood nickname "Boo-Boo" that John Stiles, our sailing friend, had given me when I was a toddler, and started being nicer to me. He was almost seventeen, and he looked like a man with his facial hair and bulky muscles. That year as I began to develop, Ken would joke with me, letting his eyes travel from my head to my toes. He would tell me I looked cute, and an uncomfortable chill traveled down my spine. Sometimes at night, he'd come into my bedroom and ask me about my girlfriends—what were they up to and if they had boyfriends. He'd tell me to invite them over more often and let him know when I did. I liked that he was being nicer, but his overtures left me feeling exposed, as if I'd forgotten to put on my shirt before leaving for school. My friends told me they didn't want to come over anymore because Ken gave them the creeps. I began to regret my changing body and I wished things could go back to the way they were before. I started spending more time at my friends' houses. When Mom would ask me why my friends didn't come over, I'd tell her there was nothing to do there or that we were going to listen to Rod Stewart at my best friend Margaret's house down the street.

That spring Mom and Dad took us to Colorado for our annual ski trip. My father drove the twenty-two-foot Winnebago motor home we'd bought from Grandma Olive, his mom. I still liked our family ski trips, but after the shift between Ken and me, I was unsure what to expect. As the trip began, I claimed my space in front of the van sitting on top of the engine cover between Mom and Dad. Ken and Will were in the back seats.

We arrived in the town of Aspen after our two-day drive. The streets were lined with high-end ski shops and restaurants that were too fancy for our budget. Traveling in our motor home, Mom only allowed us to take what she called "a poor man's bath." We'd use a washcloth to clean our pits and private parts only, and stop at a hotel to take a real shower every couple of days. We stopped at the first hotel that had a "vacancy" sign. This hotel was more beautiful than the usual Motel 6. We walked into the room admiring the dark beams protruding from the white ceiling. There were rustic tables carved out of wood and a stuffed deer hanging above the couch. The large one-bedroom suite had a small kitchenette and pullout couch. The headboard in the bedroom was made from logs with a white and black Native American rug covering the hardwood floor. Will smirked and said, "Wow, this must be how other people travel." We all laughed.

The following day after skiing, we all came back to the hotel. I watched TV in Mom and Dad's room waiting for my turn to take a shower. My parents had decided to walk around the town and stop for a beer. None of us kids wanted to go and be bored, so we stayed in our hotel room. Shortly after Mom and Dad left, Ken came into the room. "What are you doing in here?" His glance left me with a level of unease I'd never felt before.

"Watching TV," I replied. I locked eyes with Will, who was sitting on the couch in the other room, as Ken shut the door. My body froze as acid flooded my stomach. I stared at the TV so hard I tuned out his small talk. I quickly glanced at him as he walked toward the bed, sat down next to me, and asked, "Can I watch TV with you?"

My mouth moved with no sound—my words were stuck in my throat. I wished I could run to my best friend Margie's house down the street like I had done so many times before when Ken threatened me. I couldn't move, and before I knew it, he was lying next to me under the covers. I moved to the other side of the bed and felt his hand pull me toward him. I tried to pull away but he pulled me closer. What did he want? Before I knew it, he was on top of me sticking his tongue down my throat. Gross. I tried turning my head away but he yanked it back toward him.

"Just relax," he said. I tried to yell but his tongue was in my mouth and his body was pinning me down. My eyes pleaded with him to let me go, but he was determined. He held me down with one hand on my chest and unzipped his pants with the other. He pulled my pants down around my ankles and lay on top of me and pinned my arms down to the mattress. He planned to go all the way with me. I felt his gross warm penis on my stomach and realized what was about to happen. I knew what sex was and knew that this was *all* wrong. I tried to resist his strength as he slowly forced my legs open. I fought him, but couldn't get away. He was too strong.

He said, "This will be easier if you don't fight me."

His vein pulsed in his neck as he pushed his penis inside me. I closed my eyes. Tears of defenselessness rolled down my temples as his body thrust into mine. He continued on and kissed my closed lips. I turned my head so I didn't have to kiss him. I wasn't his girlfriend. I quickly became sore from his thrusting, and even though he was inside me for only a matter of minutes, it felt like hours. He finally let out a cry and stopped. By thirteen, I was aware of what this was. I knew I couldn't get pregnant—I hadn't started my period yet.

When he was done, he gave me a peck on the cheek, as if to thank me. A prickly feeling ran across my skin. I squeezed my eyes shut and pulled the covers over me. My eyes were on him as I lay in a ball paralyzed like a spider poisoned by its prey, glad that my nightmare was over but afraid of when he would strike again.

"Oh, and if you tell Mom or Dad about what just happened, I'll beat the shit out of you." His hazel eyes pierced me. He zipped his pants. I knew his threat was real, and I hated him for that. I hated him for touching me and forcing me. It was all so wrong, but I knew if I'd fought him, it would have only made my life more difficult.

As he opened the door, I peeked out at Will. He was fourteen and my gut told me he knew what had happened. I wanted Will to protect me, but his eyes told me he felt helpless too.

After Ken left, I ran to the shower to scrub him off me. I felt violated, scared, and confused. Tears streamed down my face, washing me from the inside out. Why did he do this to me? He was my brother, and he was supposed to look out for me. Did this mean I was no longer a virgin? I felt silenced and so alone.

The rest of the trip, I stayed close to Mom and Dad. I skied when they skied, I sat next to Mom at lunch, and only left the engine cover to pee or grab food the entire ride home. Telling Mom or Dad wasn't an option. I guessed they might defend him and not believe me, like they had in the past. I feared for my safety when my parents weren't around.

Over the next couple of years, Ken approached me a few more times, but I dodged his advances. He spent less time at home after Mom and Dad kicked him out for his delinquent behavior. When he did stop by the house, I avoided him, and the handful of times I found myself alone with him, I left the room or walked to my friend's house down the street.

The only other time he came close was the summer before I turned sixteen. Mom and Dad were gone and I was cleaning out the motor home for our next trip, when Ken walked up the driveway. He stood in front of the motor home doorway and the only exit. He had *that* look in his eye and I instantly felt powerless. I thought about how I could get around him as he made small talk with me. I replied with short answers. He stepped inside the motor home. "So, I was wondering if you've started your period yet?"

My palms became sweaty and my heart palpitated. "Yeah, about six months ago," I lied. I'd had one light period by then. I was a late bloomer. Looking deflated, he turned around and walked into the garage. I took a deep breath to fill my lungs and slowly calmed my nerves. He might have stolen my virginity, but I wasn't going to let him steal what dignity I had left.

Many years later when I was in my early twenties, I finally got the courage to tell my parents. Even though Mom held her stillborn secret within her, I was unwilling to hold my burden in any longer. At thirteen, I hadn't made the connection that what Ken did was rape. That understanding came years later, and by then I needed to tell Mom and Dad to help heal my pain. I had to let it out so I could let it go. The day I told my parents, I saw the weight I'd been bearing transferred to them. The fear and struggle my parents were carrying was clear. Ken scared all of us, and none of us knew how to stop him.

Ken's abuse would define me in ways I never imagined, and I wouldn't recognize the rippling effects until much later in life. When I was a teen, I became promiscuous, thinking the way to get a boy to like me was to sleep with him. I'd hop in guys' cars without knowing them, or sleep with them on first dates. I developed a hard breastplate to cover up the continued damage those relationships did to me. It took years for me to realize those weren't the guys who were good "boyfriend" material, and many more years to decipher the truth of Ken's inexcusable behavior. What I didn't yet know was the lingering hold it still had on me.

The closer I got to the hospital the more resistant I became to seeing Mom the way Will had described her. I was scared of what I'd find. I knew Ken couldn't hurt us now, but my impulse was to turn around and drive back to Mammoth. I wanted to run away like I often did as a child. What did Mom's post-surgery behavior mean for us in the future? Could we train Dad to help, or would we need to include him in the care plan? Would she regain her faculties, or was this the beginning of my needing to care for her too? I still depended on Mom, and I wasn't ready to see her in that state. I needed her to be my pillar of strength like she'd always been, the one person I'd always been able to count on.

twelve

I arrived at the hospital by midmorning, my mind dizzy with worry. My head spun faster as I walked through the sterile stillness of the lobby toward the elevators and up to the third floor. I turned the corner into Mom's room, and said hello to everyone.

Will and Dad were standing by the window. Dad wore a blue plaid shirt, and Will was dressed in a white dress shirt and tie for work later that day. Haze muted the view of Santa Anita racetrack and the mountains behind them. I hugged everyone as I made my way toward Mom. She was sitting in a hospital chair at the end of her bed. Nancy stood next to her holding her hand, a concerned look on her face. I said hello to Mom, but she remained unresponsive with a blank expression on her face.

I hugged her shoulders and kissed her cheek. "Hey, Mom, it's me, Laurie."

I stayed close to her face, trying to get her attention. She looked at me as if she were searching for my name. Unease stabbed my stomach. I turned to Will and then Nancy with a look of alarm. Will hadn't exaggerated Mom's symptoms. Mom drew figures in the air as if writing on a school chalkboard. She seemed like a different person than the one I'd left only a few days earlier. That was hard to absorb.

She said, "You know when Georgie and I go to Antarctica, we can take our boat and sail it there. Wouldn't that be an adventure?" Her eyes widened like a confused child. She was mixing her experiences together. She had gone to Antarctica two years prior with her friend Georgie, and they used to sail in Maine on a boat they'd bought. In shock, I plopped down on Mom's hospital bed. I felt like I'd walked onto a movie set watching a bad scene play out. But this wasn't a movie—this was *my* reality.

Dr. Shan knocked on the open door. He went over to shake Dad's hand, then pulled out his stethoscope, listened to Mom's heart, felt her pulse, and turned to us. "Your mom is doing better today and can go home. We should have her discharge papers ready before lunch."

I stepped closer, making sure I understood his Indian accent.

"She will need full-time care for the next several weeks. Will one of you be able to take care of her while she recuperates?" He stared directly at me.

What? I turned to Will—we exchanged confused looks.

I asked, "Can you repeat that?"

"Yes, do you have someone who can take care of your mother? She'll need full-time care for the first couple of weeks."

Questions popped in and out my head faster than I could grasp them, but I had to be direct. The most important question tumbled out: "Can Mom stay in the hospital one more night? We weren't prepared for this, and we don't have anyone to care for her."

Dr. Shan paused. "Sure, I think I can do that for you." He made some notes on the chart.

"Thank you." My muscles relaxed momentarily until the next wave of panic set in. We had twenty-four hours to find someone to care for Mom. This was uncharted territory. Where could we begin?

Dr. Shan left, and the rest of us huddled together to talk. Dad asked, "Now what's going on?"

Will and I quickly explained what Dr. Shan said and what Mom needed. He sighed and said, "Well, I don't think I can take care of her with my bad hip. If she falls, I can't pick her up." His hands slid deeper in his pockets.

Nancy patted Dad on the back. "She'll be fine, Jim. We'll take good care of her, don't worry."

I was glad that Nancy was there. We needed her help.

The three of us agreed that an in-home caregiver would be best for Mom. Dad also needed help cooking meals and washing clothes, and I didn't think he'd want to be home alone.

Will chimed in. "My friend Neil hired a caregiver for his mom a few months ago. Let me call him and find out who it was."

Quickly switching into problem-solving mode, I said, "Okay, and I'll see if the nurse's station has any resources. They must run into this situation every day."

The nurse working at the station handed me a packet full of information and lists of nursing homes, assisted living facilities, and home health care companies. How would I know which was the right company? It seemed overwhelming.

Will showed up a few minutes later with a smile across his freckled face. "I got the phone number from Neil and called the agency he used. The owner, Daniel, said he would meet us here in an hour."

"Really? That's perfect." A renewed sense of hope settled in, but thoughts and worries rattled around in my head.

I was thrilled that the agency had responded so quickly, and I remained cautiously optimistic. While I was working as a corporate recruiter, it was always a challenge to find good employees, and since I'd become a mother, at times it had been difficult to find quality babysitters too. Mom and Dad needed a babysitter who preferred to work with the elderly.

Nancy chimed in, "Before I go, I need to tell you and Will about what I discovered the other night. When I brought dinner to your dad, I went into your parents' room to grab clothes to bring to the hospital. I found a couple hundred dollars stashed in their dresser drawer. I told your dad and then we searched their bedroom and found money stashed in your mom's jewelry case and in the pockets of her purse. Your dad has all the money."

"It looks like it's time to add Will and me onto Mom and Dad's checking account and talk to the bank about limiting Mom's withdrawals." I sighed, feeling the weight of the mounting tasks resting heavy on my shoulders.

"I need to get to work. Call me if you need anything." Nancy gave me a gentle hug. "I'll stop by tonight and check on your mom on my way home from work."

I gave her a hug goodbye and thanked her for all her help over the last week: visiting Mom daily, bringing dinners to Dad, and taking him to the hospital the day of Mom's surgery. I couldn't have managed all this without her. We had an hour before the agency showed up, so Dad, Will, and I decided to grab a bite to eat in the cafeteria.

After a mediocre lunch, we returned to Mom's hospital room. Daniel, from the agency, arrived minutes later. He introduced himself, and handed us his business card. I homed in on the "PhD" after his name. He looked professional in his blue sports coat and tie and his neatly combed brown hair. He explained he was an owner of a local franchised office of a nationwide agency. He instantly put me at ease.

"So tell me what your needs are." He pulled out a notepad and pen.

We explained that we needed someone who could help Mom shower, get dressed, and keep a close eye on her. She was disoriented and confused after her failed surgery, and she was expected to improve in a couple of weeks. Daniel walked over to Mom and said hello, but she continued to stare out the window mumbling and not acknowledging him.

Will added, "She also needs to be watched at night. She hasn't been sleeping here in the hospital, and we've needed a night nurse for her since her surgery."

He looked up from his notepad. "Are there any other needs I should know about? If not, I think I have all the information I need."

"Yes, she's getting discharged tomorrow. Do you think you can find someone that will fit our needs by then?"

"I already have someone in mind and will contact her once I get to the office." He smiled with a look of assurance. "I'll call you later this afternoon to give you an update."

I knew from being a recruiter that his comment was a trained response, but it worked. Daniel left me feeling confident that he'd be able to find someone to care for Mom. I trusted him. I didn't have any other choice.

Dad's rough palm grabbed my hand. "Thanks for cutting your vacation short to come back and help. I know I couldn't do this on my own." He sighed.

I looked him in the eye. "You're welcome, Dad. Will and I are happy to help out."

Dad's lines on his forehead looked deeper.

Will turned and chuckled under his breath. "Of course he's thankful. He doesn't know how to take care of Mom. He doesn't even know how to take care of himself."

I gave Will a glare, urging him to stop. Will's continued condescending comments weren't helping. I didn't want to take on these responsibilities either, but I needed cooperation, not conflict.

After Will left for work and Dad for home, I sat by Mom on her bed and looked into her eyes. "Hey Mom, it's Laurie." I moved my head around trying to get her attention, but her glazed eyes looked elsewhere. She was in her own personal prison, and I couldn't enter.

The idea that she might not recover frightened me. When I held her hand, she pulled it away. I might as well have been a stranger. Even though the doctors told us she'd recover, I didn't trust them. They'd been wrong about her surgery, and they could be wrong about her recovery. I stared at her blank face and feared she'd never be the same. Even though I'd yearned for a closer relationship as a young child, I'd always loved her. I wanted her to recover and have another chance. Maybe her health scare would bring us closer, and I could mend some of my childhood. I wished I could make plans for her to come see the kids next week, like I had for the last fifteen years. Already, I missed seeing her bright face when I opened my front door and the girls ran into her arms. As I rested my hand on Mom's leg, I realized that none of those things were going to happen. My window of opportunity had passed, and life as I knew it was shifting. I was a mother, a daughter, and a wife. How would I juggle it all?

thirteen

The following morning after scrambling to find a caregiver, I drove back to the hospital to help Dad bring Mom home. Daniel's call the night before comforted me. He told me one of his best employees, Sue, had just ended an assignment and was available. She lived close to my parents and had over ten years of experience caring for the elderly. I trusted his word when he told me they checked references on their caregivers. Everything seemed to be falling into place the best it could.

As I drove to my parents' house, I reminisced about the years I'd sat in the back seat of Mom's car counting the buildings and houses to pass the time as we drove a similar route to the marina where we'd kept our sailboat for thirty years. Throughout my childhood, Mom had grown to love sailing even more than Dad did. She looked peaceful when she was on the water. We nicknamed her Captain Betty. By the time I was twelve, Dad worked six days a week and barely came down to the boat. One year for Christmas Will bought Mom a personalized license plate for her car with "CAPT BB" on it. As a teacher, Mom had summers off, so I'd go sailing with her while Dad worked. Sometimes we'd sail with one of Mom's teacher friends and John, our friend whose boat we'd bought.

Through the years, we'd become close family friends with John and his wife, Helen. If we hadn't seen John in a while, we'd stop by their house on our way home and visit them. They'd always give us kids treats, or Helen would show me her latest sewing project. She was a seamstress and sewed the prettiest dresses for her clients. I was always enamored with her creations.

As I was growing up, John was like a favorite uncle. When we'd go sailing with him, he'd give me candy and let me sit on his lap so I could help sail the boat. When I was little, he called me "Boo-Boo" and would always greet me before my brothers. If he didn't see me first, I'd search the dock for his boat to say hi to him. He always made me feel special.

The summer I was twelve, Helen taught me how to sew, and the following year John taught me to sail our twenty-four-foot boat. I couldn't wait to take my weekly sailing lessons. John would greet us at our boat, wearing a wool-collared shirt over a white T-shirt and wool pants that Helen had sewn for him. John's round face and thin blond hair was always under a white sailor's bucket hat to protect his fair, sun-weathered skin. You always knew which boat was John's. It was the cleanest boat on the dock, with every knot tied properly and every line secure. He was strong, knowledgeable, and had a true passion for sailing. John's strong male qualities stood out to me as I grew older—they were qualities I wished I'd seen more of in Dad, and perhaps Mom wished for that too.

John showed me how to rig the boat, tie the knots, and hoist the sails. He'd sail the boat out of the harbor and would let me take the helm once we were out on the open water. He taught me how to tack, jibe, and rescue a lifejacket as if it were a person who'd gone overboard. By the end of that first summer, I was not only rigging the boat, but I could singlehandedly sail our boat in and out of the slip. I noticed other boat owners were watching as I tacked out of the harbor with confidence. My body would tingle from the rush of energy that flooded me as I handled each turn precisely while John sat silently in the cockpit, smiling.

The power of singlehandedly maneuvering a sailboat when I was thirteen years old gave me confidence that I was good at something that was unique to me, something that neither my brothers nor my friends were good at doing. Most of my friends were taking the bus to the beach or hanging out and bored that summer. Ken was partying, and Will was working or fishing. Some of my friends said, "Gosh, you're so lucky," while others, my brothers, and a few friends brushed it off as no big deal. I didn't care what others thought about me learning how to sail a boat before learning how to drive a car. I was proud of what I'd accomplished that summer, and no one could take that away from me. But as life would have it, nothing lasts forever.

I was helping Mom make dinner a week before my sixteenth birthday, when the phone rang. "It's good to hear from you, Helen," Mom said to John's wife.

Her smile quickly faded and tears slid down her face. "I'm so sorry, Helen."

I waved my hand, trying to get her attention. "What happened?" Emptiness suddenly filled me. I knew something was terribly wrong, and it was about John.

I sat down at the kitchen table trying to piece together the one-sided conversation, waiting for Mom to hang up the phone.

"What's going on with John?" I asked. She sat down next to me and wrapped her arm around me. My gut clenched as I waited to hear her answer.

"John was riding his motorcycle and was killed by a drunk driver yesterday." John had been riding a motorcycle since gas rationing in the seventies and was the safest rider I'd ever known. He'd told me many stories about how he'd swerved to avoid drivers or how other motorcyclists drove carelessly.

Mom hugged me and told me she was sorry. After that, nothing else mattered. John was dead, and I was a teenager who didn't know what to do with such strong emotions. I'd never lost anyone I loved until then. Three of my four grandparents passed before I was five years old, and the fourth before I was born, so I had no memory of them and didn't mourn them.

I'll never forget John's funeral that crisp November day just before my sixteenth birthday. I stood between my parents next to John's gravesite. A handful of people stood around as the minister said a few words before they lowered his body into the ground. Tears fell from my face. I looked at Dad, his face drawn yet expressionless, staring at John's coffin. Not knowing what to do with my feelings, I followed Dad's cue and buried mine alongside John that day.

After Mom's hospitalization visit and failed surgery, I feared getting a similar call about her. If only I had someone like John by my side to comfort me and tell me I was making the right decisions. I missed sailing with John, but I held onto our memories and the strength he and sailing had given me.

The day Mom was to come home, Dad helped me pick her up, and we drove to their house where Suzy, our new caregiver, greeted us in the driveway. Her bright face smiled as she walked to the car and opened the door to help Mom out.

"I can help," I exclaimed, hurrying to the passenger side of the car.

"Don't worry," Suzy said. "I got this."

"Are you sure?"

"Yes, I've done this many times before." She seemed confident as she helped Mom up the porch stairs and into the house. We sat Mom down in the den and I turned on the TV. She looked more relaxed now that she was home, even though she had few words. I gave Suzy a tour of the house Mom and Dad had bought almost fifty years earlier. When I was in middle school, Mom had wanted to move north to a better community, but Dad insisted on staying where they were. He claimed that if they moved, they wouldn't have the extra money to travel the way they wanted to.

Over the years, Dad had remodeled each room and had covered every surface with wood, including the floors, kitchen and bathroom cabinets, and countertops. Dad never completed any one project before jumping to another. We lived for years with no kitchen cabinet doors, unaligned doors, and missing floor molding. Mom would repeatedly ask Dad to fix these problems, but twisting his tongue and stomping his foot, he'd say, "Betty, I'll get to it, but I'm working most weekends right now." Dad usually underestimated how long it would take him to complete a job, so he worked most weekends to try and keep up. He was a craftsman, and his customers loved his work, but he had no business sense. Now Dad took on fewer home projects, but much of the detailed work on the house was still left unfinished.

I showed Suzy her room, my old bedroom, which had become a storage closet after I'd left home over twenty years earlier. The pink walls had been painted light blue, and the stained pink carpet had been replaced by a hardwood floor. A trundle bed and an antique armoire took the place of my seventies pink and white bedroom set.

After we toured the small home that had never seemed big enough for all of us, we sat down at the kitchen table to go over the care plan that Daniel had put together. I showed Suzy where we kept Mom and Dad's medications, and made sure she knew that Dad had type 2 diabetes. I made some healthy dinner suggestions that Dad would eat, since he disliked many vegetables. I instructed her to lock the doors at night and hide the keys until Mom stopped wandering at night.

"So do you think you can handle this for us?" I asked, searching her eyes for confirmation.

"Yes, I've done it many times before," she assured me.

"And as Mom recuperates, you're okay cutting back your hours?"

"That's not a problem. I can find additional work if I need to." She seemed clear about her responsibilities and my parents' needs.

I exhaled my tension, and my shoulders relaxed. I liked Suzy's confidence. She seemed comfortable with her responsibilities, and I was glad she was willing to be flexible with us. I hoped we'd only need Suzy to work for us for a couple of months and then we'd let her go completely once Mom recovered, pushing our need for regular care out a few years. Even though Mom's memory loss had begun before her surgery, she was in the early stages and could function on her own. I worried that if her dementia progressed too quickly, they'd run out of money, and they didn't have long-term care insurance.

Mom was smart and had invested their money where they could—saving a small nest egg. She had her retirement, and Dad had his social security. They owned two rental properties, so they'd be comfortable in their retirement years, but in their planning I don't think they'd thought about long-term care, and now it was too late to buy that insurance. Mom was seventy-six and Dad was seventy-eight, and care was expensive. After I wrote the first check to pay the agency, I found new things to be concerned about. We'd need to dip into their savings to pay their caregiver's salary, and I wanted to be frugal with their money. I didn't know how they'd pay for their care if their needs were prolonged, but I knew I'd be the one who would have to figure it out.

That afternoon, I walked into my empty house. It was eerily quiet. Sharon would arrive home from Mammoth with the girls later that evening, and David was still at work. I needed to call Will to give him an update about finding Suzy and the new routine for our parents, but dread washed over me. My head wouldn't stop spinning. I wanted to collapse on the couch. Talking to Will had become a challenge. After years of distance, we'd been talking daily about Mom's health and our conversations often ended with him complaining about how inept Dad was. I picked up the phone and quickly put it back down, drained from the thought of our call.

A memory of Will and our family road trip to the Midwest popped into my head. Dad had driven our motor home to Wisconsin, Iowa, and Michigan so my parents could visit their relatives throughout the Midwest. Ken stayed home, and at age fifteen, Will asked Mom if he could stay home too, but she said no. Mom and Dad wanted to visit their cousins, aunts, and uncles—they hadn't seen them since they'd moved to California twenty years earlier. At thirteen, I would have preferred to stay home and spend my summer hanging out with girlfriends, going to the beach, and taking sailing lessons, but fighting against what Mom and Dad wanted was futile.

Will was angry he had to join us, and I became his target. One of the first days on the road, he cornered me in the back of the motor home, inches from my face. "I don't want to be on this trip, so you better not bother me or when you fall asleep tonight, I might kill you." His eyes were wild.

He'd never threatened me like that before, so I stayed close to Mom and Dad, resuming my position on the engine cover, like I had on all our other road trips. He made the same threat a few more times over our five-week trip, each time his eyes seared his message into my mind. He never followed through on his threat, but it left me on edge. Not in the same way Ken did. Ken's threats and abuse had left an unforgettable imprint on my soul.

During our later teens and early twenties, our family continued to fall apart. Will separated from our family and attached himself to some family friends. I understood why Will left, but Mom's illness had left us at a crossroads, an opportunity for us to put our past behind us. I wanted to be closer to the one sibling I still had left. I needed a sounding board as I made decisions on how to best care for Mom. David was absorbed in his career, John was gone, and with Mom slipping away, I wanted someone I could count on. I didn't want to do this alone.

fourteen

For the first two weeks after Mom was released from the hospital, Suzy stayed with her around the clock. We were pleased to see that Mom had stopped wandering at night, she was less agitated, and her memory had improved. I switched Suzy to an eight-hour day, five days a week, once it seemed safe to leave my parents alone at night. Over the next couple of months, Mom slowly regained her ability to bathe, dress, and eat on her own, which alleviated some of my concerns.

Over the next several months, I visited my parents every other week. I took Mom to follow-up doctor appointments, checked on her frequently, and made sure Suzy was taking good care of them. Mom liked Suzy and didn't seem to mind having her in the house. Dad liked anyone who made him a good meal and washed his clothes. After Mom came home, we found more money stashed around the house. That week Will and I went to their bank to add us to their bank account and put a dollar limit on Mom's withdrawals. I took control of their investments and savings and found a property manager to take care of their rental properties.

Nancy offered to help us out on the weekends without pay. She knew I was trying to stretch my parents' savings, and I was grateful for her help. Nancy cooked, cleaned, and drove Mom to their friend Georgie's on Sundays for an informal church service at her house.

Before Mom's surgery, I would see the joy on her face when she talked about the kids when she was substitute teaching, or the preschool that she'd started at her church. When she visited us, she was full of life and fun. But now, her speech was limited. I learned how to talk to her so she'd grasp for fewer words. Some days she'd smile, silently listening to our conversations, but other days she'd look sullen and withdrawn. She'd pace around the house as if she were in a labyrinth looking for a way out. Since Mom's heart attack, I didn't know how she felt about being cooped up in her own house instead of doing the things she loved.

Mom wasn't one to talk about her feelings, but after her surgery, they were etched on her face. I'd take her to lunch after a doctor's appointment or grocery shopping and tell her about the girls. She'd smile, but her eyes didn't sparkle, and I knew the lunches and trips to the store didn't bring her the same kind of joy that teaching did. It was as if she were trapped inside her own armored body, the same armor she'd built to protect herself from life's pain and suffering. I wanted to take her armor off so I could have my mother back. I would have done anything to see her smiling face and bright eyes, and to feel her warmth when she hugged me. I was not in denial. I was sad because my strong vibrant mother was fading away like a fine fabric left in the sun too long, and there was nothing I could do to change that.

The summer after Mom's heart attack, I reluctantly adjusted to *my* new normal, which included the care of my parents. David and I had made vacation plans to go to the Big Island of Hawaii with our four girls. Hawaii was one of David's favorite places, and I counted down the days until we'd arrive. I couldn't wait to smell the sweet plumerias in the air, snorkel in the warm ocean, and read a good book by the pool.

Summers with the girls always meant more driving—taking them to summer school, Junior Lifeguards, art, and acting classes. I very much needed a two-week break from the added responsibilities that were weighing heavily on me. It was a challenge to manage two households, a caregiver, and four teenagers' needs while trying to be a good wife to David. I would get up every morning and put on my good face to take on the day, but the pressures of all my responsibilities ebbed and flowed, and I began to feel the effects. Some mornings, I'd wake exhausted after eight hours of sleep. I began drinking coffee to give me energy—some days it would work, but other days it didn't. Sometimes, I'd walk around for days feeling as if a sad fog hung over my head. I chalked up my exhaustion to the constant cooking, cleaning, carpools, errands, the extra summer driving, and running two households. My body was telling me I needed a break.

As our vacation inched closer I became energized, buying last-minute items and packing for our trip. I was refreshed by the thought of having *only* two responsibilities during our trip: feeding my family and deciding which chaise lounge to lie on. Everything else was optional. I intended to enjoy each day, knowing school would start in a few weeks, and our lives would fall back into their usual patterns.

We got off the plane in Hawaii and walked toward the open-air baggage claim. As our luggage arrived, David pulled it off the carousel. I closed my eyes and felt the thick warm air on my face. My tense shoulders relaxed as "Over the Rainbow" played in the background.

Emma scowled, "I'm sweating already. Is it going to be this hot the entire trip?"

A sudden irritation arose in me, and before I could respond, she walked away to fill her empty water bottle. I hoped our trip wouldn't be spoiled with her fifteen-year-old attitude. Of course, I had behaved similarly when I was her age, but Mom hadn't set me straight—she'd let me talk back to her. As a mother now, I consciously worked to raise our kids to respect David and me and to appreciate the opportunities we were giving them. During these teen years, it sometimes felt like my attempts fell on deaf ears. I let Emma's response go. I was looking to start our family vacation without conflict and I hoped her attitude would change when we got to the resort.

By the third day of snorkeling and reading our books by the pool and beachside, we had all settled into island life. The sound of the lapping turquoise waters melted the gnawing pressure that had rested between my temples for weeks. I could see David shedding his stress too. He snapped less about the little things that would normally bother him. Emma engaged with her sisters more than I'd seen in months, playing in the pool and joining in afternoon card games.

One night after the kids went to sleep, David grabbed a bottle of champagne out of the hotel refrigerator and popped the cork. He poured us two glasses and led me to the balcony. We sat in the chairs looking out at the dark, calm ocean as I felt my drink go to my head. He rested his hand on top of mine and said, "Thank you for planning a wonderful vacation." We clinked our glasses.

I turned to him. "Thanks for making it all possible."

We sipped our champagne and gazed at the dark sky dotted with blinking stars. We discussed the logistics of our plans the next morning to drive to Kilauea National Park to see the volcano, fit in a stop at the waterfall on the way, and still make sure we got there in time to see the lava flow that night.

We listened to the soft waves gently rolling on the shore as silence settled between us. I wondered if our lives had turned out the way he'd hoped. It was a subject that had been nibbling at my mind since Mom's recent heart attack. David had very few hobbies outside of skiing with the family and fly-fishing in the summer. Whenever I'd ask him about his interests, he'd brush off my question. His dad was seventy-six and still ran their small business with no plans to retire. He didn't have outside hobbies. David had a similar work ethic, and it concerned me. I wanted to talk to him so I could make sense out of my life, his life, and our future together.

While we sat in silence finishing our champagne, I craved the connection we had when we first dated. I wanted a sympathetic ear so I could talk about the internal tug-of-war I felt about this new path with my mother. I didn't know how to start that conversation. The barrier between us seemed impermeable. As much as I wanted to start those conversations that night, I didn't. Instead, I followed David back into the bedroom where we made love. It was the only way I knew to feel close to him.

⸎

The reality of raising teenage girls along with my other duties hit me head-on once we returned home from our laid-back vacation. The day after we arrived home from Hawaii, Emma asked to go to her boyfriend Tommy's house. I agreed, as long as a parent was there. I didn't allow the girls to go to boys' homes without supervision. That was our house rule.

Emma had blossomed into a tall, slender young woman with thick, wavy brown hair and high cheekbones. She enjoyed playing volleyball for her high school and hanging out at the beach. My friends would often comment on how gorgeous she was, but I wanted my girls' beauty to come from having strong morals, values, and integrity, not just their looks. From a very young age, Emma had pushed our rules on curfews, sleepovers, and shaving her legs, and I wanted her to respect her body more than I did at her age.

Emma had become smitten with this young man, and had spent much of her free time that summer with Tommy. She'd had a couple of boyfriends in middle school, but this boy was different. He stood six feet tall, had blond hair and blue eyes, played water polo, and his bronzed skin oozed testosterone. They seemed to be serious, kissing each other hello and good-bye in front of me, which left me uneasy.

Tommy's parents owned a local retail store in town and were in and out during the day. When I first called Tommy's mom about our house rule, Emma was mortified. I didn't care. I was her mother, not her friend, and I guessed her boyfriend would be gone by Christmas.

Tommy's mother seemed to be caught off guard when I

said, "Emma isn't allowed to be home alone with a boy or with the door shut when parents are home. Are you comfortable monitoring that?" The kids were too young to have sex at fifteen. His mother paused before agreeing.

I finally agreed to drop Emma off at the Pizza Parlor a block from his house, and they'd walk to the house once his dad came home. My radar was up, sensing it was a bad idea, but I gave her a little rope and a chance to prove me wrong. As she got out of the car I said, "Make good choices."

She looked back with an eye roll. "I know."

I drove off but intuited that I should park my car around the corner of her boyfriend's house and take a look. I inched up so I could see his house, but they'd only be able to see the hood of my large Suburban. My heart began to pump as I channeled my inner detective. Within minutes, I saw Emma and her boyfriend holding hands walking down the middle of the street. I knew it. I took a second look to confirm it was them. His dad wasn't home, and they walked into his house together. Anger quickly kicked me into offense. My shaky hands started the car and I drove into their driveway. I wasn't naive enough to think that two fifteen-year-old kids weren't going to be curious about their bodies if they found themselves alone. I got out of my car and knocked on the door—no answer. I waited a few seconds, then knocked again.

"Emma, I know you're in there, please come out." I could see someone moving behind the shades of the window—still no answer. I shouted, "Emma, I know you are in there, come out now!"

She finally opened it. "Mom, you are so embarrassing."

Her boyfriend was standing in the hallway behind her, his muscles protruding from the tank top he was putting on. "Get in the car," I spat. I didn't care that I'd embarrassed her. I wasn't going to knowingly let my daughter spend time alone with a boy, especially one I suspected only had one thing on his mind. Emma climbed in looking furious. I turned to her and said, "We'll talk about this once I've had a chance to cool down."

My vacation high had vanished, and it took hours for my anger to subside. Later that night, I went into her room to discuss what had happened. She gave me a contemptuous look, expressing little interest in listening. I knew she'd continue to challenge me through her high school years. I could've used an owner's manual for my children, elderly parents, and marriage. While I waited for them to come in the mail, I blindly felt my way forward. I'd sometimes take the hard road, but my heart would always be my GPS.

fifteen

Family responsibilities continued to tug on David and me. Ten months after Mom's heart attack, David was summoned to duty when he received a call from his Aunt Ruth's caregiver. Ruth was ninety-six and had been hospitalized with a severe stroke. David sat with her in the hospital every day until she passed away three weeks later.

Four years earlier, David's Uncle Harold had died in his sleep, and Harold had appointed David as Ruth's power of attorney for health care and the executor of their will. After Harold passed, David had made sure Ruth was well cared for. He'd stop by or check in with her caregiver weekly, and we'd take her out to dinner once a month. He managed her household and finances.

I could see the added stress that he carried. He'd been promoted to Senior VP of Human Resources and Administration and managed over two hundred people. As his responsibilities increased, some nights he'd stay at the office until after I was asleep. He stopped working out and gained another ten pounds. He started relieving his pressure valve at home more often—complaining when the kids left their homework sprawled out on the counter or if their rooms were messy. My body tensed most nights when he'd walk through the front door, unsure of what mood he might bring home, but I said nothing, knowing the enormity of the pressure he was under.

Harold knew David would take good care of Ruth and his estate, and be a good gatekeeper to his wealth. David had a huge job ahead of him. He'd need to sell their rental properties, their home in Beverly Hills, and their art collection, and inform the relatives in England about their inheritances. I told David the first few days after Ruth's death, "Please let me know what I can do to help." He thanked me and told me he'd let me know. I hoped he'd open up and allow me to be helpful.

Only a few family members gathered the day we buried Ruth next to Harold. When we walked up to the gravesite, my tears surprised me. I realized it wasn't Ruth that I missed—it was Harold—and I felt guilty for such thoughts. I should have been mourning Ruth's death, but as I stared at Harold's headstone, I realized how much I missed his accepting nature and the warmth he exuded when he greeted me. I couldn't help but think about the way his face lit up when we'd come to visit or meet him and Ruth for dinner. I was overcome with sadness, not realizing until then how much I missed him and the way he made me feel—like I was family.

The kids and I didn't see much of David over the next year. I missed watching TV with him in the evenings and his presence on the weekends. He spent most of his spare time sorting through Harold and Ruth's legal and financial issues. He had to decide how to best liquidate their estate and distribute it to their heirs.

When one of his relatives in England was unhappy with his arrangement, David became irritated and looked like he might explode. I told him he was doing a great job and again offered to help. I wanted to ease the pain I saw in his eyes. It wasn't until his aunt and uncle's house sold that he finally asked, "Will you help me pack up their belongings?"

I said yes, pleased to finally be included, but David had already sold most of their belongings and didn't include me in the decision of what to keep. I'd been left out again.

David told me he'd inherited more money than what was needed to cover the girls' college educations. I asked him several times what we were going to do with the extra money, but he told me he hadn't thought about it yet.

His comment stung. I suspected David had known from the beginning how much he had inherited and was waiting to tell me. He analyzed every decision he made and never discussed anything before he was ready. I wanted him to trust me enough to discuss our future together and not make decisions on *our* behalf assuming I'd go along with them.

Early on in our marriage I'd followed David's lead when it came to our financial decisions. Now that we'd been together for seventeen years, I was looking to be more of an equal partner. I saw us growing together as a couple trusting that our goals were the same, but I began feeling our divide deepen. I assured myself he was just distracted by his responsibilities in an attempt to compensate for missing the man I loved. As the burdens wound down, we'd mend that gap.

sixteen

I was the kind of person who trusted people until they gave me reason not to, and I would soon find my trust tested. It began when I overheard Suzy, my parents' caregiver, sharing confidences at my dad's eightieth birthday celebration. She was sitting across from me at a large table when I overheard her tell a friend of ours that she had several social security cards, and she alluded to collecting unemployment while working, which I believed was illegal. After the party, I confirmed what I'd heard with her friend. If she was willing to steal from the IRS, she might be willing to steal from us.

The following week, Suzy called to ask if she could leave Mom at home and go to the bank to deposit her paycheck. I agreed and asked her to let Dad know when she left and when she returned. She said she would, and the next time I visited my parents, I asked Dad how long she was gone that day.

"I don't know exactly, but it seemed like a long time . . . over an hour maybe, and she's been leaving the house a couple times a week for the last several weeks."

That was another clue that things might not be quite right. I was paying her to care for Mom, not to leave her at home for extended errands. Dad's hearing loss left me worried that he wouldn't hear Mom cry for help, and if he did, he wouldn't know what to do. I called Nancy that weekend looking for confirmation about Suzy. Nancy was still taking care of Mom on the weekends and overlapped with Suzy on Fridays. I told Nancy about my concerns, and asked her opinion about Suzy.

"I think she's doing fine, but she left their laundry for me to do and when she left, I saw her take a basket of folded clothes to her car."

"So she did her laundry and left Mom and Dad's for you to do?"

"It seems that way."

That was the last straw. I called the agency the following day. Daniel, the owner, didn't seem surprised by my story. "It's common for caregivers to get burned out after a year. I'll look for someone to replace her."

I asked to interview the person this time. I wanted to find someone who had stronger morals and would stay longer than a year.

Mom had improved significantly since her heart attack, but she hadn't made a full recovery. She needed help with her daily medications, cooking, and cleaning, and she could no longer drive. Most parents don't give up their independence easily, and Mom had always loved doing her own thing, but when I asked her for the keys, I was thankful she didn't fight me. It was one less thing to worry about.

Two weeks later I hired Karen, the only caregiver I interviewed, to replace Suzy. Karen was a weathered, tall dishwater blond with deep crow's feet around her eyes, marionette lines around her mouth, and a voice with a smoker's rasp. The day I interviewed her, she held on to her coffee cup with shaky hands. She'd had one year of caregiving experience and had been a hairdresser. I thought that Mom needed more of a companion than a caregiver and chalked up Karen's shaky hands to interview jitters. I needed an immediate replacement, so I hired her. She seemed like a good enough fit.

When I visited, Karen was always busy cooking, cleaning, or taking Mom to the garage to help Dad. Her hands still shook. I took note, wondering what was causing it, but Mom and Dad were doing well, and the house was always in order.

Dad was upset with Suzy's departure. The first few months, he would repeatedly ask, "Why did Suzy leave us? We're nice people."

I told him, "Suzy's departure didn't have anything to do with us. She needed a change." It took him months to accept my answer and to warm up to Karen. Four months in, he began telling me how much he liked her. I asked him what had changed. He told me she was a good cook, helped him in the garage, and watered his garden. Dad had always struggled with change, but he was also a sucker for anyone who fed him and paid attention to him. Things seemed to have stabilized with my parents and their care.

A year into Karen's time with us, David and I began to breathe a little easier. He was wrapping up his responsibilities as the executor of his aunt and uncle's estate, which eased the tension at home. The kids were busy with school and their respective interests. I took that window to research a hip replacement for Dad. His hip pain had increased, and the doctor had put him on a stronger opiate painkiller. I didn't like the thought of him staying on strong painkillers indefinitely. He was eighty-one, and this was our last opportunity to explore surgery. He hesitantly agreed to a consultation, so I set up one up with the same trusted doctor who'd performed a knee replacement for Mom.

On the car ride home from the first appointment I asked him what he thought. He shook his head, "Oh, Laurie, I don't know. I'm not sure it's all worth it." Dad disliked doctors and liked the idea of surgery even less.

Mom chimed in from the back seat, "Jim, he's a good doctor, and you should have it done." My head jerked to the back seat and I grinned at Mom. That was the most coherent thing she'd said in the last six months. She apparently understood more than I'd given her credit for.

Dad sighed, "Well, let me think about it then."

A week later, Dad reluctantly agreed to the surgery, so I quickly made appointments to get clearance from his various doctors before he changed his mind. Dad was fifty pounds overweight, had type 2 diabetes, edema in his legs, and had undergone triple bypass surgery nine years earlier. Even though he was a high-risk patient, his doctors cleared him. We scheduled his surgery for early June, two weeks before school ended for the summer. A successful surgery would give Dad a chance to have more mobility and improve his health. That was the hope.

A week before Dad's surgery, I drove to my parents to pick him up for his pre-op appointment. I walked up the driveway and saw two cats sitting under Dad's truck. We hadn't had cats since I was a teenager. They scattered when they saw me, and one looked like she'd just given birth. I gagged from the stench of cat urine and feces. I held my breath, and entered the garage where Dad was making miniature lighthouses and whales to give away as gifts. He didn't seem to be bothered by the smell, so I irritably asked, "Where did these cats come from?"

"Oh, they're strays," Dad casually said.

Could Dad not smell the putrescence? When the mother cat ran into the woodpile in the garage, I looked between the cracks and saw four sets of eyes staring back at me. Shit, where did all these cats come from? My body tensed at the thought that the cats that were living in Dad's garage would now become *my* problem. Cats stayed around because they were fed. It wouldn't be easy to get rid of them.

Frustrated, I walked into the kitchen and asked Karen about the cats. She told me they'd been hanging around for a few weeks and one had just had kittens. Agitated that she hadn't told me, I shot questions at her—how many cats? Where had they come from? Who's feeding them and why?

She said there were four adult cats and probably four kittens. Nancy had been buying food and bringing a week's supply on the weekends. Mom sat at the table and stared at me with big eyes. Karen walked to Mom and put her hand on her shoulder. "And your mom loves to watch the cats in the morning. They all gather at the back door waiting to be fed, and your mom giggles while she watches them. They make her so happy."

I laughed sarcastically as more questions popped into my head. How could they stand the smell? Why was I the only one who thought this was a bad idea? I needed to develop a plan fast to eliminate these cats despite my mother enjoying them. I doubted she understood the whole situation.

I called Will and told him our dilemma. He laughed and said we needed to come up with a plan. I researched feral cats, and finally concluded that trapping them and taking them to the pound was best. Will agreed to help. We'd trap as many cats as possible while Dad was in the hospital, without telling Nancy or Karen since they wouldn't agree.

I asked Nancy to stop feeding the cats, but she saw things very differently. "They're God's children and I need to feed them."

I pleaded with her to stop, but she refused. I wanted to tell her that if they were God's children, let God feed them, but I didn't. That argument was pointless.

Really? Now I was in charge of eight feral cats? How had I suddenly become responsible for trapping and transporting these unruly cats from my parents' house while overseeing Dad's surgery? My plate was suddenly overflowing again. I wanted to rewind my life—go back to simpler times, when the kids were little, Mom and Dad were healthy, and I was happier. But I couldn't.

I spent the night at Mom and Dad's house the night before his surgery. We needed to be at the hospital early the next morning, and I knew it would ease Dad's worries if I was nearby. The next morning, we all arrived at the hospital and checked in.

Dad sat down and let out a sigh. I told him, "It's going to be okay, Dad."

"I hope so." He sounded unsure.

I went with Dad to the pre-op room while Mom stayed in the waiting room. He was one of the first patients being prepped for surgery that morning. Dad sat on the gurney as the nurse began asking questions. He interrupted her. "Oh, I wanted to show you something that's on my leg." He pulled up his left pant leg and the nurse looked at a lesion the size of a half dollar.

The nurse's eyes got bigger as she examined it. "How long have you had that?"

Dad thought about it for a moment, "I don't know exactly. . . maybe a week . . . I'm not sure."

"I need to check with the doctor on this." She quickly scurried off. Why hadn't he let me know about this?

The nurse came in a few minutes later and told me the doctor would come talk to me once he arrived. I knew it wouldn't be good news.

An hour later Dad's surgeon came in and told me he needed to cancel Dad's surgery. He had cellulitis on his leg and he wanted to admit him so they could run some tests. I asked him to explain what cellulitis was and he told me it was a serious skin infection.

I saw the concern written across his face and agreed with the plan. Mom and I stayed with Dad until he was assigned a room, and then I took Mom home and told Karen the unfortunate news. I asked Karen and Nancy if they could stay with Mom a couple nights a week and fill in the other nights. I needed to make sure someone was with Mom every night. I assumed Dad would be in the hospital for a week at the most.

Dad ended up staying in the hospital for a month as his failed hip replacement continued to morph into other issues. The surgeon handed Dad's care back to his internist, Dr. Shan, the doctor I hadn't replaced yet—a decision I continued to regret. Dad stayed in the hospital for the next several weeks while Dr. Shan figured out how to treat Dad's infection, but it wasn't getting better. The third week Dr. Shan finally brought in an infectious disease specialist who eventually diagnosed Dad with MRSA, a strain of staph that had become resistant to common antibiotics. He was finally given a new intravenous antibiotic, and Dr. Shan put him on bed rest. The antibiotics worked, but Dad developed a blood clot in his leg. At that point, I was furious with Dr. Shan for not telling the nurses to put a compression device on Dad's legs to prevent him from getting blood clots. I wondered if Dad would have had a different experience under a different doctor's care.

As time went on, my guilt would sneak in. I should have been a better advocate for Dad. I should have asked more questions and demanded better care from a doctor I didn't trust in the first place. Maybe I could have helped prevent his long stay, but I had to give myself a break with the huge list of things I was taking care of.

Summer was in full swing, and even though Emma was driving herself and Heather to summer school, I was juggling the twins' carpools for summer camps and Junior Lifeguards. Summer always meant more chores at home. The kids were free of homework, and I welcomed the change in schedule. We'd sleep in, the kids would have weekday sleepovers, and we had dinners at the beach, but that summer tested my limits. For a month, I stayed with Mom two nights a week, visited Dad at the hospital, and continued to trap feral cats before Karen arrived for work.

When Karen showed up to relieve me, she became less friendly over those weeks. I sensed she was mad at me for trapping the cats. One morning I asked, "Are you still feeding the feral cats? I thought we agreed that you wouldn't."

She snickered, "Well, Nancy's still feeding them too."

Her smug response incensed me. If I hadn't been drowning in responsibilities, I would have replaced her, but the thought of adding that to my plate was too much.

I called Will to share my frustration and asked him to keep an eye out for any odd behavior by Karen. He told me he'd noticed her jitters too. "When I'm there, she's always carrying around a plastic water bottle with red liquid in it. I think there's vodka mixed in there." He chuckled. I had never seen the plastic water bottle Will described and hadn't smelled alcohol on her breath, but something just as disturbing came to my attention the weeks after our conversation.

While paying my parents' bills one day, I noticed their credit card bill was the highest it had ever been. At first, I thought the fluctuation was due to their spending patterns, but as I examined their credit card and bank statements, I saw a few large charges at the grocery store, and their cash withdrawals had increased too. Mom still had possession of her credit card, but Karen took her shopping. Dad was in the hospital, so Karen was only shopping for two. These charges were suspicious.

That night David helped me create an Excel spreadsheet to track their finances. I sifted through everything and tallied it up. It was clear that their grocery bill for the month of June was $900 and had slowly increased every month for the last six months. My suspicions were confirmed: Karen was skimming off Mom and Dad.

When I told David, he smirked. "It sounds like it's time to fire her."

I knew he was right, but it wouldn't be that easy. Dad was going to be released from the hospital any day, and I needed hard evidence before letting Karen go. I didn't want her to do this to another family.

The grocery store where Mom and Karen shopped soon provided my evidence. Karen had been buying vodka, wine, lobster, and filet mignon—nothing my parents would buy on their own. Will might have been right; maybe she was drinking on the job. That would explain her jitters.

As I drove to the hospital to see Dad, my blood boiled. I was furious at Karen's audacity to take advantage of our family. I wanted her to pay for what she had done, and I wanted to press charges, but taking all that on felt overwhelming. Since Karen was an employee of the agency, I let it be their problem. The store manager said this wasn't the first time he'd seen this kind of theft. Preying on the elderly was a despicable thought, but it was real, and I was thankful I'd caught this when I did. Now that I had the truth in my hands, finding a new caretaker hung in the balance. The warning signs had been there, but I had shooed them away.

Now I was back to square one—finding another caregiver. Someone we could trust. I pulled into the hospital parking lot and sat for a moment. I closed my eyes and took a breath, letting my tensions subside before heading up to see my father.

seventeen

The summer Dad was in the hospital, I continued swimming upstream, my destination just out of reach. Dad came home from the hospital a week after I'd found out that Karen was stealing from us, and a few days later, Mom ended up in the emergency room with a severe urinary tract infection. It went undetected until she stopped eating and drinking and her fever spiked to 102 degrees—symptoms Karen had missed. I didn't need another reminder of why I needed to let Karen go.

The morning that Daniel, the director of the agency, planned to confront Karen for us finally arrived a few days after Mom came home from the hospital. I walked into my parents' kitchen to find Daniel at the table sipping coffee with Dad. Daniel told me that Karen was gone, and I grinned as joy filled me. Mom shuffled into the kitchen and I gave her a hug. I was thankful Daniel had handled her departure and that Mom and Dad were safe.

Minutes later, our new caregiver, Lisa, showed up. I opened the door and she stuck her hand out, offering a wide friendly smile. I immediately took a liking to her. She was a tall, slender Hispanic woman with long silky black hair that hung to her waist. Her green eyeliner highlighted her round, lively brown eyes, and her lips were ruby red. Dad's eyes immediately lit up like a kid on Christmas morning as he scanned her body from head to toe, checking out her tight jeans and heels. Even at eighty, he still had an eye for the ladies.

I invited Lisa to sit down with Daniel and me. We all talked about her responsibilities, and then I showed her around the house. I knew from my phone interview with Lisa the week prior that she had plenty of experience. She seemed eager to work, and told me how much she valued family. Having someone with strong standards was important to me. Lisa seemed like someone we could trust and who would be a better long-term fit for us . . . someone who could become an extension of *our* family.

When I left my parents' house that day, I felt lighter, relieved of some of my burdens. Lisa had asked all the right questions, responded to our needs, and had immediately taken a liking to Mom. I left that day hopeful that she could be the caregiver who would stay with us until Mom passed. After my chaos-filled summer full of numerous hospital visits, trapping feral cats, Karen's pilfering and dishonesty, managing four teenagers' schedules, and tending to the needs of a husband who expected dinner on the table every night, I simply needed a break. I desperately wanted Lisa to work out so my life could calm down.

My summer of chaos had one reprieve. Earlier in the year, Emma had asked me to hike Mount Whitney with her. She was about to begin her senior year in high school, which left me vacillating between joy, sadness, and fear. Boyfriends, teen drinking, and her desire for more independence had strained the last three years of our relationship. I worried that she might not be ready for college and the responsibilities of taking care of herself properly. The idea of hiking together was an opportunity to support her as a strong young woman and give us a common goal and a shared adventure. It might even smooth the rough edges.

When Mom was fifty-five, she and several of her friends had hiked Mount Whitney. In my early twenties then, I had no desire to take on such an adventure with or without Mom, but my daughter wanted to hike it with me, so I said yes.

When I told David our plans, he shrugged. "Well, you know I can't hike at that elevation, so count me out." He couldn't hike at high altitudes because of his asthma.

I organized a group of six of us to hike together—Emma's best friend, her mom, and two of my close friends. I got our permit and bought a good pair of hiking boots for each of us. Over that summer, I read up on how to train for our one-day summit, started a boot camp class two days a week, and planned three strenuous hikes to get into shape.

Our training hikes were my only hiatus that summer. As I climbed to the peaks and looked over the amazing vistas in southern California, I began to realize how much I missed nature and how it always had recharged me. When I was young, my parents took us camping most summers in the Sierras with family friends. We'd water ski on Mammoth Pools Reservoir on the west side of the Sierras, explore the deserted apple orchards, and fish and play in the snow-melted streams. As a child, it became a tradition that I looked forward to each summer.

The September morning we hiked Mount Whitney came

early. Rising at three o'clock in the morning, I'd hardly slept. Our group had spent the night at the portal campground to adjust to the altitude before we began our long trek to the summit. We shoved our tents and sleeping bags into the back of our cars, pulled our packs from the bear-proof containers, and used the toilet for the last time. We turned our headlamps on and began our twenty-two-mile round-trip hike.

We began at an elevation of 8,500 feet and would climb to 14,505 feet at the peak. I was already tired and cold, but my nerves fueled my adrenaline as we began our ascent into the alpine woods. The sweet smell of the fresh earth and pine trees made me forget everything that was wrong, all the things that begged for my attention. Our first stop was Lone Pine Lake where we ate granola bars and trail mix, my primary source of energy for the day. The lake was still and reflected the shadows of the trees and the light from the moon. We still had a long hike ahead of us to the top.

We continued through the meadow past Outpost Camp where the waterfall was dry and the air was crisp. The dirt trail turned to granite rocks as we passed the tree line. Emma was doing great and would often stop for me to catch up. We were making good time until we hit the legendary ninety-nine switchbacks. People who'd hiked Mount Whitney warned us they would last forever, and they did, seeming endless. My head began to feel fuzzy and my balance became unstable. I had to stop frequently to catch my breath, and Emma did too. If this was what it felt like at 11,000 feet elevation, I couldn't imagine hiking Mount Everest at 29,000 feet. We were almost to the top of the switchbacks when Emma stopped me.

"Mom, I don't know if I can keep going. My fingers are

frozen, I'm really dizzy, and my head feels like it's going to explode." Tears rolled down her pink cheeks. Did she have altitude sickness?

I gave her a hug and wiped her tears. "Do you think you can make it?"

"I don't know." She frowned.

I pulled two Ibuprofen out of my pack. "Here, take these and put your hands in your armpits to warm them up."

I didn't know what I'd do if Emma wanted to turn back. I didn't want to hike nearly the entire distance and not reach the summit. I knew we were close. I looked into her eyes. "It's only a few miles away. You got this. I'll stay with you."

She nodded, but I saw the uncertainty well up in her eyes. Her worry was getting the best of her. We made it to the top of the switchbacks and rested, looking down into the dry, barren Owen's Valley on one side and the Sequoia National Park on the other. The sky was clear with a layer of haze resting on the valley floor. It was breathtaking, exhilarating, and scary to be at that elevation.

My heart pounded in my ears, and my vision blurred. I put one foot in front of the other, concentrating as I walked on a ridge with a shear that was unforgiving. I looked back to make sure Emma was behind me. One wrong step and it would be all over.

Just before noon we'd reached the summit and caught up to the rest of our group. Emma's friend was eating her sandwich, and her mom was signing the logbook. Emma and I put our packs down, pulled out our phones, and began photographing our monumental achievement. My eyes started to tear as gratitude for our accomplishment settled in. Emma was smiling with pride. I gave her a squeeze and kissed her cold cheek. I'd made it. We'd made it. I was proud of both of us.

After fifteen minutes, we swiftly gathered our packs and began our descent. Once we cleared the switchbacks, Emma began talking to a fair-haired young male hiker we'd met earlier in the day. He engaged her in a conversation, and I quickly lost sight of them as they walked ahead, leaving me with my aching joints, burning feet, and thoughts about how my life had taken so many unexpected turns. Our group had split off, and it would be hours before I made it down. Every step hurt more than the next as my feet pounded the granite trail.

As I walked the rest of the trail alone, I listened to the whistling wind through the trees and took in the changing landscape as I made my decent, in awe of the vastness all around me. I felt a bond to my past that I'd lost through the years raising my girls. I was grateful for Emma's suggestion, my renewed connection to the joys and challenges of hiking, and my positive relationship with my eldest daughter. I didn't know exactly which path I needed to take when I returned home, but I knew being back in nature would give me the clarity to find my way.

A few months later, just before Thanksgiving, Lisa called me saying she needed help with my father. They'd had a disagreement—Dad didn't want her to put a lock on her bedroom door. I told her I'd talk to him next time I visited.

After I hung up the phone, I recalled a conversation with Nancy a few days prior. She said that Dad was having a hard time adjusting to Lisa, and the two had been butting heads about how she was running the house. Nancy also told me Lisa was very flirtatious with Dad and was concerned that he might be developing feelings for her. We both agreed that would add fuel to their arguments.

Sexual harassment was the first thought that popped into my head. I had to talk to Dad. Now I had to address two issues: the lock on Lisa's bedroom door and his feelings toward her.

In the last few months, Dad had allowed Lisa to park her friend's car in the driveway and store her extra clothes in the house and garage. When I questioned him about these things, he got mad and said Lisa had promised the car would only be there for a short time. I wanted Dad to have a say in some household decisions, but I understood why Mom had always managed everything. Letting Dad be involved was quickly working against me. I'd hired Lisa to ease my load, not add to it.

My unease with confrontation set in as I nervously told Lisa that she needed to find another home for her friend's car. She assured me she would remove it as soon as she could. Next, I had to talk to Dad about his feelings toward Lisa and the argument about the lock. When had I become their referee? It felt *all* wrong.

The following week, I took Dad out to lunch to get to the bottom of their differences. We sat in a large booth at Denny's and ordered.

"So Dad, how's Lisa been?" I asked, as if I didn't know.

"Okay, I guess," he paused. "Why do you ask?"

"I'm hearing that you and Lisa are having some disagreements."

He smirked and shook his head. "You know everything, don't you?"

"Yep," I smiled. I advised him to pick and choose his battles and not sweat the small stuff like the lock Lisa wanted on her door.

Dad stared out the window looking like a child who'd been caught stealing candy. After a little more convincing, he finally agreed to let Lisa install the lock on the door as long as she left her bedroom unlocked during the day. Dad was never able to articulate his reasoning for not wanting a lock on the door. I speculated it was his desire to have some control.

We were nearly home before I finally got the courage up to ask Dad how he felt toward Lisa. We weren't a family that talked about our feelings or about love, so I wasn't sure how our conversation would go. Just a few blocks away from home, I finally blurted out, "Dad, I need to ask you . . . do you have feelings for Lisa?" I gripped the steering wheel tighter and my foot pressed on the gas pedal.

He glanced at me, looking surprised. Seconds felt like minutes before he answered. "Well, I don't know, Laurie." He looked out the window. "Now that you mention it, I think I do." He paused. "In fact, I think I like her a lot. I don't think I've cared for anyone this much since I met your mother."

A jolt of shock ran through me. What? How could he love anyone but Mom? How could he betray Mom and me? I slammed on my brakes as I approached the stop sign and turned to him. "Dad, you can't act on this. She could sue us for sexual harassment." I held his gaze to make sure he understood the significance of my words.

His fists clenched and he let out a sigh. "Damn it, Laurie, I know! I can't act on it. It doesn't work anymore."

My ears burned as reality rushed in. Did my eighty-two-year-old father just tell me his penis didn't work anymore? I could've lived a full life without knowing that. I wanted to pretend I hadn't heard him, but it was too late. Was this really happening? I pulled into the driveway, still pondering what to say to Lisa. I had to put a stop to Dad's infatuation and Lisa's flirting.

I helped him out of the car and found Mom watching TV in the den while Lisa folded laundry beside her. I sat on the couch. "I talked to Dad at lunch today." Adrenaline pumped through my veins.

"Oh, what did he say, *mi hija?*" she asked innocently.

I never took offense at her calling me *mi hija* until that moment. I wasn't her daughter. I was her employer. After my conversation with Nancy, I no longer trusted Lisa's intentions.

"I believe Dad has a little crush on you?"

"Oh, really?" She flashed me a look of surprise.

She wasn't as innocent as she pretended to be. "I think your playful personality is being mistaken for flirtation on his part."

I suspected her actions were intentional. I asked her to stop dancing with him in the mornings and be careful about how she talked to him.

She smiled and agreed. "Okay, I'll be careful."

I left doubting that my conversation had made any difference. I called Will on my drive home to fill him in. He laughed and said, "My friend saw Lisa at the doctor's office with Mom and Dad. She was wearing a miniskirt, heels, and a low-cut blouse."

"What? Why didn't you tell me this sooner?"

"She just told me a week ago."

"I wished I had known that before today." If I'd had this information, my confrontation might have been more direct.

He apologized before we hung up. I hadn't asked for much help from Will, but after the last few years of managing our parents' finances and caregivers, and overseeing their care by myself, I could have used his support. He lived only two miles from our parents, while I was an hour away. Months would pass between his visits. He worked long hours, and I wasn't working full-time, but the recent accumulation of my responsibilities for my parents and my own family was piling up.

I knew then I should replace Lisa, but it felt like a monstrous task. She had become so embedded in the household and with my parents that it would take me months to encourage her to remove all her belongings without her knowing my real intent. I didn't want Mom and Dad's care to become jeopardized, and Christmas was around the corner. I couldn't fathom finding a new caregiver while preparing for the holidays. I made the decision to wait and see if my pep talk with Dad and Lisa would encourage them to behave. I would assess everything again in the new year. I loved making Christmas special for my girls, and I didn't want Lisa and Dad to ruin that for me.

eighteen

Over the next several months, Dad and Lisa were getting along better, which gave me a small break before the tectonic plates in my life began to shift. I didn't know at the time that the small tremors and fissures that had occurred in my marriage over the last nineteen years were about to break loose and make me question everything I thought to be true. Maybe I was naive. Maybe I didn't want to believe those early warning signs. Maybe I was just too damn busy caring for everyone else to notice.

The first shift came one evening when David came home from work and told me about his day. "Mike, the new CEO, confirmed today that he's bringing in his own Senior VP of HR and Administration to replace me, and he's starting next month." His head hung low, and I could see this was not good news for him. David had been in that role for over a year, with over two hundred employees working for him.

The hurt in his eyes was clear. We had known this shift was a possibility when the new CEO took over. A new leader would usually bring in his own executive staff. David had never been demoted before, and it hit him hard.

"Oh, I'm so sorry," I said, giving him a hug, hoping to

ease his sadness. "At least they aren't letting you go altogether."

"That might have been better at this point." He paused. "But I don't think they'd do that." He pulled away and poured himself a glass of wine.

From then on, David's bruised ego sat just beneath the surface in everything we did. I had wondered if leaving his job might have made him happier, but he was three years away from early retirement, and if he left now, he'd walk away from a huge portion of his pension plan. His golden handcuffs were on tight.

Over dinner that night, he told me he'd be keeping his Senior VP title, but he'd be taking on less appealing responsibilities like real estate strategy, risk management, benefits finance, and payroll processes, and he'd work with a reduced staff of fifteen.

Several months went by as David tried to adjust to his new position. Every morning that he left for work seemed more painful than the next. One Monday morning, he stood in front of the mirror and recited, "I love my job, I love my job, I'm so happy it's Monday," sarcasm biting each word. I could see the agony in his eyes each morning he walked out the door. I knew it must have been torture for him to walk past the staff that he used to manage every day. I worried about his well-being, but there was little I could do outside of encouraging him to go for a walk or to dinner and a movie.

As time went on, David sulked around the house, spending most weekends sitting in front of the TV and napping in the afternoons. His temper became shorter. He snapped at us more often for small things—leaving the blankets unfolded or dishes on the counter. I made sure the house was in perfect order and the girls' needs were taken care of so he would have less reason to be critical, but that only provided a small buffer. I made excuses for his behavior and walked lightly when he was home.

One day he called me at lunchtime and in a sharp tone asked me what was for dinner. I told him I didn't know yet.

He spat, "How do you not know what's for dinner?"

David worked hard, and a warm meal was important to him. There was rarely a night when dinner wasn't waiting for him when he got home. If I was out for the night, I always told him so he could pick something up on his way home.

"I haven't thought about it yet, it's only noon," I responded irritably.

My heart felt pierced. It seemed like nothing was right anymore. I thought we had set up the perfect arrangement for our family responsibilities, but now I was questioning our plan.

As David continued to bring home his unhappiness, my shoulders stiffened each night as the front door opened. He'd call from his office, letting me know he was on his way home, so I'd quickly scan the house to make sure everything was in order. I told the kids to clean up their snacks and get ready for dinner, trying everything to ease the strain. During dinner, he would complain about his day, and I'd brace myself to swallow the tension. I began to understand the pain Mom must have endured with Dad and why she left every summer for six weeks to sail with her friend Georgie in Maine.

One chilly February morning, I quickly cleaned up the breakfast dishes after the girls left for school. David and I had a meeting that day to update our will and trust for the first time in ten years. David had made an appointment with Charles Lawrence, the same lawyer who'd helped him manage his aunt and uncle's estate.

We entered Charles's well-appointed Beverly Hills office, and his assistant walked us down a long hallway decorated with travel photos of Cuba and other exotic places. She sat us down in a large conference room with a huge oval mahogany table and closed the door. I suddenly felt inadequate. I wasn't the one who sat in meetings all day with people dressed in business attire. I'd left that life behind when I chose to stay home to raise our kids. David had more recent knowledge about estate planning than I did, and I felt at a disadvantage.

Charles came in minutes later, wearing blue dress slacks and a white shirt with an open collar. He sat down across from us, and I asked him about his travels to Cuba, trying to build my own rapport. David then asked Charles about some unfinished business they'd been working on, leaving me out of the conversation. I pulled my notepad out of my purse and waited patiently to discuss our business with Charles.

Finally, Charles began asking us a series of questions in the event we both died and scribbled our answers on a yellow pad. When we finished, David closed his leather-bound notepad and I rose from the chair, thinking our meeting was over. Charles turned to David, "So one more thing—have you made your final decision to keep your inheritance separate?"

"Uh, yes," he replied, with a sheepish look on his face.

"Okay, I'll need you to answer the same questions so I can draft a different will and trust for you," Charles replied.

Everything immediately slowed down as if I were in a dream. I was trapped and couldn't move. It felt familiar, as if I'd experienced that feeling before. I realized it was similar to the feelings I'd had when I was a child and Ken raped me. I tried to speak, but I couldn't find my voice. It was as if I were in a separate room, trying to get their attention by waving and banging on the window that separated us, but they didn't hear me. David and Charles continued their conversation. I didn't exist.

I finally came to and muttered, "What? We never discussed this." I gave David a look that could have set the building on fire. It took every ounce of willpower to keep my tears hidden. I suddenly hated David for making a plan for his future life that did not include me. The inheritance was his Aunt Ruth and Uncle Harold's legacy and thus was meant for *our* daughters' college education.

Charles's eyebrows shot up as an awkward tension settled into the room. He must have realized that this was the first time I'd heard about David's decision.

David stuttered, "Um okay . . . I'll need to get back to you on some of those details." His matter-of-fact tone cut deeper. This was just another business deal for him.

I turned to Charles and glared back at David. "We need to discuss this later."

The air in the room became suffocating. I was barely able to breathe, and my world began closing in on me. Was this really happening? I stood up. "Are we done? I need some air."

I walked down the hall, passing Charles's assistant, barely turning my head to thank her. I opened the door and gasped for air in the hallway. David trailed behind me saying goodbye to Charles. I pushed the elevator button, hoping it would open before David arrived, but he caught up with me and we rode down together. I stared at the floor, unable to say a word.

On the ride home, I sat close to my door, needing to be as far from David as possible. When he stopped at a stoplight, I wanted to jump out of the car and run. I was still numb and frozen, and I had to pick up the girls from school in an hour.

All afternoon my actions were robotic while a pure, sharp anger hummed at the depths of my soul. Why had he chosen not to discuss this with me first? Why was he protecting himself, his money and future, and not the unity of our marriage? I'd never given him reason not to trust me. We had been married for twenty years, and I thought we were in this together. We'd taken vows—for better or worse, richer or poorer, in sickness and in health. What else was he up to that I didn't know? What had I done to make him want to rip open my heart and leave me lying there to bleed?

Over the next couple of weeks, I tried to make sense of the new chaos that traveled through my mind and body. From morning until night, I obsessed over his decision to look out for only himself financially, to withhold his generosity in jointly enjoying the money. I randomly burst into tears in the car or while making dinner. When I wasn't crying, I educated myself about the legal aspects of David's choice, scouring the Internet for answers. I quickly discovered that inherited money wasn't community property unless you comingled it, so I had no legal rights to make him share it. I called a girlfriend who shared in a family trust that her dad had set up for her and her sisters. She told me she and her husband always discussed and agreed upon how her inheritance would be spent or invested, and she suggested I do the same with David.

The following Friday night, David and I found ourselves alone without the children. I set the mood and mustered up the energy to have appetizers and wine set out when David arrived home with a nice dinner to follow, proving to him I was worthy of his partnership. As we finished our meal, I asked him, "Why didn't you want to discuss your inheritance with me before you made your decision?"

He crossed his arms. "Laurie, you're not bringing this up again, are you? We've already discussed this."

We'd had one brief unresolved conversation a few days earlier. "Your choice was hurtful, and I'm still having a hard time." A lump in my throat quickly formed.

"If you love me, this money won't matter," he said angrily.

Rage kicked in. "If you loved me you would have talked to me about this before you humiliated me in Charles's office."

David's voice rose. "Laurie, stop making a big deal out of nothing."

Tears of helpless anger trickled down my face as I grabbed my car keys and left the house. I felt a huge division from him as a result of what he'd done, and even more from how he reacted when I wanted to talk about it with him—it wasn't just about money. It was about how he valued—or devalued—me as a partner. I drove in circles around my neighborhood trying to see the road as sobs gathered in my throat. I eventually found myself sitting in my car in front of the black ocean. The sky was dark with no moon. I burst out crying as I felt a piece of my heart turn as black as the night sky.

Desperate, I called my girlfriend who'd given me advice a few days earlier. I told her what had happened as my tears continued falling.

"I'm so sorry he's being such a jerk about this," she said with warmth in her voice. "He'll come around; just give him a little time."

My body slowly stopped convulsing as she stayed with me on the phone. Her words comforted me, and I hoped she was right. Maybe David just needed a little more time to see how hurtful his choice was, and then he'd want to repair the damage. I knew he loved me. Why didn't he want to make things right?

I slept little the night before we were scheduled to sign our new will and trust documents. My nerves were on edge, worried that David might spring another surprise. I couldn't bear to be humiliated again.

Wearily, I asked him that morning, "So, no surprises today, right?" My stomach churned.

"No, I don't think so."

We agreed to drive separately. David had a meeting in the area afterward, and I wanted an escape car, just in case—the scab of my wound was still fresh.

The assistant escorted us to a small conference room with no windows. We sat down at the table and silently waited for Charles.

"So I have both your community and David's separate will and trust documents for you both to sign." The word "separate" left me hollow.

Charles pulled out the two documents and asked his assistant to notarize them.

David read through each page, referring back to the list of

questions he pulled from his shirt pocket. As we came to the pages that discussed who'd manage our assets in the event David died first, he asked Charles. "So if I pass first, can Laurie change the terms of the trust?"

"Well, yes, it's a revocable trust."

"Should we consider putting a clause that states that these terms can't be changed after my death?"

His words ripped off my fresh scab.

Charles responded, "By doing that, it makes the trust irrevocable. I don't recommend that."

Enraged, I tilted my head and glared. "We don't want that."

David grinned, "Well I guess, as long as Laurie doesn't have another family that I'm not aware of, it should be fine." He turned to me with big eyes. "Do you?"

I knew he was trying to be funny, but the joke fell short.

"You're the one who's been married before and travels all the time. Maybe you're the one with another family," I spat as my pulse pounded.

Charles's eyes bulged as he glanced at me, then David. A familiar awkwardness filled the room.

"Okay, I think we can move on," Charles replied as he handed David his next page.

As we finished signing our documents, I swallowed my humiliation and asked Charles, "Is there a contract you can draft stating that in the event David and I divorce, David will pay for our kids' college education with his separate assets?"

I wanted a guarantee that David would follow through with Harold and Ruth's wishes to pay for our children's college education. David had been coaching his brother on how to invest his inheritance, and he had chosen to pay for only half of his son's college expenses. After David's poor communication around his inheritance and the advice David was giving his brother, I realized that I needed to protect my daughters' future and myself. My inquiry went against everything I had valued and believed about marriage, but David left me no choice.

Charles said, "You may want to contact a family law attorney. I can draft up something simple, but this isn't my area of expertise. I'll send you a couple of referrals."

I thanked Charles, stood up, and walked toward the office door. I hadn't recovered from the last blow in Charles's office and here was another one—David's joke about my having another family. It was anything but a joke. How could he say such a thing? We rode down the elevator in silence again. As the doors opened David said, "I think that went well . . . and as long as you don't do anything stupid, everything will be fine."

Shaking, I seethed at yet another insult. "You're the only one who's making stupid decisions."

A look of surprise crossed his face. I walked to my car as I fumbled for my keys. When I got in the car, I called a marriage and family therapist who had been recommended. Tears fell from my cheeks, and my voice quavered as I left a desperate message asking for her first available appointment. My marriage was in pieces. I was too dizzy and confused to gather them all up by myself. I didn't care if David joined me for the session or not. I was lost, alone, and I needed someone's help.

The rest of the day I spun in circles, thinking about how the therapist might help David understand how hurtful his decisions were. Once he saw that, he'd apologize and right his wrong. Then we could work on rebuilding our marriage so we could have a united purpose once again.

nineteen

My stomach in knots, I entered the waiting room for our first couple's therapy appointment alone, pressed the call button, and sat down. David had a last-minute business trip, but I had an urgent need to address our problems, and I couldn't wait for him to join me. Susan, the new therapist, agreed that I could come on my own. I had only seen a therapist a handful of times in my early twenties. Within minutes, a petite, curly-haired woman with a warm smile greeted me.

"Hi, I'm Susan. Come on in." She motioned me down the corridor.

I sat down on her modern couch across from her contemporary wingback chair. Her office looked like it had recently been decorated, a contrast to the dated eighties look of the waiting room.

"So what brings you in today?" she asked kindly.

I wrung my hands. "Well, my husband and I are having marital issues, and I don't know what to do." My voiced cracked.

She asked what I thought the problem was.

"My husband has an unhealthy relationship with money, and he's controlling."

Susan asked for examples so I gave her the list: David's

decision to keep his inheritance separate and questioning most of my purchases. He hadn't worn his wedding ring in over ten years. He disliked most things I bought for the house, but he wouldn't put any effort in decorating. He hadn't bought me a birthday present on my fortieth birthday. I inhaled, realizing I hadn't taken a breath. Could we fix everything that was wrong with my marriage?

She acknowledged each problem, and before I knew it, she was sitting on the edge of her seat signaling our first session was over. I wanted to stay for the rest of the afternoon—there was so much more to say. I had to relieve the pressure valve on everything I'd stored up so my anxiety would stop gnawing at me day and night. She stood up and said, "These issues aren't a big deal. I'm sure we can work through them."

What? How could she say that? This *was* a big deal. My marriage was teetering on the brink of destruction. I'd worked so hard to create the family I didn't have as a child, and now everything I'd built was in jeopardy. Fixing it was the only option. I got in my car and drove home. Was I really making too big of a deal out of my unhappiness? My gut said no, but I felt deflated by her comment. Maybe after she met David, she'd see his controlling behavior for herself.

Two weeks later, we were scheduled for our first therapy session together. That morning David asked, "So what are we talking about in therapy today?"

I could see uncertainty his eyes.

"The state of our marriage," I retorted. "We aren't in a good place right now."

He responded with his usual silence. Perhaps that shouldn't have disappointed me, but it did.

That afternoon, we walked into the therapist's office and I introduced David to Susan. He made small talk with her as we sat down on the couch. Did she notice the distance between us?

"So what would you like to discuss today?" Susan scanned our faces.

David turned to me. "Whatever she'd like to talk about."

Did he not see *all* that was wrong with our marriage?

My lip quivered as I glanced at David. "Last week when I met with Susan, I told her that you were keeping your inheritance separate. You question most of my spending, and we can't seem to agree on furnishings for the house."

Our living room still sat empty after seventeen years. That seemed long enough. Each time I looked at it, I was reminded that his mother's living room was still empty too.

"David, do you think Laurie has a spending problem?" Susan asked.

"I think the problem is that we value money very differently."

I sarcastically mumbled, "We certainly do." I wanted to scream that all his decisions were financially based without regard to how it might emotionally affect someone—mostly me. He would only agree to purchase a big-ticket item if he thought we needed it. What I wanted to do was to make our house a home that was comfortable for our family and friends.

David said sharply, "So here's an example, Susan. Laurie just bought a cake plate and spent one hundred and fifty dollars on it." He threw his hands in the air.

I looked over at him and saw his eyes bulging, as if I'd just committed a crime. I melted into the couch, feeling small and wondering why he was reacting so strongly about my buying a pretty dish. I turned to him to defend my purchase, and we began arguing. Susan observed us for a while before she interjected, "Okay, let's look at this differently."

"Laurie, do you have any credit cards that David is unaware of?"

"Of course not," I countered protectively. I didn't have a spending problem, but David thought I did.

"David, do you think Laurie is hiding any credit cards from you?"

"Not that I know of, but how would I know for sure?"

"Because you have access to every account," I said. Tears welled up in my eyes as I wondered how we got on that subject. I wasn't the one who needed fixing, David was. How did the focus turn to me?

"Okay, we'll need to pick this up next time," Susan said as she got up and wrote our bill.

Why didn't she call David out on his behavior? Did she not see what I did? At one point in our session, I made eye contact with her, and she gave me a look suggesting she understood my dilemma. Maybe she was waiting a few sessions so David would become more comfortable with her, but I couldn't wait. My future was in her hands, and I needed results—and soon. We thanked her and walked to our separate cars. Upset and confused by our session, I drove away hoping she'd be more direct next time.

༄

During our first year of therapy, we saw Susan every other week. When David traveled, I kept our appointment, searching for my own happiness. During our sessions together, we talked about how the foundation of our marriage had been broken by the events of the past and that we were living parallel lives in the same house. Susan used the example of the Venn diagram to suggest we find more overlap in our interests since the only common denominator was our children. She suggested we have a weekly date night and consider having sex before going out. We planned weekly dates, bought new road bikes that we barely rode, and started walking together on the weekends. David seemed willing to work at our marriage, so we both followed through on her suggestions. It gave me hope. But we still continued to fight.

David and I agreed to finish decorating the empty rooms in our house, and to update our kitchen and family rooms too. During that year, we couldn't agree on the couches, lamps, rugs, or wall and cabinet colors. He wanted a say in what we chose, but we had very different tastes, and he didn't offer alternative suggestions. Exhausted by our constant arguments, I asked for Susan's help. One of her techniques was humor, using the cake plate example repeatedly to show David how he could be more generous. She didn't see the financial issues that David said I had. David didn't laugh at her humorous example, but I did.

When we discussed David's lack of interest in wearing his wedding ring or the way he told me he was keeping his inheritance separate, she told him those were examples of how he was protecting himself and was only seventy-five percent in the marriage. When Susan made that reference, I wanted to hug her. She'd finally put words to feelings I couldn't articulate. I'd given my heart to David and continued to give one hundred percent to our marriage and family, even after his choices. I was sure her metaphor would help him see his actions as clearly as I did, and then he'd want to give me the same. He was a CPA, after all.

When I'd talk with Susan on my own, I was more free to discuss how deeply hurt I was by David's choices over the years. She told me, "Give me some time to gain his trust."

I agreed. She suggested that I expand my group of friends, plan more weekend trips with my girlfriends, and get involved in more outside activities. I lit up at the thought of doing more for myself. My focus had primarily been on our family, outside of daily exercise and one girls' ski trip a year. Any other trips were with David or our family. Her support gave me the freedom to act on her suggestions.

She repeatedly encouraged me to let go of the anger and resentment I felt toward David. I wanted to, but it wasn't easy when he didn't express remorse for his actions. If he didn't see his part in our differences, then our patterns would repeat.

During our time in therapy, we'd met with a family law attorney who helped us put together a postnuptial agreement. After David's stance on his inheritance, I insisted on a legal signed document to make sure our children's higher education would be taken care of. David's brother was only paying for half of their first child's education, and since I'd already been blindsided, I wasn't going to allow that to happen to me.

Months passed, and we still hadn't completed our agreement. I nudged and cajoled David to review the emails so we could make progress, but he made little effort to get the document finished. We disagreed on many details, including what expenses would be covered and at what age the kids needed to finish their education. Each time I asked him to finish it, my resentment grew. How was I supposed to let go of my bitterness when the pile continued to grow? I couldn't work through it all.

Almost two years after the first meeting with our lawyer, we finally sat down to sign our postnuptial agreement. As we waited for everyone to arrive, my mind traveled back to a moment when David suggested we sign a prenuptial agreement before we got married. I'd refused to sign one then, and I didn't want to sign the postnuptial now, but I didn't have any other choice. I thought I'd feel relief when it was finally signed, but when I left the lawyer's office, I was grief-stricken. Having everything legally spelled out went against everything I believed marriage to be. Marriage was when two people loved and trusted each other deeply, knowing they'd look out for each other no matter what. Now my marriage was nothing more than a contractual agreement—one that had made us adversaries, not allies.

I spent the next several weeks trying to make peace with myself. That was behind us now. I had to move forward with my wounded heart in tow. I remained hopeful that with time, we'd find our way back to each other, even though the river between us had grown even larger.

Most days, when I left the couple's therapy office, I was optimistic that we were building our bridge once again, but by the next session, there was something new to address. David eventually apologized for his decision to keep his inheritance separate, but it didn't feel genuine, and I never saw remorse on his face. Was he truly sorry for leaving me out of his life?

Would it happen again? I didn't know, so I continued to expand the ways I could cope with my marriage amid my uncertainty.

I had added more yoga into my exercise routine over the last couple years. It became a safe place for me. In my first yoga classes over four years ago, I struggled as my mind raced with my to-do list, and I twitched and wiggled at the end, but something brought me back. After each class, I felt the benefits. I found myself more focused, and my central nervous system was calmer. My muscles enjoyed being stretched, my body became stronger, and I appreciated the positive messages the teachers left us with such as, "We have the power of choice" and "choose love over fear."

One summer day after class, one of my favorite teachers announced she was leading a yoga retreat in Santa Ynez. I asked my girlfriend Marsha if she wanted to join me, and she agreed. We told our husbands, cleared our calendars, and paid our deposits. I couldn't wait. This would be the first time since getting married that I'd spend four days focusing on only me.

The retreat couldn't have come at a better time. We'd just moved Emma into college, Heather was about to have her tonsils removed so she wouldn't be sick all the time, and she was preparing for her ACT college entrance exam. Jessie's soccer games were in full swing. Katie was taking tennis lessons and had committed to the ski team in Mammoth, which meant I'd be driving to and from Mammoth twice a month. My calendar was full as always, but there was little that I'd allow to get in the way of those four days.

Marsha and I arrived in Santa Ynez in the late afternoon. The hills were barren from the winter drought and the hot dry summer that had followed. The oak trees looked like green blotches painted on the hills. The retreat was held in a large house surrounded by pomegranate trees, a vegetable garden, and a patio covered with vines abundant with ripe purple grapes. Our shared room was quaint yet minimal, with a small bouquet of fresh flowers resting on the nightstand. Marsha and I introduced ourselves to the other five women before our first relaxation class. It was the perfect beginning to our retreat. As I walked to dinner, my body relaxed, and my tension began to release.

After dinner that night, we met in the living room with our notebooks ready. The warmth of the fireplace on my back relaxed me as we all sat down in a circle. Our instructor asked us to set an intention for the retreat. I'd never thought about setting an intention—my life had always been about everyone else. I wrote down, "Let go of my anger and resentment toward David." My ongoing struggle.

Over the next two days, we practiced yoga, ate our vegan meals, and picked berries. Our third day was spent in silence. I went for a hike, and after lunch we had free time. I found my-self unsure of what to do with myself. I was a doer, always checking things off my list, but I had no list, and I was lost. I'd never allowed myself to have time to relax or just be. At first, I walked in circles around the property. I observed what the other women were doing to see if their choices resonated with me. One woman napped, another was writing in her journal, a few others were painting on paper or rocks. I found a large rock in the garden and sat down at the table. I painted a rainbow on my rock and wrote "gratitude" under it. I painted a couple of pictures of the landscape. My paintings looked like a second grader had painted them, but there was something freeing about sitting down and being creative.

During our daily yoga, we focused on our intentions. In class, we'd breathe out what we no longer wanted in our lives and breathe in what we wanted more of. I found myself crying during those classes as my shaky voice exhaled, but each day it seemed that another layer was shed. I read my book, talked to the other women, and made a vision board of what I wanted to create in my life. I added pictures of travel to exotic places, family, and skiing. I added words like redefining my marriage, celebrating female friendships, joy, and happiness.

On our last night, we had a puja ceremony. Our instructors told us we were going to burn away what no longer served us. I had my words written down: "Let go of my anger and resentment toward David, Dad, Ken, and Will." Through therapy, I realized that I'd stuffed my past inside me and my marital struggles on top, leaving me combustible. I knew I wouldn't be able to let everything go that weekend—there was far too much, but it was a start. I continued to grapple with how differently David and I had honored our marriage, trying to reconcile the gut-wrenching hurt I still had. I knew I had needed to push for the legal agreements, but at what cost?

When it was my turn, I dropped the paper into the fire and bellowed, "Burn motherfucker, burn." The other women chuckled. The laughter died down and I watched the paper turn to ash as I thought about the fury I felt toward the men in my life. Dad, who had never been a strong father figure; Ken's physical and sexual abuse; Will's teasing and threats and his lack of help with Mom and Dad; David for not trusting me enough to be the husband I wanted him to be. I was ashamed of myself for allowing so much to stay unresolved for so long.

On our way home, Marsha and I talked about our experiences and what our teacher had said to us in our last class that morning: "Now that you've released what's no longer serving you, you can make room for more of what you want. So take this time to think about what you want to bring into your life."

That morning I felt full of joy and happiness. I told my friend I wanted to bring more love into my life. I wanted to stop fighting with David and take the peaceful loving energy I'd found over the last four days home and weave it into our marriage and family.

She looked over at me and smiled. "I want that for you too."

I'd never experienced the support of other women like I did that weekend. As we witnessed each other's intentions, I felt part of something bigger than myself. I left feeling that everyone understood my desire for a new life, because they were all seeking something different too. There was no judgment. No right or wrong. There was less shame and more acceptance. And for those four days, I belonged and was not alone.

twenty

In the months after my yoga retreat, I began taking better care of myself. I experimented with cooking new healthy meals with the recipes I'd brought home from the retreat. My yoga practice continued to evolve, and I experienced more joy in my mundane routine. I had more energy and needed less sleep. David and I continued therapy, and I thanked Susan for her suggestions. We'd started putting our past behind us as he began to open up.

One Saturday morning after we'd made love, we lay in bed talking about our to-do lists and the kids' activities for the day. He suddenly turned to me and said, "You know I've been thinking about what Susan said in therapy on Wednesday."

"Oh, what's that?" I looked curiously into his dark brown eyes.

"Well, I've never told anyone about this, but . . . " His lip began to quiver.

I caressed his arm and whispered, "It's okay."

His eyes filled with tears. It was only the second time in twenty years I'd seen him cry. The first was when his uncle passed away.

He told me his dad had tried to physically beat the asthma

out of him more than once, and his parents didn't treat him medically for it until he was in high school. He went on to tell me that his mom tried to protect him and his brother when his dad would get angry with them, but she was no match for him and would get caught in the crossfire. Sometimes he would strike her, too.

"I'm so sorry you had those experiences." I hugged him. "I can't imagine growing up like that."

"Well, now you know why it's hard for me to be around my parents." He paused. "That's why I never tell them I love them, like you tell your parents. I just can't."

"I understand." I knew that his parents hadn't treated his asthma until high school, but I didn't know about the physical abuse.

He rolled onto his back and stared at the ceiling. "You're a better person than I'll ever be. I don't know how you can do it."

My chest expanded with warmth. His confessions drew me closer.

"I get it. Your childhood was more difficult than mine. At least I knew that I was loved growing up, even with our family dysfunctions." I looked into his eyes. "Thanks for sharing. I know that wasn't easy, and it means a lot to me."

He hugged me before he got up to shower. I knew it was difficult for David to open up—the shame he felt was obvious. A moment of fury and a sense of betrayal washed over me because he hadn't told me these things sooner, but I let it go. I could see how deeply hurt David had been by his childhood, and it meant a great deal to me that he was sharing his vulnerability with me now.

⟨᧖⟩

Susan had recently been talking to us about our pasts and how our childhood experiences affected our current relationships. In our last therapy session, David had told Susan about some of his painful childhood memories, but he'd revealed so much more to me that morning. He seemed to be making the link between not being able to trust his parents and how that same lack of trust had unfolded in our marriage. Seeing his vulnerable side left me feeling closer to David than I had in years. I was finally getting to know my husband from the inside, and I would encourage him to share more. If he opened up, he'd learn he could trust me, and our connection would deepen. This might be a turning point for us. Our heartfelt conversation gave me hope that our marriage was finally on the right track.

My parents' lives seemed to be getting back to normal when we celebrated Mom's eightieth birthday. I had organized a brunch the week after I returned from my yoga retreat. We celebrated at a restaurant on the Redondo Beach pier. It overlooked the Santa Monica Bay and Palos Verdes, the same bay we'd sailed around when I was a child. David, the four girls, my brother Will, Dad, Nancy, Lisa, our caregiver, and her boyfriend were invited to the brunch. I arranged a boat ride around the harbor for all of us afterward.

Mom had recently started using a walker, and I expected this would be her last boat ride. We arrived at the restaurant and met Lisa and her boyfriend in the lobby. She stood up and hugged me. She wore a V-neck floral dress that accentuated her cleavage, three-inch heels, and red lipstick that matched her dress. She introduced her boyfriend, George, who thanked me for inviting him.

When Dad arrived, his eyes darted to Lisa and traveled head to toe and back again. Will chuckled as he glanced at me —we read each other's minds. Lisa and Dad had been getting along better, but I could see Dad still felt something for her.

The hostess seated us at our table in the center of the restaurant, giving Mom the best view of the ocean with birthday balloons tied to her chair.

After we ordered, I pointed to a sailboat sailing out of the harbor. "Mom, look at the beautiful sailboat passing by."

A smile crossed her face as she looked at the boat. It appeared she was searching for words but said nothing. Did she know today was her birthday? Did she realize this was the bay where she'd sailed for more than thirty years?

Our food arrived and Nancy spoon-fed Mom. She was losing her fine motor skills and couldn't cut up her own food, but Mom was able to feed herself, though it was slow going. I wished Nancy had let Mom do more for herself for as long as she could—anything that might prolong her independence— but that wasn't Nancy's nature. She liked to take care of people.

The waitress brought out the cake with all the candles lit. As we sang "Happy Birthday" to Mom, she began singing along like a child. I smiled with joy. It was the most she'd said in the last six months.

As we strolled from the restaurant to the boat for our harbor cruise, Lisa walked next to me and said, "*Mi hija*, your dad asked me last week if I would take him and your mom on a trip soon."

Lisa had just returned from a vacation at the Grand Canyon.

I said cautiously, "I'd need to think about it, but where would you take them?"

"Your dad liked the idea of going to the Grand Canyon."

"Let's talk about this next week when I come to visit." I wanted to think through her request.

Her bright lips smiled. "Okay, *mi hija*."

I still had reservations about Lisa. The last few times I'd been to the house, I'd found her putting on her makeup and curling her hair at ten in the morning while Mom still wasn't dressed and hadn't eaten breakfast. Her friend's car was still in the driveway, even though I'd asked her to remove it six months earlier. I'd recently learned that Nancy was storing some of Lisa's belongings in her garage too. She clearly was not following through with my requests, but otherwise my parents' care had been stable, and I was grateful for that.

We arrived at the boat. David and Will helped Mom find a comfortable seat, and Katie and Jessie shuffled around the boat looking for the best spot. As we left the dock, I glanced over at Mom. Her smile was wide as the wind brushed past her cheeks. Mom's smile never faded the entire cruise. It was the same grin I'd seen when we sailed together all those years.

I grabbed Mom's hand and caught her gaze. "Remember when we went sailing and there were small craft warnings up?"

She paused for a second, "Oh, yeah."

"We were probably a little crazy for going out that day," I said.

She chuckled, "You're probably right." Mom said more than she had for some time. Maybe the boat ride had unlocked something inside her.

I remembered that day as if it were yesterday. It was a cool spring morning, and I was in college. I'd spent the night at my parents' house, and in the morning Mom asked if I wanted to go sailing.

It was Saturday, I didn't have to work, and I had Sunday to study. "Sure, I'll go."

"You'll go with me?" she asked giddily.

"Yeah." It had been a while since we'd been sailing together.

Mom scurried off to change her clothes while I made us a couple of turkey and cheese sandwiches. I put them in a cooler with our Diet Cokes and two beers. Mom loved to drink a beer once we got out past the breakwater. It was a ritual.

We said goodbye to Dad and arrived at the marina. There was a strong breeze. As we pulled into our parking spot I looked at the Harbor Master's Office flags. They were stiff in the wind and it was whistling through the masts and rigging of the sailboats docked below us. A pang of fear settled in as I looked at Mom. "Do you think it's too windy to go out?"

She looked at the flags. "Oh, no, we'll be fine. We can use the storm jib."

A storm jib was a small front sail used in heavy wind. Mom was always up for a challenge, and her confidence was contagious. Most sailors wouldn't attempt sailing in heavy winds, but that didn't scare Mom—she saw it as an adventure.

We rigged the boat, hoisted the sails, and I pushed us off the dock like I'd done so many times before. I hopped onto the bow and crawled back to the cockpit as we tacked out of the small harbor entrance. We had a motor, but Mom rarely used it. After we left the harbor, we changed tack and headed north toward Marina Del Rey. Mom was sitting on the leeward side of the boat, controlling the tiller with her foot.

Mom began eating her sandwich, and I wedged our two beers between the cushion and the side of the cockpit. The wind blew her hair flat. I climbed out of the cabin and plopped myself down, holding onto anything I could find so I wouldn't fall over. The waves were rolling in from the northwest, and at times I thought the white-capped swells might swallow our boat. I sat on the windward side, bracing myself so I wouldn't slip. I cracked open our beers and handed one to Mom.

She took a sip, and her smile grew wider. "A real sailor never goes sailing without a libation."

Mom was truly in her element. After an hour, I noticed the wind had picked up even more. I thought about what John would advise as Mom checked the sails.

Mom said, "Here, take the tiller. I'm going to reef the main. I think we should head back in."

John had taught us well. Mom climbed up onto the deck and carefully supported herself as she lowered the mainsail. Waves were crashing against our bow. We needed to safely tack and head back into the harbor without the wind overpowering us. Worry kept my attention as Mom crawled back into the cockpit and took the tiller from me. I didn't want to think about having to rescue Mom if she fell overboard in high winds.

"Ready to tack?"

"Ready." I grabbed the jib sheet, waiting to pull it around to the other side of the boat.

"Helm's a-lee," Mom called out as she pulled the tiller toward her and tacked into the wind. As the boat came around, a swell swallowed the bow of the boat, splashing us as the water traveled back into the cockpit. I wiped the salty water off my face. Finally, we were heading back in.

We tacked into the harbor and let down our jib as we sailed past the Harbor Patrol. Someone was watching us through the window as we passed by. The small craft advisory flag was flying, which was a warning that winds were at a speed just shy of gale force. I had never been in winds that strong before, and had no intention of doing it again. I glanced at Mom, who had the tiller between her legs and a wide smile on her face. She seemed to think nothing of what we had just done.

Mom sailed into our slip, and I jumped onto the dock to tie the boat up. Adrenaline pumped through my veins as my feet hit the stable dock. We had made it back. I always counted on Mom's strong, steady force to guide me forward.

Today, as we continued to motor around the harbor for Mom's last boat ride, I realized how much I missed my sailing adventures with her—our many weekends to Catalina with other friends and the trip we took up to the Channel Islands when we stayed off Santa Cruz Island. Even with Mom's memory fading, I'd always carry my memories of her strength and courage with me.

That fall a few weeks after Mom's party, I sat down to pay Mom and Dad's bills. Their cash withdrawals had increased, but the receipts weren't matching up. The difference was several hundred dollars. After I'd found out Karen was skimming from us, I told Lisa from the start I wanted *all* receipts and she'd agreed, but over the last few months I'd been lax about reconciling their finances. I checked my parents' online credit card activity and noticed there was a charge in Williams, Arizona, from two days prior. Had someone stolen Mom's credit card? A sinking feeling came over me as another thought entered my mind—the trip Lisa mentioned at Mom's birthday celebration.

I called Lisa's cell phone and asked where she was. She told me she was at the Grand Canyon with my parents. Stunned, I questioned her about her negligence in not telling me. She said Dad had bugged her about it so she'd booked the trip and she hoped I didn't mind.

I wanted to yell, *Yes, I fucking mind that you took my parents on a trip without telling me! You had no right.* But I contained my outrage. "So what would have happened if you were in a car accident and you were all unconscious? How would the medics know to call me or my brother?"

"Oh, I guess I didn't think about that."

Right, I fumed. I asked her the questions that flooded my mind: "Where are you staying? How much is the hotel? And when will you be home? I need to know your itinerary."

I wrote down what she told me and asked her to put my cell number in Mom's wallet in case of an emergency. Then I asked to speak with Mom.

Mom told me she was fine and her tone confirmed it. When I asked her if she was having fun, she said she was.

Once I knew Mom and Dad were safe, I hung up the

phone, feeling naive and irate. How could Lisa take my parents on a trip without telling anyone in the family? I also had to address the missing cash. My new findings fueled my determination to get rid of Lisa. I needed to replace her and quickly, but that would be no easy feat.

One day as I was waiting for my parents to arrive home safely, I found myself down by our old marina. I parked and sat on the breakwater, watching the boats sail by and thought about all that had gone wrong. I knew I had taken the easy route with Lisa, and now I was paying the price. I should have been stronger and told Lisa from the beginning to remove her belongings from the house, but I was trying to give Dad a say. Her flirtatious behavior was a huge warning sign. I wished I'd listened to my instincts and replaced her early on, but at the time, I was juggling too many balls and couldn't add another. I had to take responsibility for letting Lisa's antics go on this long. She'd betrayed my trust too many times. I needed to develop a plan to get her to remove her belongings without her knowing my true intent. I hated to be deceitful, but it was the only way to ensure my parents' care wouldn't be compromised. I was determined to find a good caregiver; I knew they were out there, as I'd heard stories of other families who were successful in finding them.

If only I could throw my problems into the ocean and let them drift out to sea. The exhaustion from my chaotic life reminded me of how much I missed the buoyancy Mom had always given me. In recent years, I felt lost without her and wished I had her compass to guide me through these tumultuous storms. But the tides had changed, whether I liked it or not. Mom couldn't be there for me like she had been when we sailed that boat through the storm. I had to take the helm and find my own way now.

twenty-one

After I discovered Lisa had taken my parents to Arizona, I called the agency and asked for Daniel, the owner. The assistant told me Daniel had sold the business and asked if I wanted to talk to Steve, the new owner.

Steve picked up the phone and told me he hadn't gotten around to contacting all the clients to let them know about the change. I politely told him about the issues we were having with Lisa. He seemed kind and enthusiastic about helping me. He agreed that Lisa needed to remove her belongings and we needed to let her go. I relaxed in my chair as we discussed the situation in more detail, and I filled him in about Karen too.

I told him I suspected Dad was giving Lisa cash on the side. He assured me that he'd talk to Lisa. We agreed that Dad needed to stop giving her cash, and Steve offered to manage our petty cash purchases. He promised me he was managing the business differently than Daniel.

Unconvinced, I said, "You are only as good as the care-givers you provide," a lesson I recalled from my recruiting days. After the disappointment I'd had with the last three caregivers, I'd lost faith in agencies.

"Oh, that's true." My comment seemed to catch him off guard.

We discussed our plan, and he told me he'd talk to Lisa before we all met. I hung up the phone and sighed, thankful for his willingness to help me untangle Lisa from our lives.

Over the next couple of months, I bit my tongue, putting up with Lisa's laissez-faire attitude until she removed her belongings and was gone. Her messy approach and the issues with her quality of caregiving wore on me. Everything she did and said rubbed me the wrong way. Dad had put on thirty pounds in the last year, his diabetes was getting worse, and his doctor had recently put him on insulin.

While we prodded Lisa to remove her belongings, I looked at other solutions for Mom's care. I visited board and care homes and memory care facilities, but those options didn't feel like a fit for Mom. Every time I'd visit a new place, I couldn't fathom the idea of moving her. It wasn't really a choice because Dad would be alone at home, and he still needed care. I quickly realized that live-in care was still the best solution for my parents.

After Lisa removed the car, I began interviewing candidates from other agencies in addition to a couple of Steve's candidates. The only things left were her belongings in her room. Just before we'd planned to let Lisa go, she called me one evening to say that Mom had a fever.

"What are her other symptoms?" My tired body tensed.

"She's been sleeping most of the day, and I couldn't get her to eat or drink."

She went on to tell me that her temperature registered 103 degrees. I told her to take Mom to the emergency room immediately and I'd meet her there.

Why had Lisa waited until eight in the evening to tell me Mom had a raging fever? I quickly told David, said goodnight to the girls, and drove to the hospital.

Will and Dad met me there. I asked to see Mom, and found her lying on a gurney with a curtain pulled around her. Two nurses hovered over her, poking at her thin skin as they tried to find a vein to insert an IV. Lisa stood on the other side of Mom as she flinched and shivered, looking shocked.

"Her veins keep jumping," one nurse said.

"My mom has small veins and she's probably pretty dehydrated at this point," I told them.

I turned away. It hurt to see Mom's pain.

"I've never had this much trouble getting an IV in before," the other nurse said. "I'm going to see if I can find someone to help us."

The third nurse finally found a vein in Mom's ankle and administered fluids and morphine.

A familiar unease settled in. This was the third time Mom had been admitted to the hospital in the last two and half years for what appeared to be another urinary tract infection (UTI). Didn't Lisa notice the signs? This seemed to be the worst infection yet.

Mom came back from her tests looking pale, lifeless, and shivering uncontrollably under her extra blankets. I told Lisa to take Dad home. Will and I would wait to talk to the doctor. I was furious and worried. I'd never seen Mom so sick.

A half hour later, the doctor showed up. "Your mom's infection has gone into her bloodstream, and her kidneys are starting to shut down, so we'd like to admit her to keep an eye on her."

"Of course," I replied, as Will nodded in agreement.

I asked, "How long do you think she's had this infection?"

The doctor rubbed the stubble on his chin. "With how bad her infection is, probably a couple of weeks."

Will's eyes grew bigger with shock. I knew what he was thinking.

Will said, "How could she have let this happen?"

I couldn't meet his eyes—I knew he was right. "I don't know."

"And Lisa still has crap at the house that Dad let her store there. We need to get her out," he rambled.

"I know. We've been working on it."

I knew "we" meant me. Over the last month, I'd asked Will to drop in on Lisa, to be another set of eyes besides Nancy, whose assessment I found skewed. Nancy wanted to see the good in everyone and sometimes turned a blind eye when the caregivers were being untrustworthy. Will had said he'd try to stop by, but never did. So as usual I boxed up my discontentment and drove home. I kept that box tucked away until therapy each week, where I'd open it and reveal the past week's complaints.

While Mom recovered in the hospital, I split my time between visiting her and interviewing caregivers. I worried about the additional toll this infection would take on her. After each hospital visit, another piece of Mom slipped away.

During my interviews, I looked for someone with more caregiving experience. They would wear scrubs or conservative clothing and be strong enough to transport Mom in and out of bed as her needs increased. I would personally check their references.

Steve was handling Lisa's departure with professionalism, so I decided to interview a couple of his caregivers while networking and using other agencies. Based on the rate I was paying Steve's agency, his caregivers only made ten to twelve dollars an hour. I wasn't sure that would be enough to find a more skilled caregiver, but I kept my options open.

One morning I arrived at Steve's office to interview two candidates when he stopped me on the way to the conference room. He opened the drawer of a file cabinet, pulled out two files, and handed them to me.

"Look inside," he encouraged.

I opened the folder and saw an application that was only half completed—it was Lisa's. I flipped to the next page. Neither her references nor background sections had been completed.

Stunned, I asked, "Where's the rest of her information?"

Steve's eyebrows rippled. "That's all the information Daniel had on Lisa."

I opened the second folder. Karen's application had the same half filled out application—her references and background sections were blank too.

I raised my eyebrows at Steve.

"It appears Daniel didn't do background checks on either caregiver."

"I can see that," I said sarcastically. "I'd like to see the completed references and background checks on all the candidates I'm interviewing."

He agreed as he motioned me toward the conference room.

I thought about his candidness. It gave me solace to find answers to why so much had gone wrong with Lisa and Karen. I'd trusted Daniel too much. Knowing that the paperwork was never completed or their references checked explained why I'd had incompetent caregivers. But why had Steve shown me files that put his agency in jeopardy? Was he trying to make his candidates look better? I wasn't sure, but I wasn't going to trust any agency as I'd trusted Daniel.

I hired a new caregiver and finally let Lisa go. Steve told me Lisa seemed angry and surprised when he gave her the news. That night I celebrated by opening a nice bottle of wine at dinner for David and me to enjoy, but that might have been a premature celebration.

The first woman I hired I found smoking a cigarette and talking on her cell phone on her second day of work while Mom sat in front of the TV. I hired a Filipino woman next. Her English was poor, but she seemed to understand my questions. After the first day, I realized she couldn't follow through on the most basic directions. I tried out several more caregivers—some lasted a day and others a couple of weeks. Mom seemed to be confused by the rotating faces that came in and out, and Dad kept asking me why the caregivers weren't staying. Where were all the good caregivers? The revolving door made me question my ability to find good care.

One morning after the kids went to school, I plugged my headphones in and went for a long walk by the ocean. I knew I needed to accept the fact that the agencies I was using weren't the right solution for us. I remembered a caregiver who had been referred to me by a family friend. Her name was Diana, and I'd briefly spoken with her the year before, but she hadn't been available then. I decided to give her a call.

Diana had taken care of a friend's mother for two years until she passed away many years ago, and she still came by to visit my friend's dad. That was the kind of person I was looking for—someone who was caring, already vetted, and who had experience with end-of-life issues. When I called Diana, we talked for an hour. Her Peruvian accent was thick on her tongue. She'd operated a board and care home for four people out of her house for ten years, and she'd been taking care of the elderly since she arrived in the US from Peru thirty years earlier. I could hear the pride in her voice, and she seemed dedicated to her job. She'd recently divorced; her two daughters were grown, and she would be able to live in five days a week—Nancy was still caring for Mom on the weekends. She seemed like a great fit, so I arranged an interview for later that week.

Diana was early for her interview, arriving before me. I found her talking to Dad and Nancy when I walked through the door. She was a well-dressed, petite, dark-haired woman with rectangular glasses perched on the bridge of her nose. She only stood five feet two inches tall, but she looked strong. Her confidence told me she'd be able to handle the job. We sat down and talked more about her responsibilities, Mom's recent visit to the hospital, and the thirty extra pounds Dad had put on in the last year. Diana assured me that she'd change and clean Mom regularly and keep her out of the hospital. Nancy went into more detail about Mom's daily routine.

I gave her a tour of the house and told her, "I'd prefer that you wear scrubs or conservative street clothes while you work.

My dad became infatuated with our last caregiver who dressed too provocatively."

"Oh, you don't have to worry about that. I'm a Christian and a very conservative person. Many of my male patients have made passes at me, but I always keep it professional," she assured me.

I hired Diana that day and she agreed to start working the following week. I was elated. She had all the qualifications I was looking for. Maybe now I could relax a little and focus on my girls and my marriage.

Mom was on her fourth year of needing care when Diana started working for us. She settled into her new role and quickly made order out of chaos. Each time I visited, the house seemed cleaner than the week before. She was organized and had a proactive approach. Mom had never looked better. Diana washed and curled Mom's hair, dressed her in matching outfits daily, and applied her favorite lipstick. Mom seemed to notice the difference, smiling more even though her mind and body were reverting back to infancy. She'd take Mom out for short walks and sit with her in the backyard so she could enjoy the sunshine. Diana stayed on top of Mom's UTIs and took her to the urologist when they'd flare up. Mom had just begun using Depends at night, which could increase the chance of infections if we weren't careful, but Diana kept Mom clean and out of the hospital.

Dad adjusted more quickly to Diana than he had the previous caregivers. She talked and joked with him, but remained professional. Diana cooked healthy meals and assisted Dad with his portions to help control his type 2 diabetes. Six weeks after she started working for us, Dad had already lost five pounds. After six months he'd lost twenty-five pounds and no longer needed insulin.

Dad felt the difference too, telling me, "If it wasn't for my bad hip, I'd feel like I was twenty-five again."

Each time I'd visit, I would thank Diana for giving my parents the care they needed and deserved. I made sure she had everything she needed to make her job easier, and she was showing me she was trustworthy. I hoped she'd stay with us until Mom passed, whenever that time might come.

Diana kept me abreast of how my parents were doing in between my visits. She called with even the smallest of details, but I didn't care. I preferred more communication than less. Even with Diana's care, Mom's health slowly declined. After a year, Diana asked me if we'd buy a hospital bed for Mom. Her rheumatoid arthritis left her nearly immobile, and she could no longer get in and out of bed on her own. She told me it would be easier to transport Mom if she could raise and lower the bed. I found a used bed online and asked Will to help me pick it up.

Will, Mom, Diana, and I drove an hour one Saturday to pick up the bed. On the car ride home, Diana started talking about religion and said she read the Bible each night. I praised her for being so disciplined.

Diana said, "You know, God woke me up the other night and spoke to me . . . and it wasn't the first time."

Will turned from the driver's seat and gave me a look. I

grinned back at him and asked, "Oh, really. What does he tell you?"

She paused, "Lots of different things."

I had recently started my own spiritual quest. I believed we needed to learn from our experiences and listen to our intuition, something I drew upon as I raised my kids. I didn't want to disrespect Diana for her beliefs, but I wasn't even sure I believed in God, and I didn't believe God spoke directly to anyone.

After we got home and unloaded the bed, Will snickered, "I think Diana's a little crazy."

I laughed and said, "I hope not. She's the best caregiver we've had."

I thought about Diana's comment and Will's response. Diana belonged to a congregation, went to church every Sunday, and didn't believe in sex before marriage. I didn't want to pass judgment, but I took note of her comment about God. Still, Mom and Dad were receiving the best care ever. After the last year, she'd proven herself to me. She wasn't stealing, lying, or drinking on the job, and she took great care of our parents. The positives outweighed the negatives, and she deserved to have her own beliefs about God. I couldn't expect for us to be in perfect alignment, and I felt like her comment wasn't enough to change the course of my parents' care.

twenty-two

We'd signed our postnuptial agreement six months earlier, and I was glad it was in the rearview mirror, but it had left an emotional residue that ate away at my soul. I continued to struggle with the idea that my husband didn't trust me enough to discuss his thoughts prior to making his decision on how to manage his inheritance. Despite therapy and yoga, there were days when I felt like I'd never move past it. I looked for new ways to alleviate my pain. I increased my yoga practice, meditated daily, and bought crystals for our bedroom to change the energy between David and me. I prayed to a higher power I wasn't sure existed.

When none of those things worked, I signed up for a year-long energy class that met once a month. Our teacher was a PhD turned shaman who touted herself as an energy guru. She taught us about the light and dark side of our patterns, how to stay more calm and centered, and how to read and manage other people's energy. She urged us to read books about setting healthy boundaries and healing trauma, and we learned about the power of setting intentions. Through our first year, we developed rituals and burned sage at the beginning of each class. Our teacher led us on a journey with our spirit animal. Mine was a bird that flew me above the California coast over the craggy cliffs and crashing waves. She led us on a past life regression where I saw myself cooking in a house with a dirt floor. These were exercises to connect with our own inner wisdom. I stayed open to the mostly foreign concepts that she taught us—anything that might help change our patterns and create new possibilities.

I didn't talk much about my class at home. My kids and David thought what I was learning was weird, and I didn't quite know how to explain it to them. When I did share inspirational quotes with David, our therapist pointed out that he wasn't interested and suggested I stop. I was hoping we could learn and grow together, but it was a one-way message so far. As the class continued, I found it was a safe group of women whom I came to trust. We were all curious and looking to change our lives. We'd eat lunch together, share our struggles, and meet for walking dates outside of class.

In class, I found myself thinking that if David were more aware of his own energy, maybe he would make different choices. If he learned these principles, he'd stop having outbursts and blaming others, especially me, for his unhappiness. In my moments of self-honesty, I knew I couldn't fix David and I should be able to accept him as he was, but that was difficult. Instead, I worked on responding with less reactivity to his outbursts, but I still would nudge him to consider how his choices affected me. When Susan and I encouraged him, he made small changes—just enough to keep me encouraged. He stopped questioning my credit card bills and opened my car door when we'd go out on a date. He doled out positive comments more frequently, but sometimes his attempts seemed forced. My new self-awareness and healthy practices lifted my mood and changed my expectations as our progress inched along.

The spring after I started my energy class, Heather received most of her college acceptances. She was studious, possessed great retention and recall, and loved history. She'd been very involved with her Model United Nations debate team. She was deciding between Boston College, Tufts, the University of Virginia (UVA), and a full merit scholarship to the University of Southern California (USC). I booked a trip for the two of us to visit the East Coast schools. It was a welcome trip and an opportunity to spend one-on-one time with my happy, hardworking middle daughter.

Heather was the child who came out of my womb mature. She was always the levelheaded person in her group of friends. She slept through the night after four weeks, and as a toddler, she'd tell stories to her stuffed animals and dolls before she could read. She was my reprieve child, stuck between my firstborn, whom I often called "my practice child," and the double whammy of having twins. She required the least from me as a parent, and I often felt guilty for that. Even though Heather had always been self-motivated and independent, I took pride in the way I chose to raise her and her sisters. I often wished I'd had that kind of confidence and maturity at her age.

We boarded the plane for our flight to Boston. Just as the plane was leaving the gate, I patted Heather on the leg. "I'm so excited for our trip. Are you ready for this?"

"Yeah, but I'm nervous at the same time. What if I make

the wrong decision?" Her brown eyes looked apprehensive. Her usual confidence was being tested by her first important decision.

"I know you have a lot of people telling you what you should do, but you need to listen to your own gut. You've worked hard through high school, and I'm incredibly proud of you for all you've accomplished, but this is your decision, not anyone else's. You have to pick the school that's right for you. Our trip will help you figure that out." I looked her in the eye. "Trust me."

David had been pushing Heather to take the full merit scholarship she'd been offered to USC. I wanted Heather to gather information from all the schools and then decide for herself. I didn't want her to have any regrets later for feeling pushed toward a school that wasn't right for her.

Heather's eyebrows furrowed as she laid her head on my shoulder. "You always know what to say."

The next morning we woke up late, grabbed coffee and a breakfast sandwich, and agreed to walk the Freedom Trail. This was our first time in Boston, and we wanted to explore the museums, buildings, and historical landmarks that had shaped our country. We started at the Boston Common and walked briskly to follow the red brick path. We stopped at Paul Revere's house and ended at the USS *Constitution*, the oldest commissioned warship afloat. We discussed the history of what we were seeing and how hard it must have been to be a woman living in Boston over two hundred years ago.

Early evening, the sun dipped behind the buildings, and the temperatures quickly dropped, leaving us hungry and chilled. Heather looked up local restaurants and found one a mile away with great reviews. When we arrived, there were fifteen people in line outside the small cozy restaurant that was already full. We looked at each other, wondering the same thing—was it worth the wait?

Heather searched for other nearby restaurants while we eavesdropped on the couple in front of us, who sounded like locals with their heavy Boston accents. I asked if the restaurant was worth the wait.

They smiled and said it was more than worth it—the restaurant served the best Italian food in town. We passed the next forty-five minutes talking to people in front of and behind us in line. Before we knew it, we were seated at a table next to the kitchen. The warmth quickly took the chill off. I noticed my stomach growling and my mouth watering at the aroma of garlic that floated through the lively restaurant. We quickly agreed on two dishes to share and I ordered a glass of wine. When it arrived, I toasted us. "Here's to a great day exploring Boston together."

Heather smiled and held up her glass of water—the red highlights of her hair catching the light. We talked about our schedule for the next day as we devoured the fish and homemade pasta with Bolognese sauce, filling our stomachs and our hearts. As we left the restaurant, Heather said to me, "Thanks for a yummy dinner and a great day, Mom."

I wrapped my arm around her shoulder and kissed her head. "You're welcome."

Over the next couple of days, we toured three different schools, and all seemed like excellent choices. She met with older kids at a couple of the colleges, people she knew from high school. One girl said she became very homesick her first year living so far away, but another seemed to adjust with no problems. After we left UVA Heather said, "I'm more confused than ever. I could totally see myself at UVA, but how do I turn down a full merit scholarship?"

"You don't need to make a decision today, you have time. I also don't want you to make a decision based on money. I want you to choose the school that's right for you, and if that's UVA, then your dad and I are okay with that." David's aunt and uncle had left plenty of money for our children's college education.

After another visit to USC and a few weeks of deliberation, Heather sent in her acceptance letter to USC. I was thrilled that the school she chose kept her closer to home. David and I celebrated Heather's achievement together, but I didn't feel he gave me enough credit for how I raised our children.

Now that Heather had made her decision, I had two years before Katie and Jessie started their college process. After raising kids for the last nineteen years, I was ready to embark on something new. I had loved staying home and raising my girls, but I didn't identify with only being a caregiver for my parents and a mother to my girls. I yearned for something more but felt lost about what that might be. I was ready for all of us to start something new, but each time I thought about what I might want to do, something got in the way.

The one thread that kept surfacing was my crazy caregiver challenge. When I'd tell my friends what I'd been through so far, we'd laugh together and they'd encourage me to write it down, but I'd brush off the idea. I wasn't a writer, and my least favorite subject in school was English. Besides, I hadn't written much more than an email for years. Where would I even begin?

Soon, I was back in my caretaking role. A few weeks after Heather graduated from high school, Nancy called to tell me that she couldn't continue helping on the weekends due to back issues, and would work only one more weekend.

Nancy had helped us out for over four years, and I was grateful. I told her I understood, which I did, but after I hung up, I screamed, "Shit!" to a silent house. I wished I'd had more than one week's notice.

I was back at it again—interviewing people, trying to figure out who would work best with my parents and with Diana. Finding someone reliable who was willing to work on the weekends was difficult. Diana had high standards, and she wanted someone who did things her way. I agreed up to a point. If the house was clean and Mom and Dad were well cared for, that was enough for me, but Diana was picky, and no one seemed to fit her criteria.

Over the next few weeks, I went through five caregivers who didn't work out. During my search, Mom developed another UTI and wasn't responding to the antibiotics, which added to everyone's strain. The doctor had told us her body was developing a resistance to the antibiotics, so Mom's recovery was slow.

Almost a year later, I was still cycling through weekend caregivers trying to find the right fit. I used agencies, websites, and referrals, but no one stayed very long. Diana began working some Saturdays so she didn't have as big a mess to clean up on Mondays. I worried about her burning out. When I'd ask her how she was managing, she'd reassure me, "Don't worry,

I'm fine" or "I've done this for years." But each time I saw her, she looked more tired and unhappy than the last time.

Then one winter day, the agency I was using let me know they were sending someone named Bella and asked if I wanted to do a phone interview first. I agreed. I hoped having a new caregiver wouldn't disrupt our girls' ski trip to Mammoth, where we were at the time. When we spoke, her voice was soft and calming. She was an RN who specialized in helping people with respiratory problems. Her qualifications assured me that Mom and Dad would be in good hands. I relaxed, thinking my weekend might not be ruined after all.

At the end of each day, I checked in with Bella, and every time she assured me that she had everything under control and my parents were both doing well. On my way home Sunday evening she said, "I've really enjoyed taking care of your parents this weekend, especially your mom, she is so sweet and funny." She giggled.

Relieved, I told her, "I'd love it if you'd come back next weekend." Bella agreed and said she'd call the agency. Bella's interest gave me hope. I called Diana Monday morning and asked her for a report on Bella. "She did a great job. Your daddy liked her cooking, and your mommy looks good . . . oh and the place was clean when I came in. Can we get her back next weekend?" she happily asked.

The following week Bella began working for us as a regular caregiver. I learned she was from Uganda and had been here for fifteen years. She'd never married and didn't have children, which was beneficial for us. As I got to know her, I loved her demeanor. Her gentle approach gave me the comfort and relief I'd been looking for. She never rushed Mom, always telling her what she was going to do next. "Okay, Betty, dear, I'm going to help move you from your wheelchair to your bed now." Mom would stare back at Bella, acknowledging her words with a smile.

I was able to breathe again. I had finally found two reliable, skilled caregivers who worked well together. If the personal work I was doing had taught me anything, it was to enjoy the pause in life, never knowing how long it might last. My pause could be a few minutes, days, or weeks—I didn't know. The unpredictability of my life was teaching me to stay nimble, even if I didn't always like what it presented. I had a choice—I could accept or resist what was happening. Acceptance seemed to take much less energy.

PART THREE

twenty-three

S everal months after I hired Bella, I came home after dropping Katie and Jessie off at sailing practice. David planned to go out to dinner with friends that evening, and the next day I was leaving for the Esalen Institute in Big Sur. A new friend, Kelly, from my energy class, was turning fifty, and she'd invited most of the women in our class and other close friends to join her there.

I lay down on my bed and picked up my iPad from the nightstand. I knew I'd be in a better mood if I meditated for fifteen minutes. I turned it on to type in my password when a message popped up: "iPad disabled. Try in two hours." Wait, what? I tried again, then a third time and received the same message. Why was my iPad disabled? The twins had been in school all day. On my phone I researched the topic. The results said I'd typed in the wrong passcode too many times. I hadn't used my iPad since the previous day and I hadn't changed my password. Who had used my iPad? David had stopped by the house after a lunch meeting earlier in the day and left just as I arrived home.

I grabbed my phone and called David. He didn't answer, and I left a message with his assistant to call me back right away. I impatiently waited for him to call or come home, trying to contain my outrage.

Why would he be using my iPad and then lock it up? He had his own. And why wouldn't he call me and ask for my password if his wasn't working? I kept coming back to the thought that he had been snooping, which infuriated me. I had nothing to hide, but he'd crossed another line. Was he questioning that I was going away with girlfriends the next day?

I had been voicing my needs and viewpoints more in our relationship and had expanded my group of friends, which gave me more joy, but perhaps that left him with questions. We continued to bicker about how to discipline the kids, who'd pick up them up late Saturday night, and where we'd live after David retired, but that didn't mean I was having an affair. My life was challenging enough. I couldn't fathom the idea of complicating it even more. Why didn't he trust me after twenty years of marriage? I'd always trusted him when he traveled.

David arrived home a few minutes before we were supposed to leave for dinner. He walked into our bathroom and kissed me on the cheek. I pulled away.

"Were you using my iPad today? I tried to use it this afternoon but it was locked up."

"Uh, no," he stammered.

My words came out firmly. "You were the only one home today, and I haven't used it since yesterday."

"Well, now that you mention it. When I was home, the Internet wasn't working, so I tried to get on your iPad to see if you had Internet."

"Why did you use my iPad instead of your own iPad or your computer . . . and why wouldn't you call me to ask me for

my password?" I held his gaze, searching his face for answers.
"Uh, I had to get back to work for a meeting and didn't
have time." He walked into the closet to change his shirt.

I stood in the doorway and snickered. "But you tried enough
times to lock up my iPad for hours?" I tilted my head in confusion. "Do you know how many tries it takes to do that?"

"No, but we are going to be late for dinner; can we get in
the car and go?"

I followed him down the hall. "It takes seven times," I
snapped.

Why couldn't he simply tell me the truth and take responsibility for what he had done? I had nothing to hide, except
unhappy texts I'd sent to friends to vent about my marriage.
There had been more withdrawals than deposits in the emotional bank account of our marriage, and this incident plunged
us into bankruptcy. My mind said, *Don't go to dinner*, but my
body was stuck in forward motion.

While in the car, I questioned him again and he adamantly
stuck to his story. At one point he said he couldn't talk and drive
at the same time, which made me laugh, since he was an executive at a Fortune 500 company and could multitask just fine.

He wasn't going to confess. I sat in the car frozen, staring
out the window. Betrayed again. I resisted a strong urge to flee
at the next stop sign. I didn't want to be near him, but I
couldn't move. I was experiencing the same feeling I'd had
when David's lawyer told me he was keeping his inheritance
separate and when Ken abused me. Why was I frozen? Why
couldn't I leave? I was stuck in past patterns but didn't know
how to set myself free.

⤺

The next morning, I got up early and tiptoed into the bath-room. I began packing for my trip to Esalen as the pitter-patter of rain on our roof became louder. A big storm had arrived and promised to soak our drought-ridden state. I was meeting my friend Kelly and nine other women after we dropped our kids off at school. We were going to listen to a spiritual guru, Adyashanti, who was scheduled to be there for the weekend. He was one of Kelly's favorites.

David walked into the bathroom as I was packing. We ex-changed no words as he undressed and showered. My mind still buzzed from outrage. He got out and stood in front of the mirror, examining the stubble on his face.

I sat down on the edge of the bathtub as the blood in my veins pumped faster. A lump formed in my throat as I told him, "I don't think I can do this anymore." I paused, looking at the floor before meeting his eyes. "I want a divorce."

"What? Where is this coming from?" he asked, a look of surprise on his face.

"We can't seem to get along anymore, and you haven't been honest with me about locking up my iPad. The only rea-son to go onto my iPad was to look at my texts and emails. I've been nothing but honest with you our entire marriage, and yet you still don't trust me."

"I do trust you, and I think you're making a bigger deal out of this than necessary."

"No, David, I'm not."

We continued to talk in circles before I walked into the closet to grab my jacket and then take my suitcase downstairs.

I couldn't be near him any longer.

My shaky hands pulled the waffles out of the freezer and put them in the toaster oven for Katie and Jessie. As the waffles cooked, I felt like I was in a different marriage than David. How could we both see the same situation so differently? I tried to hold it together. I had no plan for how we could move forward, but I knew I couldn't live with a man who needed to snoop instead of trusting me. He hadn't learned from the inheritance decision; he chose to do whatever he wanted and make up excuses for his behavior.

I left that morning without saying goodbye to David and dropped off the twins at school in the rain. I left a lengthy message for our therapist about what had happened and met my friends for our trip. I also told my close friend Gina what had happened as we waited for the others to arrive. We'd previously confided in each other about the struggles we both had in our marriages.

Her eyebrows furrowed in surprise. "Are you okay?" She hugged me.

"Yeah, I will be." It felt like a pressure valve had been released. I was happy that I didn't have to see David for the weekend, and since there was no Wi-Fi or cell service at Esalen, we'd have a communication break.

On the car ride up, my anger spilled out as I ranted about David's behavior the night before and our recent fights. When we stopped for lunch in Santa Ynez, a friend asked, "Is this what you want your story to be, or would you like to change it? You have the power to change your story."

I pondered that thought through lunch and the rest of the drive in the rain. I stopped talking about the storm between

David and me and kept my eyes on the road. I was a positive person, and I didn't want my story to be as gray as the sky. David and I had been through so much over the last five years, and I wanted to find my own happiness. Was I making a big deal out of all this? Could I have the power to change my story? I wanted to, if only I knew how.

The next day at Esalen, our group sat in a large tent perched on top of a cliff as it rained steadily. We were listening to Adyashanti talk about grace, love, and enlightenment. The waves angrily crashed along the shore below. He read excerpts from his book, *The Way of Liberation*. One quote stuck with me as I searched for answers on how to move forward. He read, "It is your conscious and unconscious assumptions and beliefs that distort your perception and cause you to see separation and division where there is actually only unity and completeness."

I was sure it was David's beliefs that divided us, but were my beliefs also causing some of the separation and chaos? Not having a plan in place for when I returned made me anxious, and I wasn't exactly sure how to apply all these teachings to my life. But I was developing the idea that I might have the power to change the pattern. How could I find the solution? It seemed so elusive.

We listened to another session that afternoon before heading back to our sparse accommodations. When I walked through the front door, a beautiful bouquet of red roses was sitting on the table by the window. The envelope attached had my name on it. My heart softened as I read the card: "I love you and will do anything for our marriage. I hope we can talk when you get home. Love, David."

I sat on the bed and smiled. I was touched he'd gone to such lengths to send flowers to me, but that didn't make up for his distrust.

My friend Gina asked, "So what are you going to do?"

"I don't know." His kind gesture made my decision harder—I could see that he was trying again.

"Well, it's ultimately your decision," she replied.

That wasn't what I wanted to hear. I was looking for advice from my friends about what I should do. Now that my anger had subsided, could I actually follow through with a divorce? The flowers, the teachings from the weekend, and my friends' lack of guidance left me more confused than ever.

On the car ride home, the storm had ended, and I'd made the decision to hear David out. As I walked through the front door, the house was quiet. I took my suitcase upstairs, greeted the girls in their rooms, and gave them a kiss hello. I walked into the kitchen to find David sitting at the kitchen counter holding a letter-sized envelope with my name on it.

"Welcome home," he said with a grin. He twirled the wedding band he hadn't worn in over twelve years and pushed a letter across the counter toward me.

Apprehensive, I said, "What's this?"

The flowers, the letter, and his desire to wear his wedding ring were actions I'd wanted to see much earlier, but at least he was making the effort now. My guard came down. I picked up the envelope and opened it as I walked toward the couch.

"Can we talk?" I asked.

"Sure, but will you read my letter first?"

I agreed, and he sat next to me. His letter said he was sorry for the way he had handled his inheritance and if he could do it differently, he would. He expressed his regret for snooping on my iPad, and that he wished I'd have been around to talk through our differences. He'd do almost anything to save our marriage.

"Thanks for your letter." My heart opened more. I felt his sincerity. He wanted to make it all up to me.

"I meant everything I wrote in my letter," he said, choking up.

I could see the sorrow in his eyes.

"I don't want to lose you."

"I notice you're wearing your wedding ring."

"Yes, and I plan on keeping it on."

I sighed and turned to face him. "I can't keep doing this. Things need to change in order for our marriage to work. I want to wait to discuss all this with Susan this week."

"Okay, I'm willing to do that," he tenderly replied.

David took my hand and led me to our bedroom. The girls were fast asleep. David shut the door behind us, then pulled me close and kissed me with more heart than I'd felt in a long time. Before I knew it, we were entangled in bed, our clothes on the floor as passion carried us through the next hour.

As I lay in his arms, I thought about my weekend at Esalen. I didn't like that I had to push David to the breaking point to get his attention, but maybe now he'd be willing to make some changes so our marriage could survive. This was our chance to change our story, for both of us to consciously change our beliefs and habits. He'd shared his emotions with me that night and gracefully admitted he'd made a mistake. That's what I'd been asking for, and it was easier for me to forgive now that he'd shown remorse. Maybe now he would trust me with his feelings and recognize that I was his partner. I couldn't throw twenty-three years of marriage away so quickly. He was my husband, my family, and the father of my children. This could be another chance.

twenty-four

The crisis of the iPad was over, but I still didn't have answers for how I could move forward. After our reconciliation, I felt hopeful again, but I needed Susan's assistance to develop a plan to heal our marriage.

A few days after I returned from Esalen, I sat in her office for an individual session. She began talking about separating, and I interrupted her. She knew I'd asked David for a divorce, but I hadn't communicated with her since the day I left for my trip. I told her about our conversation the night I returned and how it led to us making love. Her mouth dropped open and her eyes grew bigger. "So where do things stand between the two of you?"

The look on her face led me to believe she thought I'd made a mistake. "That's what I want to talk to you about."

I asked Susan about a weeklong therapy program a friend from my energy class had recommended. She'd gone through a program on codependency which had addressed the trauma she experienced when she was little, and taught her how to use different skills when making decisions as an adult.

Susan had mentioned this type of program in the past and thought David would benefit from it. I wanted him to attend so he'd recognize how the shame he'd felt as a child still affected him. I imagined that if he went through the program and recognized his behaviors, he'd stop nitpicking about everything. He might reconsider keeping his inheritance separate and comingle the money, and he'd support me when I needed a shoulder to cry on. If he could change those things, our family might be able to stay together. I asked for Susan's support to encourage David to sign up, but she said she didn't think he was ready. We'd been in therapy for over two years—how could he not be ready?

Susan asked, "If you were looking for a partner today, do you think you'd pick someone like David?"

I answered no. But I had chosen him, and now I was trying to make my marriage work.

In couple's therapy the following day, I suggested the program, but David resisted. At the end of our session, we compromised on David starting the energy class I was taking. It seemed to me that it would take too long to see changes. I needed an infusion of hope. After finishing the first year of the energy class myself, I knew the results for David would take a while.

I left our couple's session flattened. If only I'd been stronger the night I'd come home from Esalen, I could have used that leverage to get David to enroll in the weeklong program. But it was too late now, I had to be patient and see where this new direction would take us.

I soon stopped fretting about my marriage when my attention was drawn to other worries. The week before Mother's Day, I arrived at my parents' house, and Diana told me Ken had shown up the previous day. He hadn't come around since we'd obtained a restraining order on him seven years ago.

I put Mom's flowers and card on the table as my body tensed. I scanned my body and planted both feet to ground myself, and the initial gut punch from discovering that Ken had been to the house began to dissipate. I'd been practicing skills from my energy class, but I recognized that hearing about him had triggered fear.

"Oh, really? What did he want?" I kept my voice casual.

The only time Ken came around was when he wanted something. The last day I'd seen him, Dad, Mom, Will, and I watched a judge sentence him to prison for two drug felonies. He still scared me.

"I don't know. He spent most of his time in the garage visiting your daddy. Before he left, I invited him in to see your mommy."

I wearily asked how he was.

"Fine," Diana said. "I asked him if he wanted to see your mommy, so he came in. I think she's been holding on so she could see him one more time before she goes."

My head turned. "What? Mom's not ready to die."

"The other day she told me she was."

"Really?"

Mom hadn't formed a complete sentence in over a year. I could barely get a mumbled "I love you" from her, and most days she didn't speak at all. I doubted Mom could voice her desires, but I didn't see her every day. Did she have moments of clarity I hadn't seen? I doubted it.

I was troubled by Diana's comments, so I asked Dad, Will, and Nancy if they'd seen similar behavior from her, and no one had. Why was Diana saying these things? And why was Ken coming around? I took note of the events of that day, hoping they wouldn't materialize into anything. But if history was the best predictor of the future, something was brewing.

A month after Mother's Day, Mom's urinary tract infections became more frequent, and her body continued to resist all but one antibiotic. I urged Diana to give Mom probiotics and cranberry extract, but she insisted they weren't making a difference, and stopped giving them to her. She went on to say, "I think your mommy is ready for hospice."

I looked directly into Diana's eyes. "Mom's not at the end of her life. She's still eating and drinking." Why was she pushing Mom toward her grave?

On my next visit, I sat with Mom while I waited for Dad to get ready for his doctor's appointment. I turned to her, grabbed her hand, and looked into her cloudy eyes. Her body tensed up as she ground her teeth in pain. She clenched my hand so hard her fingernails made imprints on my palm. Her arthritic hands never relaxed anymore. Concern settled in. She had been getting worse over the last month and she seemed to be having more bad days than good ones. Before I left that day, I told Diana I'd get referrals from Mom's doctor for hospice, but with one caveat: "I will do it only if they keep Mom on her current medications."

Diana shook her head. "I don't know if they will do that."

"If that's the case, then we're not ready for hospice," I sternly replied.

Diana's attitude was disturbing and the need to replace her was nipping at my heels, but the severity of her comments didn't fully register. I needed to manage Mom's discomfort. Seeing Mom in that state was my impetus to act. So, my search began for hospice providers.

The large hospice company I chose agreed to my request that Mom stay on her current medications and that she be treated for any UTIs. Less than a week later, I received a call from Bella, my weekend caregiver. It was Friday night and she never called me that late unless it was important.

"Your mom is really sick. She'd been lethargic all afternoon. She didn't eat much today, and has a fever. I think you should call hospice."

I hung up with Bella and called the large hospice office. The woman on the phone said they'd send a nurse out before nine o'clock that night. I relayed the information to Bella and waited.

Bella called later that evening and told me the nurse took a urine sample from mom. "They didn't give her any antibiotics, but she seems to be resting comfortably now."

"Are you serious?" Annoyed, I asked if Mom's urine was cloudy and smelly. She said yes. I was irritated that hospice wouldn't put Mom on a broad-spectrum antibiotic like they'd agreed to. She needed to be treated, or it would only get worse. I'd been very specific with my wishes. Had I made a mistake by bringing hospice in?

"Let's see how she's doing in the morning," Bella said softly. "I'll keep a close eye on her."

David looked up after I hung up the phone. "So, what's going on with your mom?"

"She has another infection, and hospice won't give her antibiotics as I requested," I said bitterly.

"Well, that's a problem," he said tonelessly as he filled the dishwasher.

"Now I'm mad at myself for letting Diana talk me into hiring hospice."

Silence greeted me, so I didn't elaborate. I tucked away my need for a hug or reassuring words along with other unmet needs. Mom's latest infection took precedence.

Over the weekend, I called the office each day to tell the hospice staff about Mom's worsening symptoms and ask for antibiotics. Each person I spoke with told me we needed to wait until we got the test results back before they'd give her medication. I urged them again, but they didn't agree. Instead, they sent a nurse out to check on Mom both days.

Upset by their lack of response, I asked Bella to look for some leftover antibiotics in the medicine cabinet. She found a half dozen and started giving them to Mom. I couldn't wait any longer.

Monday morning, I called Mom's hospice minutes after they opened and spoke with our case manager. After filling her in on the weekend events, she told me to call back in the afternoon to get Mom's preliminary results.

I impatiently waited until the afternoon and called. She told me, "It looks like your mom has an infection." I wanted to scream, "I know that!" But I restrained myself. "So when can you get antibiotics over to her? She's getting worse." Bella had told me Mom was eating and drinking very little.

The case manager told me they were sending over a prescription for Bactrim to treat her infection. I snapped, as my anger climbed through the phone. "Mom's allergic to Bactrim. Did the doctor even look at my mom's chart? The intake coordinator made note of it the first day she came out."

She stuttered, "I'll call you right back," and quickly hung up.

How could they be so incompetent? If I hadn't been Mom's advocate, she could have died.

Minutes later the case manager called back with a new prescription—one that Mom wasn't allergic to, but I worried it might be too late. It had been over three days since she'd developed a fever, and she was declining fast. Bella told me Mom was lethargic and lifeless, sleeping most of the day. Based on her past infections, those were signs that her infection may have gone septic. I sensed she needed a stronger antibiotic. I asked if they'd administer one intravenously with fluids to help rehydrate her, but they declined.

When I visited Mom the next day, her eyes were sunken, her cheeks hollow, and her face pale, yet she still gripped her fists tightly. I could see the pain that lay just beneath her skin. Mom didn't have much quality of life, but she didn't deserve to suffer. The hospice nurse and I agreed she wasn't ready for morphine, but she seemed close. Agony twisted me into knots as I thought about losing Mom now, and the upcoming family vacation to Australia that we might have to miss.

While I was with Mom, our family friend Nancy called to check on her. During our conversation, she told me about a friend of hers, Tina, who worked for a hospice company, and gave me her number.

Upset and desperate, I called Tina's number immediately

and told her the reason for my call. She agreed that what happened over the weekend was wrong, and we arranged a meeting for that afternoon.

Tina arrived on time and I quickly took a liking to her. Her pretty young eyes were kind. She said she would have treated mom differently and given her a preventative antibiotic while waiting for the test results. She examined Mom and agreed she had a serious infection and was dehydrated.

I asked, "I think she needs something stronger; would you be able to give her an IV antibiotic?" I couldn't let this infection take Mom without a fight.

"If you choose to switch over to our services, I can make that happen," she assured me.

"Great, what do I need to sign?" I asked with relief. Now Mom needed to decide if she was up for the fight.

After the new hospice company was in place, I filed a formal complaint with the first company. I called their corporate office and they followed up with me twice. I named employees and gave them every detail of our struggle. I wrote online reviews so other people would choose that hospice company with caution. I couldn't let this happen to someone else.

Mom started her new medication, and I vacillated each day about whether to stay home or leave for our two-week family vacation. I checked in with Tina and the nurse each day. Mom was slowly improving, but I wouldn't leave if there was a chance Mom might pass while I was away. The day before we were supposed to leave, Tina assured me Mom was in good hands, so I decided to go on our trip.

છઝ

I'd planned for the four girls, David, and me to explore the Gold Coast of Australia, including Brisbane, Fraser Island, and the Great Barrier Reef. On the trip, we experienced unusually stormy weather, which fit my mood, but when we stepped on the *Whitsunday Blue,* a forty-one-foot catamaran, everything changed. We left the marina off the central coast of Queensland, the southern tip of the Great Barrier Reef. The six of us, plus our captain, one crew member, and a German couple, set out to sea. It was the last leg of our trip and the part I had looked forward to the most. I checked in with Diana before we boarded. Mom had finished her course of antibiotics and was continuing to improve. The news reassured me.

As soon as we left the harbor entrance, the weather cleared and the wind died down. I was finally at peace with the decision to join my family on our vacation, and it felt as if something had changed the course of our trip. I sat in the cockpit and inhaled the salty air. I felt Mom's presence next to me as the cool breeze turned warm and the boat sliced through the azure blue waters toward our first island. This reminded me of my childhood, the peace and calm that sailing would bring me. The first evening, the captain nestled our boat into a small, quiet cove and dropped the anchor as we settled in for the night. We ate dinner on the deck, drank wine, and played cards until late. I slept like a baby, the boat rocking me as it had when our family would take trips to Catalina.

The next day we hiked and snorkeled and sailed to another island. On our last day, we woke up to light winds and a cobalt blue sky. We headed toward Whitehaven Beach, our last stop.

David and I sat on the windward side of the boat while the girls tanned under the sun on the bow. The warmth radiated through my body, and I could feel it reenergize me. We walked along the silicon white sand beach, swam in the crystal-clear waters, and took pictures to remember this beauty.

As the tide fell, the sand and swirling water created green and blue hues that were mesmerizing. I tried not to think about the challenges of the past or the ones to come. Staying in that moment with my family, soaking up the rugged landscape and the captivating beauty of the Whitsunday Islands was the fuel I needed. I knew my life would continue to ebb and flow like the tides of the islands and the currents in the sea. More challenges were inevitable—I didn't know when Mom might pass or if my marriage would survive—but nothing was going to take me away from the joy and beauty of that majestic day.

twenty-five

I returned from our trip to Australia refreshed, but life quickly handed me a series of events that left the Whitsunday Islands a distant memory. In the weeks following, I prepared the kids for the upcoming school year, and I stayed longer for my visits with Mom. Each time I pulled out of our driveway, I stared at my garden, which had been hard hit by our long hot summer. I'd told myself when I came home, "Next weekend I'll enjoy the garden." Even though gardening was one of my reprieves, that fall it kept getting pushed down my priority list.

When I visited my parents, their house seemed lifeless, and the air smelled stale. Neither Diana nor Bella could regulate Mom's digestive system, which seemed to prolong her recovery. Diana kept telling me Mom didn't want to eat, and she kept expressing her pessimistic views about Mom's future. I wondered how much of what Diana said to me in front of Mom registered with her.

One day, I brought lunch out for all of us so I could observe Diana and Mom. She started feeding Mom, who chewed slowly and swallowed, but after her third bite, Diana said, "You see? Your mommy doesn't want to eat." She dropped the spoon on Mom's plate and started cleaning up the lunch dishes. Mom didn't acknowledge either of us as she chewed the remaining food in her mouth.

"Be patient with her," I retorted. "She's just eating much slower now." I picked up the spoon and began feeding Mom myself. I'd heard that when someone is ready to die, they stop eating and drinking, and she was still doing both.

"At this rate, your mommy won't make it through the holidays," she responded.

"We don't know that," I snapped, "and it's not our decision."

Mom was able to swallow and eat solid foods, and I saw small signs of improvement: she was smiling more often and responding to me with her gibberish when I'd tell her stories about her grandchildren or read to her. Mom could take a turn at any moment, but those signs conflicted with what Diana was telling me.

A week later, my concerns deepened when I received a call from Tina, our hospice director. She told me that Diana had been acting inappropriately around Anthony, Mom's handsome young male nurse. She told me Diana had pulled down her shorts to show him a bruise she had on her hip and asked his opinion on how to treat it.

When I hung up, I was shocked. Maybe Diana wasn't the churchgoing conservative lady she'd portrayed herself to be. Who was this person taking care of Mom? Tina's call was another sign. The details she shared didn't line up with the kind, caring person I'd originally hired. That day, I uncomfortably confronted Diana on the phone. "You don't seem to be happy working for us anymore. Maybe it's time for us to part ways."

"Yeah, I think you're right."

Pleased that she didn't push back, I said, "Let's talk more about this when I'm here this week. I just ask that you follow through on your promise to stay until I find a replacement."

"Okay, I can do that . . . Oh, and your mommy has another UTI."

I asked her to contact hospice to get Mom's urine tested and I'd see her in a couple of days. When I hung up the phone, I closed my eyes, remembering the white sandy beaches of the Whitsunday Islands. When I opened them again, it felt like I'd just been dropped off in the desolate desert of the Sahara as I thought about starting a search for yet another caregiver.

Two days later, I drove to my parents' house to discuss the details of Diana's departure and see how Mom was doing. As soon as I entered the house, Diana told me, "Your mommy's UTI is getting worse."

I walked into the den to find Mom lying in her hospital bed. Her teeth were chattering as she tightly gripped her favorite beanie baby in her crippled hands. Worried, I called the hospice office to ask our case coordinator if they'd received the test results from Mom's urine sample from Monday. He said they hadn't. Diana listened in as I held Mom's hand while sitting on the edge of her bed.

I asked with urgency, "Is there something we can do for her? She's in a lot of pain."

He asked if Mom was still taking her daily antibiotic. I turned to Diana and repeated the question. She shook her head and said, "No, hospice told me not to."

The case coordinator responded, "No, that's not true. I

was on the phone with Anthony last week when I heard him tell Diana to keep your mom on her antibiotics."

Rage pounded in my chest. Phone in my hand, I opened the French doors into the backyard. I needed to get away from Diana. Did she really do such a thing? This was the second time she had made the decision on her own to stop giving Mom her medications. The first time had been ten months earlier when she stopped taking Mom to her rheumatoid arthritis IV treatments, a circumstance I confronted her about and tried to rectify, but unsuccessfully. She said it was getting too difficult to get Mom to her appointments. I'd given her a second chance, and I now regretted that decision.

In disbelief I asked again, "So, Diana knew that she should have been giving Mom her daily antibiotic?"

He confirmed again. I thanked him and hung up, infuriated. I walked down the driveway and around the block, trying to cool off. After a few minutes, I called Bella, my other caregiver, while Diana stayed inside the house with Mom.

Bella answered, and I filled her in on what I needed—emergency help. Could she work four days a week instead of two?

She said she'd be happy to pick up the extra hours. "You know I love your mom, but I don't want to take away Diana's hours."

Laughing disparagingly, I said, "I'm taking her hours away, not you. If you're uncomfortable, I'll need to find someone else to fill in."

Bella asked a few more questions before she agreed. I thanked her profusely. Then she confessed. "I need to let you know I'm planning on moving to Texas to live with my sister in a few months, but I'll be happy to help out until then."

I appreciated her candidness in light of my turmoil. I'd come to respect Bella for her calm, steadfast approach. She was a rare find, and I told her I was grateful to have her for as long as she'd stay.

Finally off the phone and trying to take everything in, I stood in front of my parents' house letting my temper cool. When I came in, I found Diana sitting next to Mom in the den, holding her hand and watching TV. Her disingenuous gesture made my stomach curdle.

I invited Diana to join me in the kitchen as my heart began to race again from my discomfort of needing to confront her— but she had left me with no choice. I told her I'd only need her three days a week until I found a replacement.

She sat with her arms crossed in front of her chest. "Well, I'll leave when *I* find a new job or you find a replacement."

I countered with a glare, "That's not what we agreed to. You're not going back on your word, are you?"

She stared out the window complacently, holding her cards close to her chest. She had the power and we both knew it. There was no purpose in continuing our conversation.

Later that evening, the home phone rang. Thinking it was a solicitor, I let it go to voice mail. When I heard Diana's voice, I ran toward the phone, catching the tail end of her message, ". . . and I won't be returning on Monday."

"Fuck!" I screamed.

Katie and Jessie both looked up from their homework and asked if I was okay. There was no concealing my upset. Diana had played her last hand—leaving me scrambling to find a new caregiver. Again.

⚬

In the following days, I continued screening and interviewing caregivers, but few of them met my criteria. Exhausted by my lack of progress, I finally retreated to my garden. I began pulling out my annuals and cutting back plants, preparing for my fall planting. Gardening was my place of solitude where I could think about what I wanted to plant, not only in my garden, but in my life. I irritably pulled out the dying dahlias thinking about how I'd let Diana take advantage of me. I knew confrontation wasn't my strong suit, a trait I'd picked up from Mom. She only saw the good in everyone and buried the difficult issues. I'd adopted similar patterns, and they had caused me unnecessary stress.

I'd told myself I wasn't going to let the same thing happen after Karen and Lisa, yet I'd let things creep up on me like weeds in the garden. I'd thought by accommodating Diana's requests for supplies, medical equipment, and hospice, it would make her job easier and keep her happy. I gave her the benefit of the doubt for her role as a professional caregiver, but at what cost? My plan had backfired, jeopardizing Mom's health while I was left scrambling to find a quality caregiver once again. I'd let all this go on far too long, and it weighed heavily on me. As I finished my gardening that day, I knew I should have taken charge and let Diana go sooner. It was hard to change patterns and take on more power and responsibility, but I knew I had to keep working on it. I would need to plant better seeds in my life if I wanted more happiness.

twenty-six

A fter Diana left, Bella became my rock, strong and stable during my tempestuous search for another caregiver. Bella and I worked well together, talking daily as we tried to find the right fit. This time my search was complicated by the Christmas holidays and my concern over Mom's continued decline as we struggled to manage her pain from a low-grade UTI she couldn't seem to kick. Her digestive system problems continued as well. I'd planned my upcoming fiftieth birthday ski trip with David for February. It was unclear with all that was going on if we'd have to postpone it.

One day in December while visiting my parents, I stood over Mom's bed caressing her frail arm. She looked more emaciated and seemed more distant than ever. I asked Bella if she'd seen any signs of improvement and she shook her head. My body deflated. I'd done everything in my power to care for Mom and make her as comfortable as possible. I motioned Bella into the hallway and told her I'd spoken with Tina, the hospice director, and that we'd agreed to revisit Mom's care plan in January, three weeks away. The pain from watching her suffer was unbearable. She was slipping away, and I wasn't ready to feel the grief and sorrow that was ahead of me.

After a somber Christmas with little change in Mom's health, I scheduled a meeting with Dad, Will, Bella, and Mom's hospice care team for the first week in January. The day of our meeting, a dark cloud hung over my head. I dreaded the thought of making end-of-life plans for Mom and facing the decisions that would need to be made. I gave the twins an extra kiss as they waited for their carpool and left shortly after. I wanted to arrive early and prepare Dad for the conversation that would take place about his wife. It would be so difficult for him.

I arrived to find Dad in the garage, the TV volume on high. I turned it down and told him I wanted to talk to him before meeting with hospice. He replied, "Well, your mom has been looking good these last few days. I think she's improving."

I shook my head in dismay. He wasn't willing to accept that Mom might only have a short time to live. I went inside, leaving him to tinker with the miniature dollhouse he was building.

The hospice team arrived with solemn faces, and we all sat down. Tina, the director; Anthony, our nurse; the chaplain; and the social worker arrived together, and we congregated in the kitchen. Bella settled Mom into her lift chair in the den and then joined us.

Tina started out, "We need to prepare you and the family for what's ahead." She pulled a handful of small booklets out of her leather bag and handed them to us. "Gone from My Sight" was written on the front. Above was a ship sailing across the ocean headed out to sea. "The Dying Experience" was written below. Tears formed in my eyes as I imagined Mom sailing away on her sailboat, never to return.

"This booklet is a guide to walk you through what you should expect over the next few months," she said.

Dad shook his head and stared at his lap while Will sat with his arms crossed in front of his chest. This was a conversation none of us wanted to have.

Tina continued, "We will administer drugs to keep your mom comfortable and laxatives as needed." Then Tina looked directly at me, "Are you ready to take your mom off all her other medications?"

My throat constricted. "I'm comfortable with everything except taking Mom off her Plavix." Mom had been living with a blocked artery since her failed surgery eight years prior, so she took a blood thinner.

Will chimed in, "What's the worst that can happen?"

Tina confirmed my worry. "She could have a heart attack."

"Would that be so bad at this point?" he asked.

His words were a blow to my gut. I couldn't knowingly contribute to her demise. I said, "I'll call Mom's cardiologist tomorrow and get back to you."

It was a decision I'd been fretting about for weeks. I knew hospice would recommend it, but I needed more time to get comfortable with the idea. I hoped my conversation with the cardiologist would give me the reassurance I needed. We continued talking, agreeing that adding more visits with the chaplain and social worker would be beneficial. At the end of the meeting, Will left for work, and Dad retreated to his garage, neither making further inquiries. I was on my own to oversee all of this.

I stayed to talk to Bella. I looked into her dark eyes. "I know you told me you were moving to Texas soon," I said, "but

I was wondering if you'd be willing to stay with us until Mom passes?"

She paused, looking around the room as she contemplated my question. "Yes, I can do that for you."

Once her words registered, I began to breathe again. I put my arms around her. "Thank you. I'm beyond grateful for your help."

She shyly giggled, "You're welcome. I've gotten attached to your parents."

The ease between us was deepened that day as her commitment helped to lessen my worries. I often wondered how Bella had ended up in our lives. It seemed she'd dropped down from the sky with her umbrella and landed at our front door, like Mary Poppins when she arrived at the Banks's family home. Bella was "practically perfect in every way."

Before I left, I said goodbye to Mom. The off-white walls looked gray from having the window shades half-drawn. Her eyes were like almond slivers as she floated in and out of sleep. Her frail body barely made an impression under the blanket. I scanned her body. She looked nothing like the strong, vibrant person she had once been. There were so many things I missed about her. I took Mom's hand in mine as I watched her chest rise and fall under the blanket. I found the words to say, "Mom, it's okay to let go. I'm going to be fine . . . Will and Ken will be fine . . . and I promise I'll take good care of Dad." My eyes watered as I took a breath. "So whenever you are ready, you can let go."

Mom's blue eyes opened wider as she stared directly at me, as if my words had registered. She held my gaze for a moment before her eyes closed again. In the months to come, I repeated that statement with each visit. I wanted to reassure her that everything would be okay if she passed, even though each time I said it, I was unsure of anything ever being okay again.

I arrived home late in the afternoon after the meeting with hospice, hollowed out and empty. I wanted to climb into bed and pull the covers over my head, but my body needed to shed the layers of my day that clung to me like leeches. I knew a walk on the strand would help me do that. It always did. The twins were doing their homework at the kitchen counter. They seemed settled, so I changed into leggings, laced up my tennis shoes, and grabbed my headphones. I opened the front door and to my surprise, David greeted me. He kissed my check and asked me how I was.

"Not great. Today's meeting was tough."

He stepped into the house. "I'm sorry."

He put his things down on the chair in our entry, while I waited for him to make a comforting gesture or ask me to elaborate. Instead, he asked, "Do you know if Joe's home?" Joe was our neighbor down the street.

"No, I don't. I told you, I just got home from a long day with hospice and I need a walk," I snapped, hoping he'd have more sympathy for my trying day. "You could join me," I encouraged him.

"I'll let you go by yourself."

I brushed past him and walked down the street as my tears began to fall. I wanted David to hold me, tell me he loved me and how sorry he was for what I was experiencing. My tears streamed down faster than I could wipe them away. I couldn't raise my head, afraid I'd see someone I knew in my tight-knit community. I began to sob—I didn't want to talk to anyone. I powered up and over the hill and saw the waves crashing on the shore, the hazy January sun close to the horizon. I paused when I reached the strand and inhaled the ocean breeze, letting it calm my shaking body. I walked vigorously for two miles while soft music played in my ears and the words "three to six months to live" kept popping into my head. I had to prepare myself to lose Mom while holding onto my marriage.

It had been ten months since I'd told David I wanted a divorce, and by New Year's, we'd fallen back into some of our old patterns. We continued to have small blowups about where we'd live after David retired in a year and disagreed on how to remodel our second home in Mammoth. Our constant bickering left little room for us to connect. The kids continued to be our primary common denominator. Even though we were still having sex, I'd all but lost my attraction toward him.

Over the past two years, Susan had helped me put words to my feelings, and I'd continued learning about my core essence and ego in the energy class, which helped me become more in tune with my inner self. I had gotten better at expressing desires without dishonoring David, but when he'd brush me aside, I'd sometimes explode like a shaken soda pop can. One time I threw my wedding ring at him and left in the middle of a couple's therapy session. "I'm done," I shouted as I ran out the door.

That felt very satisfying, but after I cooled down, I'd changed my mind. At times my outbursts made me feel like I was going crazy. The changes I needed in my marriage hadn't happened yet, and we'd been working hard at it for three years. I was losing hope. I tearfully told our therapist in a private session, "I'm so unhappy, but I can't lose my mom and my marriage in the same year. I'm not strong enough for that." She gave me a compassionate nod.

I would often use the phrase, "Change is the only constant in life." But these two potential changes terrified me. Most days I vacillated between numbness and bouts of hot tears at the thought of these losses. I knew there wasn't enough between David and me for me to stay for the next twenty-five years, but I couldn't leave either. I wasn't ready to accept that my marriage was slowly dying too. Letting go of the only familiar thing I'd known for the last twenty-two years was petrifying.

After my long walk, I approached our house. I nestled back into the familiar pain and put a halfhearted smile back on my face. I had to. I knew someday I'd need to face my marriage head-on, but for now I had to live the only life I knew.

My search continued over several months for the right caregiver. It had been over three months since Diana had left, and I was still cycling through caregivers. They either weren't the right fit for us or we weren't right for them, and I carried that heaviness with me as doubt got the best of me. Could I find two loving, stable caregivers? I wasn't willing to give up. I was clear about Mom's prognosis, informing each candidate that Bella would be leaving us after Mom passed and I'd still need care for Dad. I wanted them to know that our need was long-term.

Desperate to find a solution to the revolving door of caregivers, I called Carmen, a woman who'd filled in for us over Christmas when Bella visited her sister in Texas. Carmen had a full-time job, but she'd had a two-week break during the holidays and had helped us out. When Bella returned, she told me that Carmen had done a great job. Carmen had longevity with her previous families and glowing references. I liked her calm, positive demeanor, similar yet different from Bella's. With nothing to lose, I gave her a call.

When she answered the phone, my heart skipped a beat. After making small talk, I asked, "I know you have another job, but I was wondering if you might be available and interested in working for us for a few days a week?" I held my breath, ready for another rejection.

She paused before answering, "That might work for me. My job here is winding down." Her Hispanic accent was light on her tongue.

"Really?" I asked as her words slowly computed.

"Yes, I liked working for your family. Can I get back to you tomorrow?"

I told her yes, and we talked about the details. When I hung up, I stood up and danced around. Could I have finally found the solution to my problem? I stayed cautiously optimistic.

The day Carmen began to work permanently for us, I drove out to greet her. When I entered the house, she was feeding Mom her breakfast and talking to her.

"Hi, how's everything going?" I asked.

"So far, great," she said warmly.

Her wavy dark hair complemented her round face and bright smile.

I grabbed Mom and Dad's mail from the living room and sat down next to Mom. I looked through it while Carmen and I talked. Carmen continued to slowly feed Mom, waiting for her to chew and nibble her food in between bites. Mom's UTI was slowly subsiding, but her digestive system still wasn't regulated.

"Mom eats slowly these days," I confirmed.

"We don't need to rush her, we have plenty of time." Carmen smiled.

I agreed, noting the refreshing contrast between her demeanor and Diana's. I spent the next hour with Carmen as I went over the details of what to expect—their medications, Mom's health struggles, and the grocery delivery schedule.

By the time I left, I was confident that Mom would be well cared for. I could leave on my birthday ski trip with David and our friends in good conscience. Maybe the trip would help David and me reunite—we usually had a good time on vacation. I knew that skiing would free me from the worries I carried, and I couldn't wait to hear the wind whisper through the trees and taste the snow as it fell from the sky.

twenty-seven

After a long day of travel, I inhaled the sweet smell of pine and welcomed the cool air on my face when we arrived at Revelstoke Ski Resort in Canada. I had anticipated my birthday ski trip for months, and here we were. David and I had been looking forward to this trip with our good friends Bob and Jen. That night at dinner we drank sake and talked about how eager we were to get out on the slopes and explore the mountain the next day.

The morning after we arrived, I pulled the curtains open to view the mountain. The snow looked hard and crusty—not soft and powdery, as the reviews had touted. Revelstoke was known for its powder and high annual snowfall. My excitement dulled as I checked the weather forecast: no snow for the next couple of days. I announced the bad news to the group.

"Maybe it will be better at higher elevations," David said.

Jen, our fiery redheaded friend, giggled, "Don't worry, we'll have fun regardless."

Bob nodded in agreement. The three of them were looking at the bright side of things, but my gut told me otherwise. I hoped they were right. At some resorts in Canada, it could be raining at the bottom of the mountain and snowing at the higher elevations.

Our trip was the second part of my fiftieth birthday celebration. After the way my year had started with Mom being
put on hospice and my arduous search for a caregiver, I was
looking forward to enjoying time with good friends and losing
myself in the Canadian powder. Our week consisted of one day
of ski lessons to teach us how to ski powder at the resort, one
day of snow-cat skiing, and two days of heli-skiing in the backcountry.

Heli-skiing is an adventure sport that to some might seem
extreme. A helicopter delivers you into the wilderness to ski
fresh, untracked powder in the trees. I first learned about heli-
skiing watching Warren Miller ski movies back in the eighties,
and I'd always dreamed about trying it. It took twenty years to
achieve that dream. The first time I heli-skied, I went on a
three-day trip with a girlfriend. Heli-skiing isn't for the faint of
heart, and you have to be comfortable taking the risk of skiing
unknown terrain and potentially being caught in an avalanche.
David, Bob, and Jen were all strong, advanced skiers, but they
had never done this before. David had never expressed interest
in adventure skiing before this, so I was thrilled that he wanted
to share this experience with me.

Jen, Bob, David, and I rode up the gondola together. I
looked out the window, scanning the runs and the hard-
packed snow, thinking about how global warming had affected
our world. California had been in a drought for four years, and
the weekend of my first birthday celebration in Laguna Beach
was unusually hot—the thermometer had registered over ninety
degrees in mid-November.

I smiled as I stared out the gondola window, remembering the celebratory group dinner three months ago with my girlfriends. I had brought in a chef to cook for us on Saturday night. We ate on the balcony in sundresses without a patio heater. The breeze that usually cooled off the beach was still. After dinner each friend toasted me. The warm air and their kind words wrapped around me like a weighted blanket, comforting me. My girlfriends were my likeminded, chosen family who loved and accepted me for who I was and were available to me in every way. Since the foundation of my marriage had begun cracking, I'd spent more time cultivating these relationships. We supported one another during our struggles and would make time for walks and phone calls. These relationships had been paramount, and that night had left me speechless and filled with love.

Here on the mountain, the four of us got out of the gondola, put on our skis, and skated to the next chairlift. The snow was still hard and icy. Bob asked the chairlift operator, "What happened to the snow conditions?"

The lift operator told us it had rained the past week, and it hadn't snowed since. We skied the rest of the morning on slick snow, and at lunch I checked the forecast again. The storm was still out a couple of days. The next day was much the same and when our snow-cat day was canceled, we took the day off and explored the quaint ski town. Jen, Bob, David, and I discovered an old ski jump that we climbed, and found a great café for lunch. We finished off the evening at a restaurant, drinking, laughing, and planning our next ski trip to Niseko, Japan. David and I were having a great time together.

The next morning, I opened the curtains to see snow floating down from the sky. Goosebumps traveled up my arms. This was the day we were going heli-skiing and the mountain was blanketed with snow. I felt like a kid who'd just been told I was going to Disneyland, but I didn't need Mickey Mouse—I had fresh powder and the backcountry.

"It's snowing, you guys!" I turned to everyone standing in our small kitchenette. "Let's get ready, the powder is waiting."

"Can a girl have her cup of coffee first?" Jen chuckled.

Bob said, "I'll put some on for us."

David laughed. "Laurie would be the first person on the mountain if she could."

I smirked in agreement. He knew me well.

We arrived at the heli-skiing lodge where our guides taught us basic avalanche rescue skills in the snowy field next to the helicopter, a requirement before skiing. The guides gave each of us a backpack that included an avalanche transceiver, a probe, a shovel, and an avalanche floatation device in case anyone in our group was trapped. They made us practice by burying a transceiver and dummy and having us locate it. Once our transceivers pinpointed the general area, we pulled out our avalanche probe and started probing in a spiral pattern, a body's width apart. Once we located the buried dummy, we started shoveling, starting downhill from the probe and potential victim, clearing the snow away. We rotated positions so no one person grew too tired. Finally, we saw an arm and cleared the snow from the dummy's face and pulled it up to safety. After we finished, the guides assured us that they'd only be taking us to low-risk areas. Even with those words, my body hummed with anxiety—more than a foot of snow had fallen the night before. Were we really safe?

Just as we finished our training, the clouds lifted and the guides divided us into groups. Our two guides motioned for our group of eight to climb into the helicopter. As we lifted up, my stomach sank and I grabbed David's arm. Even though I'd been in helicopters before, they still made me queasy. As we flew to our first drop, I looked out the window at the white jagged peaks that looked like they were covered with whipped cream and dotted with green trees. The sun had burned the thick clouds away. It was a bluebird day.

The helicopter landed far above the tree line. The propellers blew snow off the top of the mountain. My stomach sank again, but I was eager to click into my skis. I knew the snow would be completely different from the hard-packed, groomed runs we'd skied at the resort. There were no marked trails, and our guides warned us of obstacles under the snow. One wrong turn and we could be buried. I stepped into my skis, put on the backpack that held my safety equipment, and glanced down the mountain. You could barely make out the large boulders that were covered with what looked like a layer of marshmallow creme. The snow glistened in the light. The guide gave us our instructions: "Give ample space between each skier, ski to the left of my tracks, and if you fall, my partner in the back will help you up."

I motioned David to go first as I let my fears fade. I checked my backpack to make sure it was secure, then pushed off the top with my poles, getting my speed up so I could develop a rhythm as I floated through each turn. My cheeks began to burn from the cold air. As I skied up and over the snowy landscape, the trees seemed miniature far below. With each turn, my worries from home drifted away, and the earth cradled me in its arms. I knew Mom's absence on this earth would strike me hard, but that day I slipped into a contented rhythm that nothing could disrupt.

We skied a few more runs in the same area before stopping for lunch at the bottom of the hill. The guides shoveled snow to create a table for our food, and we sat leaning against our skis that were stuck into the snow. David asked the guide a question and then began to laugh in response. It was wonderful to see him relaxed and having a good time too. I soaked in the landscape, taking in the picturesque mountain ranges that stretched endlessly as far as the eye could see. A few scattered clouds sat on the horizon. I tuned into the vastness, at one with myself.

After lunch, we returned to the helicopter. I sat next to David, and as we took off, I looked over his shoulder out the window, holding onto his arm. I grinned and gave him a kiss on the cheek. "This is a little slice of heaven." He smiled and squeezed my arm in return. I felt connected to David in a way I hadn't since the night I'd come home from Esalen. Everything felt right. I knew that my worries and struggles would return, but nature was giving me a fresh perspective and a sense of peace within.

When David and I arrived home, I was tired yet rejuvenated. Heli-skiing was much more physically challenging than skiing at a resort. We had to take our skis off after each run, walk through deep snow, climb in and out of the helicopter with our ski boots on, and carry the extra weight of our backpacks as we skied unknown terrain. It was exhausting but deeply invigorating and worth every ounce of extra energy it took to experience the wilderness of the backcountry as few people did.

At home I unpacked, did laundry, and shopped for groceries. Katie and Jessie were due to return from their school trip to Cambodia, Vietnam, and Thailand that same week. I was eager to hear about their trip.

The next night David and I sat down at the dinner table with the twins as they told us about how they went to a floating market in Thailand, crawled into an underground tunnel in Vietnam that had been used during the war, and announced that their favorite country was Cambodia. They both wanted to go back. Jessie said, "It was my favorite trip I've taken so far."

"Oh, really, why is that?" I asked inquisitively. David and I had taken the kids on an annual two-week trip for the last six years—Costa Rica, Europe, Alaska, and Australia.

"Because we were with some of our closest friends."

I chuckled. As a child, I often wished I could have brought a friend on our ski trips, but none of my friends had the money or the interest. David and I were raising our girls differently than we were raised, offering them experiences that would expand their knowledge of other countries and cultures. As their mother, I was pleased that they were learning independence and acceptance from these adventures. They were lifting their wings. As we sat together as a family, I felt the warmth of knowing that I'd helped to open up worlds to them that David and I could only dream about at their age. Together, we had given our kids a foundation that would benefit them for the rest of their lives.

twenty-eight

For a few years, I'd been working hard to learn the lessons my life and family were putting in my path. Sometimes I welcomed those teachings, and other times I wished for a different life. The summer following our ski trip, I received a few lessons that shifted my perspective in ways I never could have expected.

Bella discovered what had been causing Mom's digestive problems. She thought it was an overdose of the stool softener and asked if we could reduce her medication to see if it helped. I researched the side effects on the Internet—an excessive dosage could cause vomiting and diarrhea. I stared at my computer as guilt settled in. Why hadn't I checked this earlier? If I'd known about the side effects, I could have stopped Mom's suffering months ago. Anger quickly joined my guilt. What did Diana know? Had she intentionally given Mom a stronger dose? She repeatedly told me it was Mom's time to die and she'd stopped giving Mom two other medications. As mad as I was with myself for not acting sooner, I was thankful that Mom was no longer under Diana's care. After that, I began referring to Diana as the Angel of Death.

It didn't take long for Mom to respond. A month later she stopped vomiting and her appetite slowly improved. The experiment worked. As Mom's suffering subsided, she began eating more. I was grateful that Bella had caught this when she did. Staying observant with Mom's care was more important than ever, especially with her recent prognosis.

One hot summer day a few weeks later, an unexpected guest showed up at my parents' house. While I was catching up on the past week with Carmen, I noticed someone standing next to Dad in his garage. As I looked closer, I realized it was Ken, my oldest brother. I hadn't seen him in years. His gray temples were prominent against his dark hair, his T-shirt protruded from his ample middle, and his black-rimmed glasses made me question who it was. Ken. My hands became clammy as I paced around the house, a clear sign that my fear of him was still trapped inside me. I'd only had two brief encounters with him since my wedding twenty-four years ago, and I thought I'd healed from the effects of his abuse. As I paced in circles that day with Carmen, I realized very little had been resolved.

She gave me an odd look. "Why don't you go talk to him?"

She didn't know our history. "I don't know if I want to." I bit my nails and continued to pace. Why was I still so scared of him? I was no longer the little girl he'd threatened or the teenager he'd molested. Intellectually, I knew that, but my body sensed danger. I overrode my thumping heart and decided to face him. I couldn't let him have power over me anymore. I wanted to run away, but I opened the door and walked toward him, my knees quivering.

He turned to me in mid-sentence. "Hey Laurie, I was stopping by to pick up a few things that Dad kept for me."

He acted as if he'd seen me last week. My exterior façade was cool, but my heart continued to pound in my chest. I put my hands in my pockets so they wouldn't shake. I noticed that he stuttered and abruptly ended each sentence, seeming to be unable to finish a thought. I wondered if he was high on meth, his previous drug of choice. A wave of nausea washed over me.

Ken took out his phone to show me pictures of items he'd sold on Craigslist. I suspected many were stolen. In the past he'd stolen valuable items and sold them to buy drugs. It seemed like a hard life, far removed from mine.

What did he want with us now? He'd been stopping by more often over the last few months, and here he was again. I was leery of him.

He got choked up when he talked about Mom. "It doesn't seem right. She's done so much for others, and she was so active." His lip quivered.

The depths of Ken's emotions surprised me. I didn't remember witnessing that before.

While I had his attention, I changed the subject. "So how long have you been clean and sober?" My knees had stopped shaking, but the blood still pumped fast through my veins.

He said a year, but I didn't believe him. Dad stood by, moving his head back and forth, listening. He seemed to be struggling to understand our conversation. Ken told me he wanted to make a new life for himself. I encouraged him but wondered if he'd ever have the willpower to kick meth, one of the most addictive drugs on the streets. I suspected he was still using.

"If you want to stop by occasionally to see Mom and Dad, I'm okay with that, but if you fall off the wagon again, you have to stay away." My gut twisted like a pretzel at setting a harsher boundary.

"Okay, I can do that," he said. "Mom and Dad deserve that."

I agreed, pinning my gaze on him. I wanted him to know I meant it, even though the little girl inside of me was still scared shitless.

After Ken left, Dad asked if everything was all right. I assured him it was and repeated my stance on Ken's visits. Dad said, "Okay, I see now. I don't hear everything clearly."

When we were growing up, Dad had never been able to stand up to Ken's disruptive behavior, and I doubted he would now. As I walked back into the house, my pounding heart slowed, and my chest expanded. I was free to breathe again, pleased with how I'd handled Ken. Now he needed to respect my wishes and take me seriously.

Another insight came weeks later. I was driving Dad home from a doctor's appointment when he turned to me in the car. "Well, thank you for everything. I wanted to tell you before I forget."

"You're welcome, Dad." I put my hand on his shoulder. For years, the caregivers and I had encouraged him to show more appreciation. Our cajoling was paying off.

"I don't know what I'd do without you," he said with a sigh.

"Lucky for you, I'm not going anywhere." I smiled.

"Well, we almost didn't have you in our lives, you know."

"What do you mean?"

"You know that we adopted another little girl soon after we adopted Ken, and she was taken away from us."

"No . . . what? When?" This was news to me.

He told me her name was Julie and they brought her home when she was three days old, just like the rest of us. Dad said they were excited to have a girl after Mom's first pregnancy ended in having a stillborn baby girl at eight months. "It was rough on me, but more so on your mom."

My parents had never told me they'd adopted another baby girl. If I'd known this when I was snooping through my parents' dresser drawers and found photos and baby shower cards addressed to "baby Julie," my childhood would have made more sense.

Dad continued, "The family drove up in a big black Mercedes and took the baby away and never offered to pay for the hospital bills." Paying for the hospital bills was part of the adoption arrangements.

I kept asking Dad how this affected Mom. I wanted to know what she was thinking and feeling at the time. I imagined the pain she must have felt as the car drove away with *her baby*. I could see Mom rolled up in a fetal position bawling her eyes out. I wanted more understanding in hopes it would unlock something inside me, but Dad continued to focus on how they'd never offered to reimburse them for the hospital bills. Dad wasn't in touch with his own feelings, let alone talking about Mom's.

"I'm glad it worked out, because we wouldn't have had you."

"Thanks, Dad."

Dad remembered that the umbilical cord of their stillborn baby had been wrapped around the baby's neck.

"Oh, how awful." The thought of giving birth to an eight-month-old stillborn sounded unbearable. After having my own children, I couldn't fathom the thought of not being able to feed, hold, and nurture my own child. The pain Mom must have gone through and continued to carry must have been piercing.

I drove into the driveway and asked one more question.

"Why did you guys decide to adopt us instead of trying again?"

"I had a low sperm count, and we had already spent a lot of money and time trying to get pregnant, so we decided to adopt."

I walked him inside the house and said goodbye. As I drove home, I kept replaying my conversation with Dad as the puzzle pieces of my childhood began fitting into place. I couldn't believe that I'd lived into my fifties and had just found out about this. Did Ken or Will know about Julie? Mom had not just lost one, but two baby girls by the time I arrived.

As we were growing up, she made sure we all felt loved, but for me there seemed to be a distance I could never understand. I wished Mom had held me closer and protected me when Ken threatened to hurt me. I wanted Mom to guide me about boys, shaving, and what was happening in my body when I began to bleed. I wanted her to acknowledge what I saw my brothers doing when I told her instead of saying, "Oh, I don't believe that." She chose to see the good in them and others, but failed to see their flaws.

I now understood that Mom's full-hearted love had never been in my reach. I suddenly remembered a reoccurring nightmare that Mom would have when I was growing up. She'd wake up in the middle of the night screaming, "Oh, oh, oh, my

God!" She'd run down the hall checking on each of us kids to make sure we were all in our beds. She'd kiss us on our fore-heads before tucking the sheet around our shoulders. Her nightmares scared me as a child, but now they made sense. Her fear of losing another child probably replayed over and over in her dreams.

If only Mom could have told me about these losses when I was an adult, but her self-preservation was too strong, and I couldn't fault her for that. I wasn't unlovable. Those losses weren't her fault, but they got in the way of her giving me love the way I'd wanted it as a child. I used to blame myself: if I'd been a better student, kept my room cleaner, or partied less in high school, maybe she would have loved me the way I wanted and needed. As I drove home, the conversation began to settle in me, and I understood my parents better. The burden of the past began to lift.

That afternoon in yoga class, the teacher asked us what we wanted to work on. I spoke up with, "Heart opening." As we flowed through class, I reflected on my conversation with Dad and how I'd stood up to Ken and Diana. I pushed away my false beliefs that I had no voice or power, and found more strength in each pose. Toward the end of class, our teacher asked us to move our mats to the wall so we could practice forearm stand, a pose I'd been working on for years and had never mastered. I followed our teacher's instructions, starting off in dolphin pose, then kicking one leg up, then the other. My feet found the wall behind me, and I held the pose. Each second felt like a minute, but I did it. Once I came down, my teacher said, "Great job, Laurie." I beamed. I left class wanting to bottle up the love and strength I'd found that day so I could pull it out the next time I needed it.

twenty-nine

Nine months had passed since the family first met with hospice, and after adjusting Mom's medication, her health had continued to improve. Her face filled out, and she began smiling more often. Sometimes she'd stare at me for long periods of time. I might get a smile, but other times she looked at me like I was a stranger. When I saw Mom's nurse, Anthony, at the house he'd always say, "Your mom is stable, and all her vital signs look good."

On each visit, I'd thank him and tell him that was great news. But was it? I'd prepared myself for Mom's passing and braced myself for the emotional toll it would take: memorial service arrangements, paperwork, and difficult conversations around Mom's death. Her unstable health and dementia had left her with little quality of life. She simply existed, unable to do anything for herself. It didn't seem likely that the active, vibrant mother I once knew would have chosen to live life in this prolonged state. What would she tell me if she could communicate her own wishes? If she could have predicted this kind of life, would she have changed her wishes in her will?

The unknowns of this awful illness were draining me and at times keeping me from moving forward. I didn't want to commit to much outside of caring for my family. I had no roadmap, no friends or family who'd navigated this path before—no one to give me advice. So I waited in limbo to see if nature would take its course, or if Mom would continue to endure.

With my uncertain future, I continued with a third year of my energy class. I needed all the support I could get, and many women in our group had formed close friendships. We planned day hikes in our local mountains, celebrated birthdays, and laughed and encouraged each other through our struggles. During each monthly class, I'd pick one new thing to incorporate into my life. I was eager to learn new ways to communicate and respond better when something upset me. I was desperate for new tools—anything that might help ease my tension and shorten the long cyclical patterns that had developed between David and me.

One Friday in September, the focus of class was to stay centered so we could respond calmly and not react with anger. I was eager to hone these skills. When triggered, I was capable of staying calm for a while, but too often I'd back into a defensive response. Our teacher explained how to envision new outcomes. Then we worked on developing creative responses, new ways we might achieve our desired results. It all sounded so easy. The times when I was grounded, present, and calm, my energy would shift, and I'd achieve the desired results, but I wasn't successful all the time.

In the afternoon class that Friday, I role-played with our teacher. She took on my role while I took David's. I gave her the details of a recent argument that had upset me. To prepare our energy for this exercise, we clapped our hands in a circle around our body—this was supposed to protect our aura. Then she instructed me to visualize a root extending from my feet down into the earth and attaching onto a solid ball to help ground me. In the role-play, we argued like David and I would, but she'd reply calmly instead of reacting defensively. Then we switched roles, and I played myself using words similar to hers. This time, I didn't feel the jolt of electricity through my body when David's words triggered me. I kept thinking that if I could control my reactions, the cycle of our arguments would lessen. I knew these tools would be useful.

When I came home that afternoon, my body was tranquil after our day's work. David arrived home shortly after I did and asked me if I'd be ready to leave at five thirty. We had plans to take our close friends Sam and Sharon out to dinner for Sam's birthday.

"Our reservation isn't until seven and I just told Sharon we'd pick them up at six thirty." I turned and walked into our closet.

"I don't understand. Last week I emailed everyone telling them to be ready at five thirty." His response was charged with irritation.

I stayed calm. "You told me our dinner reservations were at seven and the restaurant is only ten minutes away."

Not expecting to use my new skills so soon, I observed David's reaction play out like a movie in front of my eyes. His anger began to heighten as he waved his hands. "You had no right to tell her that. This was my invitation, not yours. I made plans for us to have champagne on a rooftop with them beforehand." His words were like those his mother would say.

I meandered into my closet. "Well, you should have communicated that to us today."

He bellowed, "You screwed up my plans that I worked hard on all last week!"

My eye's widened in disbelief. Why was I to blame for his lack of communication? I stayed cool. "And what's your part in all this?"

He didn't reply, so I grabbed my shoes and walked downstairs. I waited in the entry as my gut began to bubble and churn. The shockwaves from David's ranting began rippling through my body. I paced around the house, stopping at the bathroom to check my makeup, trying not to let his blaming affect my mood, but it had already seeped in. I'd been looking forward to our dinner until this erupted. Now I was on edge, unsure what to expect from the evening.

At the restaurant, David's negative attitude continued. He complained to the waiter about waiting ten minutes for our reservation, the slow service, and his meal arriving cold. He engaged Sam in his rant, but I was unwilling to buy in. Sharon gave me a glance that told me she was wondering what was happening too. Later, when we went to the bathroom together, she told me David had never communicated his plan to them. We walked back to the table, and I ordered another glass of wine, hoping to make the dinner more palatable.

After the dinner, we dropped off our friends and drove home in silence. That night I clung to the far edge of the bed as my mind looped about the events that had unfolded. It didn't seem like any amount of work I did would help solve our differences. The cracks in the foundation of our marriage continued to widen, and I couldn't build a bridge fast enough. David's retirement was months away. Would we make it that far?

୧୬୭

Three days later, after a few conversations and little resolution about our dinner debacle, I told David about a six-month writing course that I wanted to take.

For years, my close friends and David had told me that I should write a book about my crazy caregiver stories. At first, I laughed and brushed it off, but later I gave it a name, *The Caregiver Chronicles*, though never writing a word. Expressing myself was something I'd only begun to do since I began therapy. I had always been better with numbers in school. I wasn't a writer. I was a mother, wife, daughter, and caretaker. But while I was sandwiched between cooking, cleaning, and caring for everyone else, something remained unsettled inside me. I thought that sense of unease was because I was in an unhappy marriage, but when I sat still with that subtle feeling in yoga or meditation, I knew there was something more I was meant to do. But what? I had few skills after being out of the workforce for so long, and I wasn't interested in a retail job. David had encouraged me for years to be a flight attendant for the benefits, and I'd looked into starting a nonprofit, but that seemed like a large undertaking. Fortunately, I didn't need to work, but I remained lost and confused with no idea what I wanted to do or where to begin.

The previous year, when I was at my annual yoga retreat, a fellow yogi and writer also encouraged me to start writing. I took the leap. That weekend I put pen to paper for the first time and wrote about Mom's visit to the hospital after her heart attack. The more I wrote, the more I realized how much was locked up inside me. Shortly after that, I signed up for a beginning memoir-writing course through UCLA extension, and continued writing my caregiver chronicles as I learned the craft of writing. I was nervous about my ability, but when I was writing, I experienced a calm focus and found words to help me make sense of my experiences and my emotions. Writing became a form of meditation and, like yoga, the more I got involved in it, the more I craved it. I signed up for another class, and as it was ending, a friend told me about a six-month course that sounded perfect for me. I liked the challenge writing brought me, and it fit into my schedule. I decided to make the commitment, but I wanted to tell David about it first.

The morning I explained the class to him, I added, "So, I'm going to need more help around the house." I'd been learning to ask for what I needed. Surely he'd be willing to support my interests after I supported his career for twenty-four years.

He stared into the bathroom mirror, rubbing the midnight shadow of stubble on his face. "As long as it doesn't interfere with the class I want to take."

"Oh, what class is that?" I asked. He hadn't shared the idea of taking this class with me.

"I don't know, I haven't signed up for it yet."

I bitterly snapped, "So you can't help because of a class you haven't even signed up for?"

Silence filled the room. After a few tense minutes, I continued. "I have supported you your entire career. It would be nice if you could support me in something I want to do."

Stone-faced, he turned to me.

"How have you supported me?"

All the techniques I'd learned in my energy class flew right out the window. I blew up. "Dinner is always waiting for you five nights a week, the bills are paid, the house is clean, and our laundry is done. I listened to your stories when you came home from work. Oh, and I raised our daughters while you worked eight to eight and traveled regularly. Now, I'd like to finally do something for myself, but you can't seem to put someone else first, just yourself."

The injustice of it all burned right through me. I could see that he'd never truly valued my contribution to his career or our family. Why was I so naive to think he'd want to support my interests? The truth was excruciatingly painful to hear, but I had to face it. I walked downstairs and made myself a cup of tea. My marriage was going up in flames. I picked up my cup with my shaky hands and stared out the kitchen window. What was ahead of us? What was my future?

The next day in therapy, David offered the same arguments about my class, and Susan had little new advice for us. We were living through Groundhog Day for the hundredth time. We'd been arguing more in spite of all the work we'd done on our marriage. Halfway through our session, I put my head in my hands, trying to hide my discouragement. I tuned out the rest of the session. I had nothing to add.

Hopeless, that night I lay in the guest bedroom sobbing, my pillowcase soaked with grief, shame, and fear. For the last four years I'd tried to repair my marriage. I'd communicated my feelings, listened to his point of view, and tried to find common ground so we could stop our destructive cycle, but nothing had worked.

At three in the morning, after listening to my third meditation tape trying to find some peace, it hit me: I couldn't blame David for everything despite wanting to. I'd put myself in this emotional desert, and I could remove myself. But first, I had to let go of the ideal family photo I'd created in my head so many years ago. Being a good person, wife, and mother wasn't enough. If I were ever going to find happiness, I needed to let go of everything I believed in and take a gigantic leap into the unknown. Alone.

Once I knew what I had to do, I was finally able to sleep.

The next morning, after the kids left for school, I asked David if we could talk. I was leaving that morning with Heather to visit Emma in Chicago, where she'd been living and working since she'd graduated from Indiana University. I sat down on the soft couch in the formal living room we barely used, and David sat in the chair across from me. I scanned the room— there was the imported rug, the glass lamps, and the custom window treatments we'd fought about when we decorated that room. I swallowed our history and looked into David's eyes. "I was up most of the night crying and I realized . . . that I can't do this anymore. I want a separation."

His eyes conveyed his shock. He said, "Uh, okay. If that's what you really want."

Thank goodness he wasn't fighting me.

Exhausted and defeated, I said, "It is, and I'm going to tell Emma and Heather this weekend. And when I get back, I want to sleep in separate bedrooms until we can figure this out."

He sat in silence and looked around the room like he was searching for words. "Shouldn't we get Susan's input first?"

Numbed out, I told him I'd call her to get suggestions before I left.

We sat quietly for a few minutes before he stood up and walked toward the front door, his shoulders hunched. He stood shaking his head as if he were stunned. Then he left without saying a word.

After the front door closed, I sat on the stairs, hollowed out and relieved, finally able to breathe. I had taken the hardest first step.

The morning after Heather and I arrived in Chicago, I sat on the couch in the hotel room and asked the girls to join me. Emma perched on the edge of the bed and Heather was on the couch next to me. I put my shaky hands in between my crossed legs and scanned their faces as their smiles washed away.

My lip quivered, "Dad and I haven't been getting along lately, and we've decided to separate for a while. One of us will start sleeping in the guest bedroom when I get home until we can figure things out."

Emma said, "We know you've been having issues for a while. Last summer when I was home, I could see the tension between you."

The girls were taking this well and clearly had seen more than I'd given them credit for. Heather nodded in agreement, "We don't live with you guys anymore, but how is this going to affect Katie and Jessie?

I sighed. "I'm not sure, but we're going to tell them when I get home. I wanted to tell you in person while we were together."

Another step forward, this time with no tears.

Heather added, "We know you've been in therapy for a while and if you can't work things out, we just want you both to be happy."

I stood up, motioning the girls toward me and hugged them tight. "I love you both very much."

They murmured they loved me too before Heather pulled away, smirking. "Okay, are we ready for a little retail therapy now? I think we've earned it after that conversation."

We all chuckled and headed out for our day.

The rest of the weekend I tried to keep my head above the fog. I faked laughter at the comedy show we attended and laughed when the girls told me a funny story. Even though the girls had taken the news well, my joy was dulled by the seriousness of the situation. I struggled to stay present. My mind kept drifting off thinking about what was next. How would we tell Katie and Jessie? Who would be the first to offer to sleep in the spare bedroom? Would David be willing to move out since I was the primary parent? Would we fight about that too? David sent a few texts, but each time I told him I needed space and to please only contact me if it was an emergency.

I wanted to savor every minute with my girls. I had given everything I could to them, and now that they were adults, I was enjoying the fruits of my labor. Our time together and their embrace would soften the hard blows I knew would come.

thirty

The night I arrived home from Chicago, David greeted me in the entryway. I kept my distance as awkwardness hung between us. I said hello to the twins, who were doing their homework in the kitchen and took my suitcase upstairs. When I came back down to catch up with the girls, Jessie ran past me straight toward the bathroom, her hands over her mouth. I heard the lock click behind her. I gave Katie a look, asking what was wrong. She shrugged her shoulders. In the bathroom, it sounded like Jessie was throwing up and gasping for air.

I tensely knocked on the door. "Jessie, are you okay?

"Open the door, honey." I jiggled the handle while listening to Jessie vomit. Worried, I grabbed a paperclip and unlocked the door. She sat on the floor hugging the toilet, dry heaving. Shit, what had I done? Did she know about our separation?

I kneeled down to her and held her hair back. "What's wrong? Are you sick?"

In between breaths she said, "I have an AP biology test tomorrow . . . and, and I have no idea what's going on in class." She stuck her head back in the toilet. She pulled it out, taking a gasping breath, "And . . . and I don't know what to study."

Thanking God this wasn't about David and me, I gave her a

hug. Then my thoughts shifted. Was school causing all of this?

"I can't take this test tomorrow," she sobbed.

I sat on the cold tile floor and wrapped my arms around her. "It's going to be okay. I'm here for you, and we're going to get through this together."

I didn't know then that she was having a panic attack. Jessie stopped throwing up just as David opened the bathroom door. "What's going on in here?"

I gave him a look that said don't say anything that might upset her. "Jessie's concerned about her biology test tomorrow." I motioned him to leave.

He stood with his hand on the door molding, staring at us. As she rested against me, I thought about the conversations we'd had since the beginning of the school year. She was a junior and had been worried about studying for the ACT test, applying for college, and making a decision about which school to attend while taking several advanced placement classes. I reassured her that we'd take it step by step, but she was clearly still upset.

Finally, she stood up and walked back to the counter where her homework waited. I filled her glass of water and kept an eye on her as I cleaned up the kitchen.

After getting Jessie to bed that night, I asked David, "Did you say anything to Jessie about us?"

"No, why?" he asked, raising his eyebrows.

"I was wondering if her panic attack had anything to do with us."

"Nope, I didn't say a thing."

That night I lay awake for hours wondering if separating from David was a mistake. This was no longer about what was

best for me. I had to think about the effect a separation would
have on all of us.

The next morning, I sent a text to our family therapist to
schedule an appointment for Jessie, and to my relief, she fit her
in right away. The following week, Katie saw me walk out of
the guest room early with my pillow in hand. Her surprised
look suggested it was time to tell the twins we were separating.
That evening we invited the girls to talk. David sat next to me
with his hands folded in his lap. Katie and Jessie settled themselves across from us. I nudged David to start the conversation,
but he gave me a blank stare. "Go ahead."

I exhaled to try to control my unease. "Your dad and I have
something to tell you." I scanned the girls' faces. Their smiles
quickly faded. "As you may have noticed, your dad and I
haven't been getting along, so we've decided to separate. And
until we can figure things out, one of us will be sleeping in the
guest room."

A look of shock crossed Jessie's face. "What? When did
you decide this?"

Katie replied, "Jessie, haven't you noticed that one of them
has been sleeping in the guest room for the last week?"

"Nooo," she sighed.

"We are in the process of figuring things out and will let
you know as soon as we do."

I answered a few questions before they went back to doing
their homework, but David stayed silent throughout the conversation—a small reminder that I was on my own with the
communication too.

A few nights later, Jessie crawled into my bed and whispered, "Mom are you awake? I need to talk."

Startled, I woke. "What's wrong?"

She began to cry. "I'm not happy and I haven't been for a while."

My mind tightened with worry that her anxiety was slipping into depression. I could see that she'd taken on too much during the school year. I held her until she fell asleep, recognizing that Jessie's well-being had to come first during this difficult time.

Over the next several weeks, Jessie's panic attacks continued daily. I took her to therapists and psychiatrists, and David and I visited her school, seeking to reduce her school load and her stress. We put Jessie on medication, took her out of advanced biology, and guided her to cut back on her social life. We learned she was struggling with separating from her identical twin sister, trying to keep up with her older sister, and feared the uncertainty of making the first biggest decision of her life—her choice of college.

David and I continued seeing Susan separately and together each week. I grew more indecisive about our separation. The idea of a separation was having a big impact on Jessie. Susan told me I didn't need to make a decision about my marriage right then. She encouraged David to sign up for the weeklong intensive therapy workshop I'd urged him to take two years prior. He planned to go on a work-related conference afterward, leaving us apart for almost three weeks. The idea of a long break left me relieved. I'd been so focused on Jessie, I hadn't had time to sort out my thoughts and priorities.

The day David left, I took my wedding ring off for the first time in twenty-four years. I didn't tense up around dinnertime in anticipation of his arrival, and the house felt more spacious. I sang my favorite songs a little louder, drank a glass of wine while I made dinner, and watched mindless reality TV shows in the evenings without any eye rolls or interruptions. How freeing it was to experience more room for myself as I tried on what it might be like to be on my own one day. But would I like this permanently and not be lonely? I was afraid to trust the contentment I was experiencing.

While David was away, Bella gave me two months' notice that she was moving to Texas in mid-December. The day she announced this, sadness filled me. I had been so focused on my own struggles that her announcement took me by surprise. It had been ten months since hospice had told us Mom only had months to live. Clearly, she wasn't going to leave us yet. I asked Bella if there was any way we could persuade her to stay, and she softly said no.

I didn't know if I believed in guardian angels, but if I did, Bella was both Mom's and mine. I would be forever grateful for the timing of her arrival, her willingness to take a job well under her skill level, and her flexibility. Her kindness left a stamp on me, giving me a renewed sense of faith that there were good-hearted caregivers out there. They were just a rare find.

Toward the end of David's time away, I went on my annual yoga retreat with my two close friends Sharon and Marsha.

There was so much uncertainty in my life with my shaky marriage, my concern for Jessie's health, and the need to start searching for a new caregiver that I felt like a piece of taffy being pulled apart. For those three days, I left my indecisions behind and focused on me. That weekend at the retreat, I thought about what was in my highest good. When I sat still in meditation, it became clear I had to stop trying to change David so I could feel safe. I hadn't admitted it to anyone, but I knew in my heart that I loved David, but I was no longer in love with him. Leaving my marriage felt like the key to my happiness, but it would require taking another step forward, and that stepping stone was wobbly. Did I have a right to disrupt other people's lives for my own happiness?

On the drive home from the retreat, Marsha asked what I would tell David when he arrived home. "I still don't know," I replied. "I want to hear what he has to say when we're together again." I had to be open to hearing David out. Maybe he'd had a profound shift, and our marriage would change. Maybe when I saw him, I'd realize that I missed him. Or maybe I'd feel the same as I did before he left.

As we drove down the 405 freeway, the reality of life came rushing back in. Slogging through the grief, pain, and endless negotiations of a divorce coupled with the uncertainty of Jessie's well-being overwhelmed me. I needed to search for a new caregiver, and Mom's health still hung in the balance. Maybe it was best to give Jessie stability while we got her health issues under control. The consequences of my choices were complicated and would affect so many.

I held on to the love I'd cultivated at the yoga retreat and the support of my friends as I contemplated my future. Getting to the other side of my divorce would be long, arduous, and require so much strength. I could see the other side, but I couldn't see how to get there. Maybe David's return would help clarify things.

I gave David a brief embrace when he arrived home from his trip. He looked at me with sorrow in his eyes and asked if we could talk after dinner. I agreed, curious about what he had to say. I then thought about our time apart for the last three weeks. After the first week of intensive therapy, he had called me. "This was the most difficult week I've ever experienced, and I can't wait to share what I learned with you." That day, I froze as I held the phone in my hand. I hadn't missed him and I wasn't ready to hear from him yet.

Now that he was home, it had been two weeks since that phone call. When I saw the remorse on his face, I was ready to listen. That night we sat on the couch in our bedroom. The twins were still doing their homework downstairs. He pulled out a piece of paper with his methodical thoughts neatly written out. His face appeared softer. He told me about the three different phases of the intensive therapy program he'd attended. In the beginning, the leaders showed him how his experiences as a young child had influenced how he made decisions as an adult. He stared into my eyes. "My therapist helped me see how my dad's stern parenting style and the weeks my mom spent in her bedroom regularly left me uncared for as a young child." He took off his glasses. "I had to take care of myself from an early age."

He realized the early loss of connection with his mom along with watching his dad treat his mom poorly led him to unconsciously repeat a similar pattern in our marriage. David became teary-eyed as he continued. "I knew I didn't have good role models growing up, but I didn't realize until now the effect that it had on our marriage."

My heart opened. He explained that over the next two days, the therapist prepared him and the group for the third phase—the experiential part of the program. David had to choose a person who'd caused him pain as a child to sit across from him and role-play. He chose his dad. The instructions were to tell "the father" how David felt about how he treated him growing up. Then he was supposed to tell him what he wished had been different. He told his "father" it wasn't okay for him to physically hurt him, and how painful it was when he didn't help him get medical assistance for his asthma. How it hurt to be ostracized by the other kids in school when he couldn't play sports like the rest of the boys his age. He told him he deserved to be treated better.

David softly said, "It felt good to tell my dad those things even though he wasn't physically there. He paused. "And we all had to watch everyone in the group go through their own experiences."

He looked out the window into the dark sky. "There was one woman who had a similar childhood to yours . . . she had been abused by a family member when she was young. Watching her walk through her exercise of sharing how it felt to be a child who suffered abuse helped me understand how your childhood affected you." His pleading eyes looked vulnerable. I'd rarely seen him like that.

I choked up, unable to respond. He finally understood what I'd gone through as a child.

"I've never cried so much in my life. By the end of the week, I don't think I had any tears left."

His comment struck me. I'd only seen him shed tears three times during our entire marriage, so I knew he must have experienced a great deal of pain. "It sounds like you got a lot out of the program."

"I did, and you should consider going . . . I think it would help."

I told him I'd think about it. I didn't want him to know I was already considering it after talking to a friend who'd been through the same program. I wanted to talk to our therapist first.

For the next hour, David told me stories of his childhood that I hadn't heard. I reached over and caressed him, hoping I could comfort him.

"I feel like all the therapy came together for me in that week. One night, I read an entire book on codependence. It helped me connect the dots between how the skills I used to survive my childhood continued in adulthood. My parents were either fighting between themselves, fighting with my brother, or they weren't around. I never knew what to expect."

He shook his head. "And there's more you still don't know about."

My body stiffened as a feeling of betrayal set in. I'd shared everything with David from the beginning, and I wished he had too. I knew it was difficult for him to talk about his past, but what else hadn't he told me? I continued to listen, not reacting to the idea he'd withheld important information from me. Again. David had always been harder on his mom, which led me to believe she'd been the culprit of his childhood pain. But after his stories that night and learning that his dad tried to physically beat the asthma out of him when he was a young teenager, I saw deeper truths and wounds.

"The retreat also helped me better understand how my upbringing created the way I viewed you and our marriage. I took my cues from my dad instead of Uncle Harold."

Harold adored his wife Ruth, and he made sure she was always taken care of. He'd sometimes take her to the hairdresser and often compliment her. I moved from the couch to the floor to sit cross-legged near him. His sincerity was touching, and I was pleased that he wanted to share more with me. It was the kind of connection I'd been yearning for, though I'd realized only recently how important it was. By understanding how his past had shaped him, I hoped I could better understand him and have more empathy.

Susan had warned me he'd be raw when he returned and suggested that I be gentle. Feeling tender toward him, I said, "I'm glad you were able to link those pieces together, but I need to know what will change in the marriage."

His face looked blank, as if he didn't have an answer. I knew this was the first time David had addressed his unhappy childhood, but I was disappointed that he wasn't able to articulate the changes he planned to make. I needed to see him shift his reactions to his family. Would he control his temper? Could he continue to share his past with me? Would he discuss his thoughts first before making a decision?

At the end of our conversation that first night, I thanked him for sharing his experiences and we embraced. As we separated, David stared into my eyes. "I'm not ready to give up on us. I love you."

I cautiously welcomed the sincerity in his words and the warmth of his hug. My previous self would have taken him back right then, but I was working on changing my part in our cycle. If I forgave him prematurely, before I knew it, we'd slip back into our old patterns. Would things change enough for me to fall back in love with him again? Only time would reveal the answers, and all I could do was live every day differently.

thirty-one

O ver the next month my indecisiveness felt like a roller
coaster ride. I changed my mind about my marriage by
the day, hour, minute. My moods were determined by how
close I felt to David, how Jessie was doing, and how my search
for a new caregiver was progressing. It helped to see that David
was changing. He began helping with the laundry, cooked
dinner on Sunday nights, and was more involved with the
twins. Even with the changes he was making, I worried if I'd
ever be able to love David the way I once did. In becoming the
dutiful wife, mother, daughter, and caregiver, I had lost myself.
Could we regain the love we had while I searched for my new
self? Would David accept the new me?

Susan, our therapist, continued telling me in my private
sessions, "You will know when it's time to divorce." I hated
hearing that when I expressed my doubts and confusion,
though I knew she was right. I signed up for the same codependence workshop David had attended and told him that I'd
make a decision after I returned.

I woke up early the morning after I arrived in Wickenburg,
Arizona, nervous about the workshop and the week ahead.

After listening to both David's and my girlfriend's experience of the workshop, I knew it was going to be an emotional week. The weight of the Christmas holidays was waiting for me when I returned home. As I got dressed that morning, I wanted my week to be over, but I knew the only way to the other side was through. There was no going backwards.

I arrived at the center, checked in, and sat in their large new conference room, gazing out the large windows overlooking the well-manicured grounds and the desolate cactus desert in the distance. I glanced at my folder of materials and watched people trickle in. I wondered why each one was there.

The center treated a gamut of issues including childhood trauma, substance abuse, depression, eating disorders, and sexual issues. I signed up for the workshop that focused on childhood trauma, the same one David had attended. A dark-haired woman with a soft round face walked up to the podium. She wore a long black skirt, cowboy boots, and chunky turquoise jewelry. She welcomed everyone and gave us an overview of what we could expect. She'd be my group therapist for the duration.

She talked about the importance of confidentiality and asked everyone to go around the room and say what workshop they'd signed up for. Some said substance abuse, others childhood issues. One man said he had sex addiction issues. My body tensed. I wouldn't feel comfortable discussing the abuse I suffered from Ken if he was in my group. After that, several therapists arrived and we were assigned to smaller groups. Thank goodness they grouped me with four other women.

After lunch, we met with our small group in a cozy room with shades covering the windows—it would be our home for the next five days. Our therapist asked each of us why we were there. A thin blond woman said her husband was a sex addict and alcoholic. A divorced woman from Wyoming had a teenage son in the drug and alcohol treatment center there. Both women had signed up for the workshop after visiting their family members the weekend before.

When it was my turn, I confessed that I was adopted, I'd been sexually abused as a child, and my husband and I had been struggling for years in our marriage. The therapist responded, "Your therapist at home suggested we work on your adoption issues. Is that right?"

I stuttered, "Ye-yesss, and also my abuse." The pang in my stomach grew. Even though I knew my past had affected my life and my marriage, and contributed to my loneliness, the thought of revisiting those experiences sounded like a form of torture. At the same time, I knew I had to resolve them to move forward.

The other women continued sharing their reasons for attending. After listening to their stories, my experiences seemed mild in comparison. Did I really need to be here?

I spent the next two days learning about codependence and answering questions about what my childhood was like and how my past had affected me. I used a feeling chart with eight basic emotions and guidelines on how to communicate feelings like, *when I saw . . . it made me feel. . . .*

Our therapist had us check in with our feelings three times a day. This came easily to me after over four years practicing yoga and three years in my energy class. The first three days were in preparation for the experiential portion of the workshop. We would sit across from an empty chair that represented someone who'd caused us pain, the role-playing exercise David had talked about.

By the time we started the experiential phase, I understood how my fear of being alone had stemmed from my adoption. Not looking like anyone in my family and not feeling connected to anyone but Mom had left me searching for belonging and connection most of my life, often in the wrong places.

I let two other women in the group go first. We quietly watched each person communicate the hurt they'd carried toward the person who'd traumatized them. We shed tears for each other as each of us addressed the grief that had been buried deep inside. After each woman's turn, we each told her how we felt as we observed the role-play. After four days of constantly discussing our feelings, I was drained.

At lunch that day, I sat with our group on the patio, warming my body in the sun after being in a cool dark room all morning. One young woman who'd taken her turn that morning said, "I've made my decision . . . I'm going to leave my husband."

I sat across from her, staring into her determined eyes, her light-brown hair shaping her face. She was in her early thirties, married with two young children. I wanted her strength, her decisiveness. I wanted that feeling of certainty and knowing. I wanted her conviction. Would I develop the same clarity after this workshop?

The next morning on our last day, I took my turn. By then, I was anxious and ready for all of it to be over. My therapist allowed me to focus on two issues, so I had two experiences to play out. The first was my adoption, and the second would address my abuse.

I sat in the chair, put both feet on the ground and my hands in my lap. I closed my eyes and took a few deep breaths. This preparation was familiar since I'd done similar exercises in our energy class to help calm my body and my mind.

"Okay, when you are ready, open your eyes," she whispered.

She handed me a baby doll wrapped in a blanket. "I want you to hold this baby. We are going to pretend it's you as a newborn."

I cradled the baby as if it were my own. I wanted to give my younger self the love I'd given my own children. The love I'd yearned for as a child. I'd never claim to be the perfect parent, but I tried to give my girls the kind of love I wanted when I was a child. A more connected, protective kind of love.

"Now, what would you like to tell yourself?"

Tears formed under my closed eyes and my words spilled out. "I want you to know that you are loved and wanted . . . and you deserve to be here."

The room was quiet as my therapist calmly said, "Yes."

I continued, "Someone should have been there with you in the hospital, so you weren't left alone the first three days of your life." Tears dribbled down my cheeks.

"And I want you to know, you don't need to feel alone anymore. You are a smart, funny, caring person, and you deserve to have your needs met."

I looked down at the baby, visualizing the love I was giving myself as an infant. Warmth traveled through my body.

"Is there anything else you'd like to say?" the therapist asked.

I sat for a minute surrendering to the warm tingling sensation that had taken over, touching parts of my soul that had lain dormant for years, my own words mending my brokenness. I waited to see if something else surfaced. "No, I think that's all."

After handing her the baby, I continued to sit with a calmness I hadn't felt in so long. She told me to stand up when I was ready.

I walked in circles, shaking my legs out, and took a few deep breaths before sitting down again.

"Okay, tell me when you are ready."

I wiggled in my chair, putting my feet back on the floor, my hands back in my lap. "Okay, I'm ready."

"Now, what would you like to say to your brother?"

I exhaled deeply. I imagined him across from me. "Ken, what you did is despicable."

She said, "Tell him what he did to you."

My words came tumbling out. "It wasn't okay that you physically and sexually abused me. You had no right hurting me and taking advantage of me when you should have protected me."

I told him his abuse had affected my marriage and changed how I saw my relationships with men. I'd been promiscuous during my teens and early twenties because I thought that's what men wanted. I threw wadded up tissues at him and yelled, "You didn't have the right to invade my body without my consent. It wasn't my fault and you . . . should have . . . known . . . better!"

Tears dripped down my face and onto my legs as I collapsed in my chair. I slowly sat up, my eyes closed. No words were left.

The therapist softly said, "I'd like you to stay seated for a couple of minutes."

I sat with my eyes closed. My body continued tingling from the shame and anger that had been stirred up. I envisioned the negative energy traveling down my legs and seeping into the floor, a technique I'd learned in my energy class.

Then she asked, "Tell me how you feel now."

I continued sitting there with my eyes closed. "Better," I murmured.

"Okay, I want you to slowly open your eyes. Look at the chart and tell me how you feel."

I glanced at the chart and checked in with my body. "I feel relieved and sad."

"Yeah, that's good," my therapist quietly acknowledged. "Just sit with those feelings before you get up."

I rose from the chair after the tingling in my legs subsided. I looked around the room and saw sorrow on everyone's faces. They felt my pain as I had felt theirs.

One other woman went after me, the last person that day. When it was over, we said goodbye to each other. Our therapist told us, "Over the next couple of weeks, you may be a little more emotional than normal, so be kind to yourself. The work you've done will take time to settle in and take shape."

I gathered my belongings and walked outside. The clear dry air passed through my lungs, cleansing me. I walked around the grounds one more time, scanning the dry desert, searching for the resoluteness the young mother in our group had the day before. I wanted answers for David, my family, and me, but nothing came at that moment. I knew I needed to give everything more time to unfold.

◦€๏

A week after I returned, David and I met with Susan. She asked me what I learned while I was away. "I have a fear of being alone."

She smiled and said, "Yes."

I went on. "I also learned that my fear of being alone stemmed from my adoption, and feeling like I didn't belong in my family." I stared at the floor, swallowing the lump in my throat, "And the sexual abuse added to that and was still affecting me." My voice trembled.

David sat quietly and listened. I went on to tell both Susan and David that I still hadn't made a decision about our marriage, and I needed more time. I requested that we continue to sleep in separate rooms. Susan advised us that when we tell Katie and Jessie, to keep it simple.

The next day in my individual therapy session, I sat on the couch telling Susan what I couldn't admit in front of David the previous day. "I realized that my desire to create the family I didn't have as a child caused me to ignore my own needs throughout my marriage."

Susan nodded in agreement.

"And my need to keep my family together has added to my loneliness."

She agreed again.

After therapy I went home and did some chores. While I watered my garden and pulled the wilting flowers off my plants, I thought about my confession earlier in therapy. Why was I staying? Was I using Jessie's health issues and my need to keep my family together as my excuse? Why was I so afraid to leave my marriage? Trustworthiness, honesty, and mutual respect were the keys to keeping my marriage alive, but we had lost those years ago. When I took my vows, I envisioned a unity of marriage in which we nurtured and protected one another. We had done that at times, but I wasn't sure what we had now would be enough to keep us connected in the way I needed.

I snipped off the last flower from my hydrangea and stared at its brown leaves. I had no fear of flying in a helicopter to ski fresh powder, sailing a boat in a winter's storm, traveling to developing nations, or hiking to the top of Mount Whitney, but I was afraid of being alone. Would I feel more alone if I left? Having felt alone for most of my life, the thought of experiencing more of that kind of pain seemed unbearable. I gathered the dead flowers into a pile and put them in the trashcan. Being alone forever sounded like a prison sentence.

thirty-two

C hristmas quickly became my priority, and I threw myself into the trappings of the holidays—shopping, decorating, and making Mom's spritz cookies. As I stayed busy with all the preparations, the state of my marriage stayed at the forefront of my mind. The only gift I wanted that year was clarity, but it must have been on backorder. Avoidance became my mode for dealing with David. But one evening he pragmatically asked, "When are you going to come back to our bed?"

Wincing at the direct question, I stopped in my tracks. It wasn't a surprise, and he deserved an honest answer. I'd finally admitted to Susan the week prior that I still loved David, but I wasn't in love with him. I'd felt the loss for years, but I could only admit it out loud now.

My throat restricted. "I don't know."

"Heather will be home from college soon."

It had been two and a half months since I'd asked for a separation, and David and I were still taking turns sleeping in the guest bed. Heather would need it when she came home in a few days.

"I know."

I owed David, my kids, and myself a clear answer. I worried how my uncertainty contributed to Jessie's anxiety, even though her panic attacks had lessened. She was making progress, but it was slow, slower than I'd expected.

I told David, "I'll tell you tomorrow. I need to sleep on it."

I didn't want my ambiguity to strain our family time during Christmas, nor did I want the girls to associate the holidays with their parents splitting up. I hoped my individual therapy session scheduled for the next day would help me get clearer about my decision.

He grabbed my forearms and looking sincere he said, "I promise no intimacy until you are ready."

My constricted throat softened. "I appreciate you saying that."

I was relieved. I couldn't jump back into being intimate too fast like I'd done last time.

I spent the next day and my time in therapy gathering my jumbled thoughts. David was trying to change. His outbursts were less frequent, and we were having weekly conversations about our relationship, which had started after his retreat. Those things had helped me to feel closer to him. But why was it necessary to push him to the brink in order for our relationship to change? It was the second time that I'd walked to the edge of a cliff, and both times I was ready to take that leap. Putting everything on the line seemed to be the only action that caught his attention. I was glad to see his efforts, but each time our marriage weakened, and so did my love.

After sorting through my confusion, the following evening I made the choice to put my family first and agreed to sleep in the same bed as David. A week later we made love for the first time in several months. Over the last seven tumultuous years, my desire for David had waned, which at times made our lovemaking a chore. That night felt different. After we pleased each other, we fell asleep in each other's arms. When I woke the next morning, I tried to conjure up the last time we'd fallen asleep like that. I couldn't remember; it had been years.

That night, David told me again he didn't want our marriage to end. I couldn't exchange the same sentiments, and finding the solace we once had seemed further from my reach. But I had to hold on to the thread of hope that our renewed connection would be enough to carry us through each day. My decision may have been made out of self-preservation, but it was the only way I could stay and give Jessie the time she needed to find a better balance in her life. And maybe through it all, I'd find my way back to David.

We announced the news to the girls on Christmas Eve, during our drive home from visiting my parents. I told them that their Dad and I were going to give our marriage another try. It was the right decision for our family.

Heather didn't hesitate. "We want you to do what makes you both happy." The twins agreed with Heather. Her words struck me. The times I'd been the happiest lately were when I wasn't with David. I wasn't sure what happiness looked or felt like in my marriage anymore, and I appreciated them giving us permission to try and find it again.

When we were almost home, I told David, "Oh, get off at the next off ramp so we avoid all the airport traffic ahead."

David scoffed, "Wait, what? No, I'm going my usual way."

Emma snickered, "I thought you guys were trying to get along?"

And there it was again—that small shard of disagreement

slicing through my previous statement for the girls to see. They knew us better than we knew ourselves. I slid down in my seat trying not to show my reaction, my hope sinking again.

The day after Christmas, a late and unexpected gift arrived. The four girls and I joined Mary, my birth mother, for breakfast. It had become an annual event for all of us over the last ten years.

Mary met us in Manhattan Beach. She looked the same as the year before except the lines on her face appeared deeper. She wore a red holiday cardigan, blue slacks, and a long gold chain around her neck. She was always well dressed, with her short blond hair and thick eyeliner accentuating her blue eyes. Our waitress seated us at a round table in the middle of the restaurant with swags of garlands spilling over the serving tables. Mary brought gifts for us as she did every year. That year they were floral enamel bracelets.

As thoughtful as her gifts were, I sensed the girls weren't excited about them, so I guided the conversation to something interesting. "We went to the Galapagos Islands this past summer. It was an amazing experience."

Mary smiled. "Really, what did you girls like most about it?"

The girls told her about the unique and abundant wildlife we'd seen. Emma told her about her new life in Chicago, and Heather shared her excitement about her upcoming semester abroad in Paris. Katie and Jessie told her about the colleges they were considering.

After breakfast, the four girls left together for the restroom, leaving me alone with Mary. She hesitated, then touched my arm and looked into my eyes. "I'd like you to know that I never wanted to give you up for adoption." She paused as her hand slid down my arm and squeezed my hand. A look of anguish crossed her face. "I didn't feel like I had a choice. Very few women had children out of wedlock back in the sixties."

The girls meandered toward us. Unsure of what to say next and aware we'd be interrupted in a moment, I stuttered, "Thank you . . . I know." I squeezed her hand in return as we walked toward the lobby. I was speechless. Her confession caught me by surprise, and I needed time to think.

The sadness in her face turned to relief when she said, "I've been wanting to tell you that for years."

"I could only imagine how hard that must have been." Heaviness sat in my chest.

She nodded with understanding and a look of regret.

I thought about the difficult decision she'd been forced to make, a decision that I never had to face. The idea of carrying a child for nine months and handing it off to a stranger, not knowing if you would ever see your child again, sounded unbearable. When I imagined being in her shoes and having that deep, raw, unconditional love being taken away from me, my eyes welled up. Nothing could be more painful for me than losing a child.

The girls met us in the lobby and we all said our goodbyes. The girls walked toward the car.

"Thank you again for sharing . . . I know your decision wasn't an easy one."

"You're welcome, and I meant what I said." Her voice was still thick with emotion.

"I know . . ." I hugged her goodbye as the weight of her words sunk in.

Over the next few weeks, I kept coming back to our conversation, replaying her words—"I never wanted to give you up for adoption. I didn't feel like I had a choice"—my body absorbing each word, repeatedly. I'd always sensed that she wouldn't have given me up unless she'd had no other choice. Women were ostracized for having children out of wedlock back in the sixties, but hearing those words directly from her settled something deep within me. Perhaps I'd been waiting to hear them my entire life, but I didn't know it until then. It was a reminder that I was loved. I was wanted. I deserved to be here.

That December, something inside was set free. The door to my past that had imprisoned and silenced me for years was open. Mary's words, my week of intense therapy, and my deeper understanding of how my past had shaped me gave me the freedom to walk out and explore the world in a new light. The flowers were more vibrant, the evening stars brighter, the ocean air a little sweeter.

thirty-three

Katie brought worry to me the evening our family returned from our holiday trip to Mammoth. I sat with her in an examination room at our local urgent care, waiting to be seen by a doctor. Her swollen neck blended into her face, and her red cheeks radiated heat as she wiggled uncomfortably on the hard examining table. She'd slept most of the five days of our vacation, barely able to ski. On our last day, I knew it must be more than strep throat or the flu.

A handsome, tall young doctor walked in, examined her, and after running a few tests, diagnosed her with mononucleosis. I was relieved but still concerned about how this illness might affect her already compromised immune system. Over the last three years, Katie had developed allergies and asthma, which turned into chronic sinus infections. Her tired body had just begun feeling better after frequent doctor appointments, multiple rounds of antibiotics, and immunotherapy shots. Now another illness.

The doctor sent us home with a prescription for rest. Time and sleep were the only cure. Like Jessie, she was in the middle of her junior year of high school. I worried that she too had taken on too much with her heavy course load and activities that school year. Her immune system was fragile, and this was how stress showed up in her body. As I helped settle her in bed that evening, I thought about the unconditional love I had for each of my girls, the same kind of love I'd felt from Mom when I sat on her lap and she showed me how to sail or when she held me and kissed my forehead when I was sick. When I first became a mother, I had no idea what motherhood would demand of me—all the sleepless nights, worries, and guilt about not being perfect. Now it seemed natural to know what to do, though I guessed that worry would always be part of the equation even after they were grown. I kissed Katie and told her I'd check in later.

The next day I called Katie's doctor and asked for a note so we could modify her school schedule. We had to put her health first. Over the next month I dropped her off late and picked her up early. I was apprehensive about how she was going to manage her commitments to work at the local temple, the Model United Nations debate team, and her advanced placement classes.

A few weeks later, after I picked Katie up from school, she said, "I forgot what it feels like to have energy. I've been tired for the last two years straight." Tears slid down her cheeks.

I put my arm on her shoulder. "Your health is more important, and you don't need to work."

"I know, but I like my job," she cried.

I repeated that statement multiple times and offered to pay her to be free of work pressures, but she didn't accept.

That evening while making dinner, I thought about how my admiration for Mom grew stronger after David and I had started our own family. I reflected on the challenges Mom faced raising the three of us after losing a baby at eight months gestation and taking the leap to adopt. She'd managed Ken's delinquent behavior; taken us to our music lessons, church, sports, activities, and orthodontia appointments; and given us the things we wouldn't have had if we'd stayed with our birth mothers. She'd offered unconditional love when I was a selfish teenager. Mom had always made her children a priority.

When I was an adolescent, I saw her struggle, but I never heard her complain. She disregarded the social norms of being a stay-at-home mother and went back to teaching when I was in kindergarten to help make a better life for her family. When Mom realized she'd need more money to retire comfortably, she got her master's degree in education.

I'd adopted similar traits, overcoming obstacles and differences in the name of family with few complaints. But at what point did this mentality no longer serve me? Where was the breaking point? When I was younger, I didn't understand why Mom didn't divorce Dad, but now I saw the ways you had to compromise. Work it out somehow. We all have reasons behind the decisions we make, even if others don't see them or agree.

During the next year, Katie's mono turned into chronic tonsillitis, and she developed abscesses that sent her to the emergency room several times, followed by two surgeries. Stark differences continued with David and me around how to treat Katie and deal with the minutiae of living life together. Jessie's anxiety lingered, but she kept learning how to manage it. Even though our marriage was far from ideal, like Mom, I put my family first—giving the twins the stability of one home while their health improved and nurturing them until they graduated from high school. It was the only choice for me.

❦

After the holidays, Katie and Jessie's first day back to school was David's last day at work. After thirty-five years of working for the same company, he'd officially retired at age fifty-eight. David had dedicated his life to his career and had worked hard for our family. I was happy for him. He deserved this, but I worried that more time together would polarize our already noticeable differences. I cherished my alone time during the day and rarely felt lonely. I kept myself busy—focusing on my writing course, paying bills, and managing my kid-related volunteer commitments. David's hobbies were volunteering as a board member for a local credit union and for the Homeowners' Association for our rental property, skiing with the family, and fly-fishing a few times a year.

Susan and I had encouraged him to take up new hobbies outside of the house in anticipation of his retirement. At first, he said he'd think about it. Then he told us, "I'm not going to commit to anything for the first year after I retire. I need time to decompress." He missed the cue that spending more time together might create more opportunities to get on each other's nerves. I wished he'd taken up golf, tennis, or cycling, or anything to create a better balance between us. There was some relief when he rented office space down the street, a place for him to go as he transitioned into retirement.

Months later, he stopped using the rented office entirely. One afternoon, we were sitting in the shared office in our home, our backs to each other. After being with him for several days without much of a break, his grunting and sighing made the hair on the back of my neck stand up. I turned to him.

"Will you agree to start going to your office twice a week? I would like to have some time alone in the house."

He turned toward me and laughed. "I got the office because I thought I'd have a hard time with this transition. I never thought you'd be the one having a hard time with my retirement."

My tension boiled over. "Well, if you aren't going to use the office, I will."

"You're not allowed to use the office. It's a one-person lease," he quickly retorted.

Irritated, I got up and walked downstairs to make tea, feeling like an expired product left sitting on a shelf. My needs weren't even considered. I stared out the kitchen window, sizzling with pent-up resentment. My choice to stay was being tested again. I thought about our continued struggles that had bubbled up since his retirement, making me question whether I could make it through the girls' senior year, a year and a half away.

The longer I was in therapy, the more I understood that David was more like Dad than I'd ever realized. I'd learned that we might unconsciously marry someone with similar character flaws as our parents to resolve childhood issues. David continued to put his needs first. My father was similar, but he'd throw temper tantrums and stomp his feet when he didn't get his way. Mom had taken care of Dad, his business, the house, their finances, and the children. I'd done much the same, even though I wanted to think I was different from her. Mom had endured everything until her body froze from all she'd held inside, her mind gone. Long ago, I promised myself I wasn't going to allow my marriage to mirror Mom and Dad's, but here we were. I didn't want to end up imprisoned in my own body like Mom. Would that happen to me if I stayed? I couldn't bear to think about that. While biding my time, I'd imagine what my future might be, not knowing when it would begin.

thirty-four

W hen you are a caretaker, you're on duty even when things seem to be going well. No matter what else I was doing, my obligations to Mom and Dad were always perched in the back of my mind. When there was a lull, I appreciated the minutes, hours, or days between each predicament, knowing I could be summoned at any moment.

One spring morning, four months after David retired, I received a call from my parents' caregiver, Kay, at six in the morning. She told me that she wasn't coming to work that day. I'd hired Kay after Bella left, despite my intuition that she wouldn't be a long-term solution; she was the best solution at the time.

From the beginning, Kay had flip-flopped. One day she'd tell me she needed more hours but didn't know if our job worked for her. Shortly after that, she'd say she liked working for us. The day she called at the last minute, I let her go.

Carmen, my other caregiver, was kind enough to cover Kay's shift while I searched for someone else. By then, Carmen had been with us for several years. She'd never called in sick and was always willing to help out in a pinch. We'd built a trusting relationship, and I was grateful that I could count on her. Determined to find someone similar to Carmen and Bella, I began interviewing caregivers again.

Spring led into summer as I replaced one caregiver after another. I tolerated little, and when my negative thoughts of not finding a caregiver popped into my head, I found it easier to push them aside. It was my responsibility to make sure my parents were cared for. After all, they'd adopted me, loved me the best they knew how, and sparked my love for nature, skiing, and sailing, gifts my friends had gone without as we were growing up. As grateful as I was, there were times when the burden became too heavy for me to carry alone. During those moments, I'd break down and cry. Eight years had passed since Mom's health had begun to fail. I never thought I'd be managing their care for this long. I'd asked for more help from Will, but he fought me when I asked him to do the weekly grocery shopping. He eventually gave in, but I knew he'd never be the brother who'd show up to help as I'd hoped.

Ken's presence in our lives continued to complicate matters. Although he helped out around the house—running to Home Depot to get supplies for Dad's projects, fixing the dishwasher, and cleaning out Dad's fishpond—there was a price to pay. He'd sometimes boss around the caregivers, and I'd have to intervene. And there was his addiction. After almost a year of sobriety, Ken ended up back in jail, waiting to enter court–ordered rehab once again. After forty years of substance abuse, addiction was hard to overcome.

I was disappointed but not surprised to hear the news from Ken. He told me he wanted to stay sober this time. He wanted to get a good job so he could start paying into social security. I encouraged him to take care of himself.

David and I were in Boston for a college tour when Ken called to say he was finally being admitted to rehab the next day, and he wouldn't have contact with us for sixty days. Relief and frustration twisted inside me. He agreed with my decision to replace the caregiver and rambled on about his big plans to change his life when he was released, but I tuned most of it out. At the end of the conversation he said, "Anyway, I should go. I love you. I'll call you and Dad when I can."

I stuttered, "Okay," and slumped in my chair. Our hotel room was quiet and everyone was sleeping. Did he just tell me he loved me? Did he think those words would erase our past?

As we were growing up, my brothers rarely, if ever, told me they loved me, and only as adults had Will and I exchanged those words. After the call, anger still burned inside me. Should I have told him his past behavior had hurt me?

I couldn't say "I love you" to Ken. I was livid that he brushed over the pain he'd caused, and I was mad at myself for not saying, "Don't tell me you love me until you've apologized for what you did in the past." I didn't know if I could ever reconcile my feelings for him. As I sat in the adjoined sitting area watching my family sleep, a pinball of pain bounced around inside me, reminding me of all he'd done to me, how he'd stolen my innocence and created anxiety that was still not resolved. I thought I'd put the pain behind me after years of working with Susan and the intensive therapy I'd done, but as I sat there reeling with many feelings and memories, I knew those wounds were still with me.

In the weeks after that conversation, I found myself uncontrollably snapping at David for things I normally didn't focus on—his not bringing in the trashcans or throwing away the stack of newspapers that had piled up. One day after snapping at him, I blurted out, "Get used to it, this is the new me."

Surprised by my own attacks, I brought up my irritability in therapy. Susan helped me recognize that when Ken didn't take ownership for his actions, it reopened old wounds. She suggested I call Ken's treatment center to see if I could meet with him and his therapist to talk about the abuse while he was in rehab.

"Ken may never own up to what he did, and you should prepare yourself for that."

I released a heavy sigh. I knew she was right, but I wanted to try. I knew what Ken did was wrong, and his actions had caused me to feel unworthy for too long. If Ken confessed and apologized, maybe then it would free me from being trapped in ongoing patterns.

A week later, I called Ken's coordinator at his inpatient rehab program. I told him about Ken's physical and sexual abuse and asked if I could address these issues while Ken was in the program. He told me he'd ask his therapist and get back to me.

"We only have our patients for a few months. It took me years before I was able to apologize to the people I'd wronged."

"I understand, and I'm okay either way." That wasn't actually true. I knew a conversation might not happen, but I needed to know for myself.

The following week Ken's coordinator called me back. "I talked to Ken's therapist and also sat in a group session with him. We asked Ken about his family and if there were any issues that needed to be resolved. He said there weren't. We both agree that Ken isn't ready yet . . . you may need to wait a while longer."

I sank down in the couch as he went on. He told me if Ken continued to work the twelve-step program, he might get to the point where he could make amends—that was step eight. Ken was only starting step four.

I hung up the phone and stared at the picture of Mom and Dad on my bookshelf. Furious, I screamed and fell to the floor. I wanted Ken to confess, but it wasn't going to happen. He wasn't capable of it, and he might never be. After raging, crying, and pounding the floor, I got up. I started the laundry, watered my plants, and straightened up the house, hoping that staying busy would ease my pain. I wanted to escape my past, but it was still raw and real within me. I had to accept that my work on this would need to continue.

thirty-five

T he following year would be the twins' last before they left
for college, a year marked by college application due dates,
holidays, college acceptance letters, senior prom, Heather's
college graduation, Katie and Jessie's high school graduation,
and our annual family vacation.

I focused on launching the twins, who begrudgingly allowed me to teach them how to do laundry and cook basic
meals. We went shopping for their last winter dance, senior
prom, and dorm room decorations. We got our nails done together, and I curled their hair for the last time on graduation
day. I was just as ready for the girls to leave for college as they
were. I'd spent almost half my life raising my kids, which was
the hardest yet most rewarding job of my life. I cherished that
last year, knowing I'd never get that time back again.

Through it all, my marital struggles seemed to escalate,
and everything became fair game. I didn't do anything right.
According to David, I shouldn't join the book club I wanted to
join. Even grocery shopping became an issue. And there was
the fight at the Hollywood Bowl.

Each June, we attended a jazz festival at the Hollywood
Bowl that had always marked the beginning of summer. We

always loved going with our friends Carol and Bruce. We'd listen to jazz music, visit, and enjoy the gourmet food our friends always brought. At one point when we were listening to a band, I was texting the twins and other friends who were there to coordinate meeting up later. David reached over and tried to grab my phone out of my hand. His look of disdain communicated that he was unhappy that I was texting.

I left our box seats and walked around the venue for an hour, thinking about how agitated he'd been earlier when we were packing up and how adamant he was about leaving at a specific time. When I came back to our seats, his face had a sneer. I knew he was unhappy I'd left him and our friends for so long. I couldn't let that go and asked to talk to him in private.

I sat on a cement wall along the path and faced him with a surge of anger, barely able to speak. He didn't have the right to tell me when I could and couldn't text. I asked, "What's going on with you? You've been unhappy all day."

He held a glass of wine in one hand and the other was on his hip. He aimed a contemptuous look at me.

I continued, "I've been communicating with our kids and my friends who we're meeting up with later . . . I don't appreciate you treating me this way."

He leaned in inches from my face. "You are being disrespectful to our friends and me."

I held my own though my stomach tightened. "I didn't do anything wrong. Why are you ruining our day?" I took a gulp of wine, hoping it would calm my nerves.

"I don't know what you're talking about." He paused, scanning me with his eyes. "You're just drunk," he said dismissively and turned to walk away.

"Fuck you!" I spat, surprised by my own outburst. I'd never said those words to David before.

I wasn't drunk. I hadn't had a drink in more than an hour. I sat on the wall, my hands shaking. That familiar need to flee took over. I had to get away from him. I opened an Uber account at that moment as my heart was pounding. I thought we were past this kind of struggle. How could I go back to our seats and face our friends when he'd treated me so rudely in front of them? What must they think of us? I didn't want to stay, but did I really have the guts to leave? As I finished setting up the new Uber account so I could leave on my own, I glanced up and saw David walking toward me. Shit. I tucked my phone in my pocket.

His face was drawn with remorse. "I'm sorry, I shouldn't have said those things to you. Will you come back to our seats?"

I bluntly asked, "Why should I—so you can treat me that way again?"

He reached toward me and with pleading eyes asked again, "Will you please come back? I'm sorry."

Every bone in my body said to leave and go home. The day had been ruined not only for me but for our friends. I knew they'd understand. All our friends knew our marriage had been tumultuous. David's behavior sent me over the edge. But why couldn't I leave him or the venue?

I returned to the concert, but it was ruined for me—and for all of us. When I sat down, our friends told us they were going to leave. I apologized for ruining their day. After they left, I suggested we leave as well.

It didn't matter what happened after we arrived home,

because it mirrored all our other disagreements. I had become less tolerant of our fights, which in turn caused him to become more defiant. The pattern felt like a cyclone we couldn't seem to escape. I was saddened by the state of our marriage, and I noticed the impact it was having on the kids. When the girls were around, they had been calling us out more when we fought in front of them. It really hit home when the twins gave us his and her voodoo dolls for Christmas. I laughed after reading the funny comments written on the body of mine: *stop acting like a jerk, buy me jewelry, take me to a chick-flick, take out the trash,* and *listen to me.* His said, *stop spending money, take the trash out yourself, pick up after me,* and *stop nagging.* But a pit grew in my stomach—our issues were so much greater. Were we hurting them by staying together?

After our spat at the jazz festival, I told Susan I wanted to leave the marriage. She asked, "Are you sure you're ready to follow through?"

Susan knew me. I'd threatened to leave multiple times before, wanting to get off the dizzy, broken carnival ride. I knew the next time I said those words to David's face, I'd need to have the courage to follow through.

After I cooled down, I thought about Katie's health issues, Jessie's anxiety, Mom's volatile health, and the revolving door of caregivers. Katie and Jessie's graduation was approaching, and the caregiver I'd recently hired looked promising. Mom's health had been stable for the last year.

My heart hurt constantly, and the thought of repairing our relationship was further from my reach. When I thought about the true state of my marriage or our future together as empty nesters, another piece of my soul slipped into a dark and lonely place. In order to stay, I had to shift my state of mind, spending most days pretending my marriage wasn't falling apart.

I mourned the upcoming loss of Katie and Jessie as their senior year progressed. I cried in yoga class, in the car, and in the aisles of Trader Joe's as I purchased their favorite snacks. I pushed thoughts aside about what life would look like for David and me after losing our last two buffers. I continued my writing class and explored additional volunteer work while keeping up my family responsibilities.

One day a friend asked me, "What are you going to do when you're an empty nester?" Her expression was filled with sorrow.

I was taken aback at first. Why did my friend seem to have such sadness for me? As much as I'd loved staying home raising the girls for the last twenty years, my identity wasn't tied to them. My life wasn't coming to an end. These changes could signify a new beginning. Being a free spirit at heart, I began to think about what I wanted to create for myself.

As graduation approached and other friends asked "what's next" I began saying, "I'm not going to be an empty nester. I'm going to be a free bird." That had the right tone. I'd do my happy dance and throw my hands up in the air.

We were all ready to adapt to the next stage. I trusted that my kids would call me when they didn't feel well, needed decorating advice, or just had a bad day and needed to vent. The twins would soon begin their new lives and grow into adult women, and I planned on living my life more fully.

❦

The summer flew by with graduation parties, moving Heather to Washington, DC, where she'd secured a job, college orientations, and a family trip to the Dalmatian Islands off Croatia. Before we knew it, David, Katie, and I were moving Jessie into USC. A week later, David and I flew to Ann Arbor with Katie and settled her in at the University of Michigan. We hugged Katie goodbye, and as we walked down the dorm hallway, David said, "Oh, this is a sad day" and kissed me on my head. I nodded in agreement, not shedding a tear. They had already fallen.

Taking the recommendation of a friend, we planned a trip immediately afterwards. We flew straight to Chicago and spent a long weekend with Emma and her boyfriend, Ethan. Two weeks later, we went to see Heather in Washington, DC. Everyone was settled in their lives. I admired my girls for leaving the community they were raised in and exploring other cities. It was something I'd wanted to do but never had the courage. We'd taught them to be curious about the world around them and not be afraid.

On the plane ride home from DC, I found myself unable to read, write, or watch the movie. I stared out the window at the dark sky and pondered what I was feeling. All the girls were settled. Even though I showed others my happy, free bird persona, deep down I was lonelier than ever. I'd poured everything into my family, and I was proud of each of my girls. Being a mother had taught me how to be a better person, to love unconditionally, and to listen to my gut instincts. Tears welled up, but I quickly wiped them away before David noticed.

I looked over at David, then out the window. What would life look like once we got home? Would we get along better on our own? David was staring at the small screen, engrossed in his movie. What did he think about our life now that the girls were out of the house? I didn't ask. I put my headphones on, turned on a meditation recording, and closed my eyes.

thirty-six

One early December evening four months after taking the twins to their new lives, I strolled along the shoreline alone. The tide was low, and a prism of light spread across the cloud-covered horizon. The sun set slowly into the sea. Birds pecked at the sand in the shallow waters that ebbed and flowed. The calm quiet ocean resonated within me.

I wrapped my sweater more tightly around my body as the crisp air crept in and the colors faded. I thought about all that had happened in the last four months since I'd become a free bird.

In the weeks following our trip to DC, David and I continued our usual pattern of arguing. One day I found him snooping through a box of gifts I'd bought. I questioned him when I caught him in the act. He denied that he'd done anything. It was yet another invasion of privacy that reminded me of all the other times he'd done something similar, including the time he took it upon himself to find my birth mother. Our differences had become even more polarized now that the kids were gone —we had no buffers to dilute our conflicts. During one of our last arguments, I'd told him, "I will eventually gain the strength to leave you."

He stared at me as I turned to walk out of the room.

Within days of saying those words, I looked at my Facebook account, and a photo of Emma, Heather, and me popped up on my newsfeed, a Facebook memory from two years ago. The photo was from the weekend I told Emma and Heather that their dad and I were separating. I stared at the screen as a familiar hollow feeling settled into my gut. I examined the photo more closely, running my finger across the computer screen. We were standing on a bridge by the river, the city lights outlining the skyline behind us. I was smiling, but as I examined my face, I saw the sadness behind my eyes. That sadness was still with me now, and my feelings about David hadn't changed. I quickly clicked out of Facebook, closed my laptop, and went downstairs to start dinner. I tried to leave the image behind, but it stayed etched in my mind.

In therapy that week, Susan suggested we sign up for a weekend couple's workshop. Even though I agreed to go, I sensed it wasn't going to save our marriage.

That evening, David crawled into bed next to me with his iPad in his hand. "Here's the retreat that Susan recommended for us. Read this." He pointed to a paragraph in the middle of the page.

One sentence popped out. "Both people need to be fully committed."

My body froze as my mind stumbled on the word "committed." That wasn't the reality of our marriage.

I quickly handed David's iPad back. "I can't look at this now."

I rolled over, turned out my light, and pretended to sleep as I deciphered my body's reaction.

I understood more deeply how my marriage was contributing to my loneliness, and I was exhausted from our constant fighting. I had a choice: I could stay in my marriage or I could find the courage to leave. David would never be the one to end our marriage. Sometimes it occurred to me that he liked the chaos between us. Maybe it reminded him of his childhood. Maybe he was angry with me for wanting something other than what he had to offer.

I had to let the truth back in now that the kids were gone. The only way I was going to find happiness was to leave. That didn't have to take away from all we'd created together: four beautiful daughters, memories of fabulous trips to parts of the world most people only dream about visiting, living in a beach community, and having a second home in Mammoth. These were things many people strive for, but they were meaningless without a deeper connection with someone you love.

I knew what I had to do.

The next morning I woke up early, my eyes heavy and swollen from crying. I grabbed a cup of tea and sat on the couch as the dawn light filtered through our backyard. A multitude of emotions ran though me—sadness, trepidation, uncertainty, guilt, and relief. The strength and courage I'd searched for all night came and went. I didn't want to cause David pain. We'd both been through so much, but if I were going to be true to myself, I had to make a decision I knew would hurt him. When I heard his footsteps upstairs, I met him in our office.

I sat down on the couch adjacent to his desk. Adrenaline raced through me. Can I really do this? That day we were supposed to commit to a ten-day ski vacation in France with another couple to celebrate David's sixtieth birthday in February, five months away. If I didn't tell David today, I'd need to stay through the holidays and into February. The thought of staying felt like a noose wrapped around my neck.

I told him softly, "We need to talk before we meet with Susan this morning." We had our weekly couple's session in an hour, and I guessed he was tired of hearing those words.

"Okay," he responded hesitantly.

"I didn't sleep at all last night and . . ." My eyes trailed down to the floor before meeting his. "If I'm honest with myself, I'm not committed to this marriage. I want to cancel our ski trip to France in February, and I want a physical separation."

With a tilt of his head he said, "Wait . . . what . . . why?"

"I can't do this anymore." Tears streamed down my face.

His face had a look of confusion and disbelief. "Where is this coming from? I thought we were doing better."

"David, this shouldn't be a surprise. We fight constantly, and it's making me crazy . . . and after twenty-six years, our marriage should be easier."

He slid down in his chair and hung his head. With a look of acceptance and defeat he said, "I feel like I'm losing you."

I didn't respond. If I had, I would have said, "You lost me years ago." He asked a few questions and I replied with few words. Then I simply said, "Let's finish talking about this with Susan this morning."

I sent Susan a text, letting her know what to expect. *This time I'm not changing my mind.*

In therapy that morning, David's demeanor changed. Determination rested in his eyes as our session began, a pattern I'd seen so many times before. I knew he wasn't going to make any of this easy for me.

I put my shaking hands in between my legs and repeated to Susan what I'd told David that morning: "I want a physical separation."

He sat up straighter and the tension heightened. David brusquely said, "If we get a divorce, I want to keep the house."

I turned to him without hesitation. "Okay, I'll move out."

I was startled by my quick response, but I felt the solidity of my decision settle into my body. I looked at Susan with confidence before turning back to David. His eyes were wide, and clearly he was shocked. His expression told me he couldn't quite believe what was happening. Two years ago, I'd asked him to move out because I was still raising the twins and wanted to stay in the house, but we'd reconciled. This time was different. David could keep the house. I had everything I needed.

When our session was over, David walked out the door. Susan opened her arms, gave me a hug, and whispered, "You're going to be more than okay."

I met her eyes and said, "Thank you for everything."

A late December evening as the sun was setting, I sat on the beach until the sky became dark before making my way back to my apartment. I had found a new place a few days after I told David I'd move out. I turned around for one more glimpse at the ocean. I'd finally done it. I had left my lonely marriage and hadn't once regretted my decision. I knew life would continue with ups and downs. Mom, Dad, Ken, and Will would require my attention, but I could shape my own happiness. I would continue working to resolve my childhood issues, and I'd need time to heal from my twenty-six-year marriage. I knew I'd make different decisions once I was ready to start dating again. But for now, I felt free.

I walked up the steps and opened the front door. My heart swelled. Not because of the life I left behind, but for everything that had brought me to this point and for all that I had yet to learn. I finally found my way home—to me.

"We must be willing to let go of the life we planned so as to have the life that is waiting for us."

~ Joseph Campbell

Me, Ken, and Mom standing next to our van.

Will, me, and Mom standing behind us.

Mom sailing with Ken, Will, and me on John's boat, 1968 or 1969.

John Stiles and Mom, March 1969.

Mom sailing with a beer in her hand.

epilogue

I made the short hike up to McCloud Lake with my five-year-old adopted Siberian husky, Lu. Jessie had talked me into getting a dog when our world was shutting down from the pandemic. Three of my daughters would be coming home for the summer and were eager to help me pick her out. The girls and I instantly fell in love with her—Lu was now part of our pack. While she frolicked in the lake, I found a shady area to sit and took a sip of water. My eyes traveled up to the peaks and ridges above the lake, the deep blue sky above. Snow was still present in some of the cracks and crevices in midsummer.

I smiled, feeling warmth travel through my body as I watched Lu play. I'd not only given her a new life, but I'd given myself one too.

Over a year had passed since I'd awakened one morning in my small apartment, my lower back muscles squeezed tight. It was a familiar pain. I'd experienced something like it several times during the past six years. I got up, went to the bathroom, took two Aleve, and went back to bed with an ice pack on my back. I expected the pain would pass like it had so many times before. When I woke up a couple hours later, the pain was worse.

There was something really wrong. I phoned my doctor who called in a stronger prescription, but before someone could pick it up, I passed out on my kitchen floor. When I woke up, my back had seized up, I was barely able to move, and my small apartment began to spin around me.

After I left my marriage, my go-to word had been *yes*. I said yes to writing courses, starting a business, cochairing a local youth program, socializing with friends, and dating. I'd also pushed for a divorce and negotiated the largest and most complex financial transaction of my life. Two weeks earlier, I'd told a close friend, "I have nothing to complain about, but I'm stressed out." I knew then I'd taken on too much, but I didn't know how to back out of it all. My body did.

After crawling on my hands and knees back to bed, I waited to see if my dizziness would subside, but it didn't. I called 911. I stayed in the hospital for the next four nights. The doctors treated me with Dilaudid, an opioid that was seven times stronger than morphine. My blood pressure dropped along with my oxygen levels, and I needed help getting to the bathroom. The doctors chased my symptoms and gave me one medication after another. I begged the doctors to let me go home so I could rest more comfortably. Once my vital signs stabilized, they discharged me. I left the hospital with painkillers and a walker, and I looked six months pregnant from the water weight I was carrying. Like Mom's had, my body was keeping score. This would turn into a hard and painful lesson, one I should have seen coming, but like many life lessons, it had blindsided me.

Over the next two weeks, my friends took turns caring for me. Someone was with me day and night, and friends brought daily meals. Simply taking a shower exhausted me. The first night I came home from the hospital, my right knee became red, hot, and swollen, and I barely slept from the severity of my pain. Within days, the swelling moved to my left ankle and then to my upper back. I developed an air pocket on my chest. I couldn't keep food down and began passing out again. Almost two weeks after my first hospital visit, I was readmitted for an additional three days. They drained fluid from the lining of my lungs, took an MRI, a CT scan, and X-rays. An infectious disease doctor visited me daily, saying they couldn't find anything wrong with me except that I'd become very anemic. Finally, a rheumatologist diagnosed me with an unnamed virus with reactive migrating arthritis. My illness got my attention.

I took everything off my plate, pushed back my move-in date to my new house, and rested. Regaining my health became my priority. While I rested and healed, I accepted that I'd pushed my free bird status too far. It seemed that the stress I'd put myself under had compromised my immune system, and I'd contracted a virus that made me feel like my entire body had been short-circuited. Now I knew how the arthritic pain Mom had lived with felt—it was excruciating. Fortunately, after running a myriad of tests, my rheumatologist told me that I didn't have an autoimmune disease, and my symptoms should dissipate with time. They did gradually go away, and I got stronger over many months.

As my body was healing, I went back into therapy. A friend recommended a therapist with a PhD who was somatically oriented and specialized in deep attachment work. After I left my marriage, I had taken a break from therapy. I could see that was a mistake and this illness was a call to continue my healing process from the inside out.

Like most therapy, experiencing the benefits takes time. I have continued to shed the layers of my resentment toward David, and he has done the same with me. Over the last six months, David told me several times that he should have appreciated me more. He said with sincerity, "I didn't respect all you did for our family . . . in fact I acted like a fucking jerk." In a later conversation he admitted he hadn't been equipped to stop our cycle of arguments. I sat with those statements and cried with relief, and I was grateful for a deeper understanding of him. I let his words settle the tragedy of our broken marriage and the brokenness that was still inside me. I never expected to hear him apologize. His words were a gift that would continue to heal me.

Therapy has also helped me to manage loss. When Mom passed after her thirteen-year battle with dementia the month after the pandemic hit, I curled up in a fetal position on my bed and cried. I lay with myself and let the grief move through me, releasing it when the waves hit me. Therapy at deeper levels has been teaching me new techniques on how to release emotions in my body that in the past I carried with me.

My past has molded me into the person I am. I continue to be better equipped to face the inevitable unknowns. I've learned that I can choose how to move through this one precious life. I choose self-care, awareness, courage, and joy. I don't need to know what's ahead, because the path of self-discovery will lead me to where I'm meant to be.

acknowledgments

I am grateful to so many:

My late mother, Elizabeth (Betty) Charlotte Menzies. Your strength, courage, and love will live within me forever. I wish you nothing but peace. Thank you, Dad, for taking us on our family adventures and for sharing the stories of my childhood. They helped bring this book to life.

To my four beautiful daughters, you are my daily inspiration. May you always be true to yourself. The answers are within you.

To all my dearest friends who lived this story with me: Sharon, Marsha, Gina, Kim, and Michele. Thank you for the many shared conversations, laughter, and unwavering support. My deepest gratitude to my Mala Soul Sistas and everyone who cared for me when I was ill, visited me in the hospital, brought me meals, and picked me up off the floor when I couldn't get up by myself. I am forever indebted to all of you. Let's continue this spiritual ride together.

Laura Roe Stevens, your words of encouragement helped me put pen to paper for the very first time. Thank you.

A very special thank you to Linda Joy Myers, president of the National Association of Memoir writers, writing coach, and author of *Don't Call Me Mother* and *Song of the Plains*. I'm beyond thankful for your dedication to the craft of memoir and for helping me bring my jumbled story to life. You believed in me when I wasn't sure I believed in myself.

I must not forget Brooke Warner, Crystal Patriarche, and the entire team at She Writes Press and BookSparks. Thank you for giving me and so many other women writers the outlet so our voices can be heard. I'm forever grateful.

ABOUT THE AUTHOR

Photo credit: Bradford Rogne

LAURIE JAMES is a recovering caregiver, wife, and mother. She has successfully launched her four daughters into adulthood and has been the primary caretaker for her elderly parents. Laurie has learned through therapy and other healing programs that she has everything she needs within her to create the life she desires, and she wants to bring that knowledge to other women. She is training to become a Martha Beck certified coach and expects to receive her ICF (International Coach Federation) credential by July 2021. Laurie enjoys coaching women who are searching for happiness and helps them discover what that means to them. An active community volunteer, she cochairs a youth program for high school students, exposing them to a variety of career paths before they apply to college. She's an active member of a collaborative giving circle that pools donation dollars to help Los Angeles–based nonprofits.

Laurie graduated from Cal Poly Pomona with a BS in business and held a position as a corporate recruiter before she stayed home to raise her children. She lives in Manhattan Beach with her adopted husky, Lu. A native Californian, she's a lover of yoga, hiking, skiing, sailing, and adventure travel. Stay connected with Laurie at www.laurieejames.com

SELECTED TITLES FROM SHE WRITES PRESS

She Writes Press is an independent publishing company founded to serve women writers everywhere. Visit us at www.shewritespress.com.

Loveyoubye: Holding Fast, Letting Go, And Then There's The Dog by Rossandra White. $16.95, 978-1-938314-50-6. A soul-searching memoir detailing the painful, but ultimately liberating, disintegration of a twenty-five-year marriage.

Scattering Ashes: A Memoir of Letting Go by Joan Rough. $16.95, 978-1-63152-095-2. A daughter's chronicle of what happens when she invites her alcoholic and emotionally abusive mother to move in with her in hopes of helping her through the final stages of life—and her dream of mending their tattered relationship fails miserably.

There Was a Fire Here: A Memoir by Risa Nye. $16.95, 978-1-63152-045-7. After a devastating firestorm destroys Risa Nye's Oakland, California home and neighborhood, she has to dig deep to discover her inner strength and resilience.

Seeing Red: A Woman's Quest for Truth, Power, and the Sacred by Lone Morch. $16.95, 978-1-938314-12-4. One woman's journey over inner and outer mountains—a quest that takes her to the holy Mt. Kailas in Tibet, through a seven-year marriage, and into the arms of the fierce goddess Kali, where she discovers her powerful, feminine self.

The Full Catastrophe: A Memoir by Karen Elizabeth Lee. $16.95, 978-1-63152-024-2. The story of a well educated, professional woman who, after marrying the wrong kind of man—twice—finally resurrects her life.